They Shall Bear You Up

They Shall Bear You Up

Memories of a Catholic Priest

Fachtna Joseph Harte

OPEN BOOK
EDITIONS
A Berrett–Koehler Partner

They Shall Bear You Up
Memories of a Catholic Priest

iUniverse books may be ordered through booksellers or by contacting:

iUniverse
1663 Liberty Drive
Bloomington, IN 47403
www.iuniverse.com
1-800-Authors (1-800-288-4677)

Because of the dynamic nature of the Internet, any web addresses or links contained in this book may have changed since publication and may no longer be valid. The views expressed in this work are solely those of the author and do not necessarily reflect the views of the publisher, and the publisher hereby disclaims any responsibility for them.

Cover photo: Killala Town taken from the west entry

ISBN: 978-1-4620-3627-1 (sc)
ISBN: 978-1-4620-3629-5 (hc)
ISBN: 978-1-4620-3628-8 (e)

Library of Congress Control Number: 2011919555

Printed in the United States of America

iUniverse rev. date: 12/03/2011

Dedicated to the memory of

my parents, Timothy and Elizabeth Harte, who were truly a lamp to my feet and a light to my path.

**For to his angels he has given command about you,
That they guard you in all your ways
Upon their hands they shall bear you up
Lest you dash your foot against a stone**

— Psalm 91

Contents

Preface

⁂

This is a priest's story. Some of the happenings recollected here come from notes taken at various times throughout my priesthood, and others rely on memories that have been engraved within my soul.

Each priest experiences a different kind of adventure in his life. Perhaps because of the clergy scandals of recent times, the vocation of priesthood has taken a fall. Occasionally parents will even discourage their sons from entering the priesthood or will encourage them to at least delay it until they have experienced the secular life for a while. It is not unlikely that vocations go astray and men who might have contributed to the establishment of the kingdom are lost to some other profession.

Personally, in the autumn of my life, I am filled with satisfaction about my life's journey. "To walk with Christ" every day of the year is a privilege that has to be unrivalled. The apostles had that privilege! They woke up in the presence of the Lord every day. So did I as a priest. The story you are about to read has to do with answering the call. It has to do with walking the roads with the Lord, proclaiming His Kingdom, listening to Him in one's heart, going among His people with compassion and love, and—yes!—climbing the hill of Calvary with Him too. No life is bereft of the cross.

"I will not call you servants but friends," He said to His followers at the Last Supper. Since birth the Lord has been my friend, and that friendship has increased and multiplied with the reception of holy orders. It has been a great life, and I am glad that, despite the twists and turns in the road, I finally reached ordination and a life that was full to the brim with the absolute euphoria of working to bring about the kingdom of God.

The words of Emily Brontë apply: "I've dreamt in my life dreams that have stayed with me ever after, and changed my ideas: they've gone through and through me, like wine through water, and altered the color of my mind." To dream of what you can do for God is the best dream of all. This book records some of those dreams and the story of a walk with the Lord.

Acknowledgments

Thomas P. Moran (Moran & Kidd, attorneys at law), Clarence Geis, Gregg Dobbs, Father John E. McMullan—advisors and enthusiastic supporters.

Chapter One:
The Longest Night

"The sun halted in the middle of the sky. Not for a whole day did it resume its swift course. Never before or since was there a day like this" (Joshua 10:13). This is Joshua's description of the longest day "when the Lord delivered up the Amorites to the Israelites." There is nothing in the Bible about the longest night!

I am going to tell you it was the night of August 14–15, 1939. I was nine years old then. Despite my young age, my parents had allowed me to join them on their pilgrimage to Knock Shrine in my native County Mayo—an all-night vigil that began at dusk and ended at dawn. At the age of nine, I knew that for dawn to come the sun must rise and the moon must get out of its way. But that night the moon simply stood still. How I longed for the comforts of a bed and blankets! There never was a night as long as this.

I was standing with my parents near the gable end of the church, site of the apparition of Our Lady on August 22, 1879. In the intervening years, Knock had become a place of pilgrimage visited by thousands of people from all over Ireland. Crutches hung in various places as a reminder of the power of the Virgin who had literally sent patients home without any need for the crutches that helped them get there. The apparition had taken place on the evening of August 22, but for some reason, most likely that it was a holy day, the all-night vigil had developed on the eve and morning of August 15, the Feast of Our Lady's Assumption.

On the morning we were there, it had just been announced that Mass would begin at dawn. After being up all night for the first time in my life, how I longed for any sign of that morning sun that would herald the dawn! It would just have been my luck that my first night up would coincide with the moon standing still and holding up the arrival of the sun for the first time in the history of the world.

Photograph of author's parents taken c.1927.

"Look to the east," my dad encouraged. In due course it happened. The moon got out of the way! The first rays of a new day began to come above the horizon. A bell rang to announce that Mass would shortly begin. We were standing outside with the crowds awaiting the start of Mass at the spot Our Lady had appeared. The priest came to the altar at the gable end. My father stooped down and whispered that I should ask God for what I wanted most. "We have been here all night honoring His mother, and ask her too for what you want."

The very first words of the Mass in those days were *Introibo ad altare Dei*, or, in English, "I will go unto the altar of God." That was what I wanted most! To go to God's altar as a priest. I whispered my petition to the Mother of God. And I kept it secret, of course!

After Mass that morning, we departed for home. I don't recall the journey because, like Robinson Crusoe after his shipwreck, Mary Queen "sent the gentle sleep from Heaven that sped into my soul." But the Mother of God had heard my petition. My journey to priesthood would possibly be a little different than that of most others. That was of no importance to me. I would have been a deliriously happy youngster had I known my prayer was heard.

There was really nothing very unusual about a nine-year-old making a pilgrimage and praying the rosary. Praying the rosary together as a family was the normal ending to our day. At nine I was well aware of God's presence in my life. And I had a yearning to please His mother too. I'm sure that yearning was absorbed in me by our nightly recitation of the rosary. Looking back, although I had no notion how it affected me and entered into my soul, it left a happy memory of a tranquil and effervescent home.

And so this story begins at home. It was a wonderful home—a place of peace, contentment, and love. It was a place to be remembered forever. It was a happy home, and it still holds a special place in my heart. It stands a few miles from the Atlantic Ocean on the north Mayo coast, just a short distance from historic Killala and the pier at Kilcummin where a French force landed in 1798 to help an Irish revolution. My father would know Kilcummin and its quiet and friendly people well. He was principal teacher of their school for a quarter of a century.

That was long before the modernization of Ireland.

When I go home—to the very same kitchen—it is now equipped with all the paraphernalia of modern times. The open hearth is no more. Gone too is the crane that hung across the turf fire and served to hold the utensils in which the breads were baked or the food was cooked. Naturally the kerosene-oil cooker, which put forth so many wonderful odors of my mother's cooking, is no more either. The kitchen is comfortable, with the "comforts" of modern times, still beautiful in its own way. But it is not the kitchen of my childhood!

The house is centrally heated now. Sometimes my mind wanders back to the old days, when the family was gathered of a winter evening around the blazing turf fire, which provided the only heating for the house. But in those days it was normal to have just one peat fire in the home, and most of the heat was therefore in the kitchen.

There were eight of us children, five girls and three boys. Mary Teresa was the oldest, followed by another sister, Ita Bernadette. Then came Patrick Enda, and later I arrived on the scene. I was followed by Aidan, the last boy in the family, and later by Carmel, Anne, and Monica. Both my parents were teachers, but when my mother married, she quickly gave up her profession in order to care for her family.

My earliest memories go back to the building of our home in 1933. It was located at Moneen, just three miles from the historic town of Killala. The word *Moneen* comes from the Gaelic for "little bog" or "little meadow"—you can take your pick. The present home replaced the old home, a thatched three-room cottage my father had purchased from a local farmer as well as the little farm that came with it. It bordered my grandfather's own farm, which in time my father came to own. Indeed, our new home was one of the first two-story homes in the neighborhood, with a slated roof and decorative front walls.

My father had qualified as a primary teacher in Waterford College, and his first position was in the quaint town of Baltimore, not far from Skibbereen and perhaps forty miles from Clonakilty in County Cork where he was born. "The sack of Baltimore" is still remembered in Irish lore, keeping alive the recollection of that terrible evening when Algerian pirates came ashore on June 20, 1631, sacked the village, and made off with almost all its inhabitants, the majority of whom were never seen again. It is believed that they finished their lives as slaves in North Africa.

The revolution of 1916 changed the lives of many Irishmen, including my father. His family was involved in the war for Irish freedom, and one of his brothers, Patrick, was arrested while playing a football game in Clonakilty. Patrick was an officer of the original Irish Republican Army in the most rebellious county in Ireland. To this day, Cork is known as "the Rebel County." Toward the end of July 1920, British troops captured him, along with a companion, Tom Hales, and brought him to the mansion of a landowner in the area. Here he was severely tortured. With his face smashed in and his nose broken by a soldier's rifle butt and almost every tooth gone, his nails were removed one by one with a pliers in order to get him to give information on his companions. He refused. Later on, after a British court had found him guilty, he was sent to Pentonville prison in England. The severity of his torture took its toll, and he died some short years later, never having recovered from the ordeal. Tom Hales lived to tell the tale, which he narrated on his release from Dartmoor prison later on. The story is retold in *The IRA and Its Enemies*, by Peter Hart (Clarendon Press, Oxford, 1998). There are many Cork locals who believe that the recent movie *The Wind that Shakes the Barley* told in its own way the story of the capture and torture of Patrick Harte.

Toward the end of World War One, the British government opened its jails and sent volunteer criminals to repel the Irish revolution. The British called them auxiliaries, but to the Irish natives they were known as the "Black and Tans" by reason of their uniforms. Being natural criminals, now given unrestrained freedom, they ran amok throughout the countryside. Civilians going about their everyday affairs were not spared by their rampaging. They left an unenvied record of murder and mayhem in their wake and are to this day remembered for their deeds of infamy against innocent civilians.

Following Patrick's arrest, the hated Black and Tans arrived in Clonakilty one evening, in search of my father. Fortunately, he was out of town, and the Tans wrought their "revenge" on some other poor unfortunate. When Timothy Harte got home, he was advised by his friends and a local priest to get out of County Cork as expeditiously as possible. His escape—with the help of the priest—took him to an island off the west Mayo coast where he was to become the principal teacher in the small island school.

There's a movie called *The Great Escape* that reminds me of my own father's journey to freedom. His priest friend advised him to head west, where a teaching post would be awaiting him. He took a bus from Clonakilty to Tralee, having been warned to be careful of Limerick City, where the Tans were rampant at the time. All went well until his Tralee bus arrived at the outskirts of Limerick City. There in front of it was a roadblock with a group of auxiliaries standing on the roadway, signaling the bus to stop. One of those "criminals"—because criminals they were!—boarded the bus at the rear, where the bus entrances were placed in those days. My father was sitting toward the front, not quite sure what was happening or if they might be searching for him. But as if through some angelic intervention, the leader of the group called off the intruder, and the entire band jumped into their truck and rode away at reckless speed.

Everything else went well until he got to Westport a couple days later. There he began to inquire about the whereabouts of his destination—the island of Innishkea. "There is no bus there, sir; it's an island, you know," someone said roguishly, "and you'll have to take a hackney car to the dock to meet the boat." With little choice he took the hackney car, paid a moderate fare, and found himself in a seemingly deserted area with a few homes looking out upon the Atlantic Ocean. Nor was there any sign of an island out there! The boat was no steamer! Apparently it was a modern-day outboard, or something akin to it; he remembered the spray washing over the few occupants as the boat wended homeward. His arrival signaled the end of an era: he was not "on the run" anymore, and there was little danger of the Tans or any British soldiers coming ashore.

It so happened that a young woman came to teach on Innishkea too. Her name was Elizabeth O'Neill. It was love at first sight. The couple were married in Binghamstown in west Mayo and in time went on to have the children mentioned above. Somewhere or other there is an irony in the name! Bingham was an English landlord, an avaricious and unfeeling man. In order to hinder his tenants from taking their livestock for sale to the neighboring town of Belmullet, he erected a barrier through which the cattle had to be driven after a tax on each had been rendered. To this day, the Gaelic name for Binghamstown is *An Geata Mor*, translating directly into English as "The Large Gate." And so an Irish citizen recently "on the run" was married in a village whose name recalled the injustices against which he had railed!

My father was a quiet man, not given to boasting or quarrelling. He had a great love for Ireland. A compatriot and cousin of the great Michael Collins, he was always saddened by the Civil War that followed the successful Easter Rising. To him Collins was a hero. "We beat the might of the British Empire," he would say, "and then sadly we turned our guns on ourselves." He would rail against the stupidity of those who could not see the political intent of everything Collins did in his life.

"Collins died at thirty-two," he would say, "and how could anyone not understand the life he dedicated to Ireland's freedom?" According to DeValera and his followers, Collins erred when he took part in signing the treaty that gave an Irish government control over twenty-six counties but left the six northern counties of Ireland to be governed by Orangemen loyal to the Union Jack—this despite the fact that over 80 percent of the population had approved the treaty in a public plebiscite. Indeed, Collins had requested not to be included in the group traveling to London at the time of the treaty, as the British had not the faintest notion of what he looked like. DeValera insisted that Collins be a member of the deputation to London, and the rest is history. A vicious Civil War ensued at DeValera's instigation, a war in which Collins lost his life.

In my younger years, my father kept a small revolver. Following the Civil War the country was divided, and it was well known which side my father had been on! On his arrival in north Mayo he was regarded as a "blow-in" who didn't really belong. His partiality to Michael Collins also became known. Civil wars come from dangerous and irrational thinking that does not end with the conclusion of armed skirmishing. Indeed, I remember my early years of primary school. I should mention here that we did not attend my father's school as children but were enrolled in Kilfian school, a school closer to home and within the parish in which we resided, though still two miles walking distance. Roadside workers would call me a "blueshirt" as I walked home from school with my companions. I really did not know what they meant, nor did my parents alarm me by telling me. Here was a child of six being badgered by adults because they judged his father on the wrong side in an irrational civil war.

Many years later I would find out about Blueshirts. After ten years of pro-Treaty government DeValera's party was elected to power in 1932. Pro-Treatyites were naturally disturbed at the turn of events. When Eoin O'Duffy was removed as chief of police almost as soon as the new government took office, there was an outcry that those who had not sided with DeValera would all suffer recriminations. O'Duffy himself began a protest movement, encouraging those who took umbrage at what was happening in the country to gather at town meetings wearing blue shirts for the purpose of identification. The movement eventually came to nothing, but the name "blueshirt" was now attached to anyone who was seen not to favor the DeValera government. For the roadside workers, the six-year-old son of Master Harte was a blueshirt! And the same Master Harte had involved himself in the struggle against Britain, though not one of the workers most likely had ever had their finger on a rifle.

First, as already mentioned, my father taught on the little island of Innishkea, off the west coast of Mayo, where islanders remembered him for many a year. Years later a school came vacant at Banagher near the town of Killala; it was a mile or so removed from the historic site of a French landing to help the Irish in the uprising of 1798. My father applied for the school. Another applicant expected to receive the post, but the local parish priest who was manager of the school preferred my father's qualifications and appointed him as principal. Following my father's appointment, all hell broke loose. A boycott of the school was recommended but failed, and for a quarter of a century Timothy Harte was the principal teacher of Banagher National School, close to Kilcummin on the shores of the Atlantic. His wake and funeral Mass were crowded with past pupils who remembered him with affection.

When my father left the island of Innishkea to take up his new teaching post, my mother resigned from her duties on the island too. Indeed, she was glad to do so and throughout the rest of her life reminisced on the perils of the boat journey from the mainland to the island. They were taken by rowboat over treacherous waters, to the mainland and back, journeys my mother never quite forgot—journeys she endured with the rosary beads in her hands. In 1927, those waters were the site of a terrible drowning tragedy that took the lives of several fishermen who were caught in a sudden night storm at sea.

I was the fourth child in my family, two girls and a boy having been born previously. Not very long after my birth my father purchased a farm that adjoined our own and quickly decided to build a new home. The decision was made that our family would move to my grandmother's while the new home was under construction. Her cottage was just a few minutes walk from where our new home was being erected. Here I find my first memories. The cottage had a large kitchen and two bedrooms as well as a dining room. There were roses on the whitewashed walls outside, and a neatly trimmed box hedge separated a little front garden from the street. There was a stile with steps in order to get into the little garden, and on that stile I spent many an hour viewing the surrounding countryside at the age of three! To this day, I recall the morning I "disappeared" in my nightclothes and my mother found me by the roadside "inspecting" the new home. I remember being swept into her arms and being carried back to breakfast, though I had little understanding of what all the fuss was about.

While we lived at Grandmother's during the building of the new home, happenings both sad and glad took place. A younger sister (Carmel) was born. And a younger brother died at the age of two. I remember the grief that struck the home. About four o'clock in the evening, when my little brother Aidan had trouble breathing, the doctor was called. He came to the house and prescribed something that had to do with the vapor from a steaming kettle being loosed around where the sick child lay. My other older brother and I were sent to bed early that night, but I remember the concern of my mother and the fear that showed itself on her face. The doctor had determined my brother had diphtheria, a disease of the time from which there was little escape. And it was also contagious.

By morning my brother had died. My father went to the parish priest, who assured him he now had an angel in heaven. It was my first encounter with death, though its awful finality had not yet struck me. That would come much further down the road and many years later. Aged four, I was not allowed to see my dead angel brother. There was no Mass for him, it being understood that a young child would journey straight to heaven. In today's Church there would be a Mass for the consolation of the parents and perhaps to assuage their grief. The Mass, after all, is Christ's great gift to us. It enables the true believer to feel and be consoled by His Divine presence.

Chapter Two:
Memories

Example, they say, is better than precept. To this day, I have vivid memories of my mother kneeling on a chair in front of a picture of the Sacred Heart, in my grandmother's home during the days after my brother died. Even as a child I took note of the streams of tears running down her face as she confided her troubles to God and tried to accept the cross that had been thrust into her life. Naturally, I had no recognition of what she was really doing, and it was only years later that the memory also became a lesson in faith.

Nor do I have any idea why this particular image has stayed with me all those years. Most likely it was to be for me a moment of grace that would endure a lifetime. In the seminary I would study about the problems of holy Job and come to realize too the statement of Saint Paul that to those who love God "all things work together unto good." The Son of God would carry a cross and would be asked to endure a horrific death. In her own way, my mother experienced and realized the will of God in her life and united herself with the suffering Christ. She was no theologian, just a woman of faith. She had never studied Saint Paul, but here she was, just after the burial of her baby son, carrying out what Paul had written to "make good what is wanting in the sufferings of Christ."

I grew up in a loving home, and whenever I think of it that home always included the presence of my grandmother, Mary O'Neill, known to us as Nan. Indeed, when I was a child she could have had Nan as her

Christian name, her only name! I must have been eight years old before I found out her last name was O'Neill.

If there are angels in childhood, Nan was the one. She advised, but she never found fault; her love was the stuff that dreams are made of, and she was a pillar of assurance whenever assurance was needed. Saint Paul must have had a woman like her in mind when he wrote his dissertation about "love." In the early years, Nan lived in a beautiful thatched cottage about three minutes walk from our home. That cottage was second home to me.

Nan was so gentle and kind. She was compassion itself. She loved to sing. To this day, "The Stone outside Dan Murphy's Door" warbles within my memory. She was also a good cook, especially when it came to confectionaries and sweets. Often, at a mere suggestion, she would whip out a pan, a pound of butter, some sugar, and presto—we were eating butterscotch. And it was much better than any store variety. Butterscotch was not her only talent however. She made all kinds of jam tarts, cakes, and scones. Those scones were a source of disappointment one Sunday evening. I had been at her side as she applied her skills. Everything smelled so good. Then my mother arrived in a tizzy. (There were no phones in those days.) Company had unexpectedly called, and she "had not a thing in the house." Did Gran have anything? We lost the scones!

While Gran lived at this house she locked the door every midmorning and spent most of the day at our home. Her husband, John O'Neill, had died some years previously, indeed previous to the time we spent living with her while our new home was being built. She had a cat that made the journey with her. The cat would sit on the wall outside and appear to be awaiting the walk up the road. The cat stayed the day too, returning with my gran in the evening. The cat, however, never walked on the road but always chose to walk on the stone wall by the wayside. I remember once asking my father why the cat never walked on the road. It was then I learned that cats like to keep their paws clean, and besides they feel safer and more in charge when they look down from a higher position. God made all His creatures with their own particular features.

But whenever I walk this road now, memories come out to greet me of a loving grandmother who made me feel special. And with the increase in modern traffic it certainly would not be a safe road for a child to walk in his nightclothes before breakfast. And when I walk the road, I can see in my mind's eye the roses blooming on the wall of her cottage, the box hedge that surrounded the little garden in the front, and the garden at the back with apple trees, pear trees, blackcurrants, and raspberries.

John O'Neill had been a member of the Royal Irish Constabulary. This was the police force of the British government. Its members were to uphold the law. They were always a target for the fundamentalist "patriots" who saw no good in anything British. Many of that police force lost their lives during the Revolution of 1916–1921, killed by their own countrymen for wearing a British uniform. My mother would tell the story of how she had been denied as a twelve-year-old from being granted the prize that went with first place in an Irish dancing competition, the reason being advanced that she was the daughter of a policeman who wore a British uniform. Later in life the same lady was remembered by her pupils in an elementary school in which she taught as the teacher who "taught us rebel songs." Throughout the revolution many of those same policemen became "double agents," because their profession allowed them valuable information that was passed on to the revolutionaries. It would seem that the British were never able to resolve this problem from within. And to disband the force would have left the country without any police force at all.

I never knew my grandfather O'Neill. I was but two years old when he died at the age of sixty-seven, in the year 1932. He had contracted cancer of the lip, which in time killed him. But his reputation lived on as a man of tough spirit, who put up with little nonsense and who did not suffer fools gladly.

Some of his genes must have been passed on to my mother. She might be said to have had little patience for those who contributed to life's follies. She had her own sense of humor, but although she had a hearty laugh and could certainly enjoy a joke, her humor did not match my grandmother's. She was a strict disciplinarian. Add to this a keen faith and a lively love for the Lord that was there for all to see.

But one asset of my mother remains in my mind to this day. She loved company, she loved a chat, and if you were going to be her friend you had better be able to converse. And believe me, she had lots of friends. Indeed, in her own way she taught me to be boldly curious. As a youngster, whenever I went somewhere on my own, she would always inquire about what "news" I might have heard. If the information was sketchy, it brought further inquiries with an admonishment that I should have asked further questions of my friends. So in my early years I learned that I should never be afraid to ask.

War broke out in September of 1939. Certain commodities quickly grew scarce. Some trades were just about going out of existence. Among them was the "thatcher." Thatched homes should have been redone every five or six years. The thatch really came from straw that was sold for the purpose. The thatcher was a rare artisan. There was a scarcity of straw, now used for cattle feed because of the war. It was hard to find the artisan either since thatched homes were now being replaced and going out of existence.

It was decided that my grandmother would leave her home and come to live with us. My father felt she would be safer with our family, and the problem of the thatched roof would go away. The house would be demolished. Looking back on it all, I remember my delight that Nan had moved in. It never occurred to me that perhaps there might have been pain in her heart as she left her independence behind, as well as the memories of bringing up her family of three in a quaint and comfortable home. And my own daily journey "down the road" was also over.

Nan was not the kind to sit around. She was no Norman Rockwell grandmother, sitting on a chair! When she moved in, she assumed certain tasks of her own. These kept her busy from morning to night. She slept little, so her first chore in the morning was to rekindle the fire and in her own way bring the house to life. She was up before anybody else had stirred, and she was the last to retire. The open hearth had an ash pit as part of it, and at day's end she would cover the fire with ashes. This served to keep the coals burning all night, so that when she came back in the morning, the fire could be rekindled with ease. That done, she lit the little red lamp under the picture of the Sacred Heart in our kitchen.

She brought her sewing machine with her to our home. She was the perfect seamstress. When something needed to be mended, Nan was sitting in front of her sewing machine, her foot on the pedal, her right hand guiding the wheel. To me it was all very mysterious and impressive, all the more so as my mother had never learned to use the machine. Nan was the only one who had that power. It turned out to be my luck.

It was a Sunday morning. We had gone to early Mass as usual. In my very young days, we had a horse and buggy to take us the two miles to the church. While the family was young, this served a purpose. We were all together, and we grew up with a Sunday morning discipline of attending Mass. But the procedure also entailed having the horse ready, harnessing him, and getting him yoked to the buggy. This entailed a certain amount of preparedness. My father was no horseman and had never managed horses. Another man had to come by and get the transport ready. Not too many men were prepared to get up early on a Sunday morning to get this chore done. By the time we were ten, we were either walking to Mass or cycling.

I must have been at least ten at this particular time. After breakfast my mother told me to change out of my Sunday clothes. In those days everyone going to Mass was dressed in what was known as "their Sunday best." Casual wear had not yet arrived on the scene. Breakfast after Sunday Mass was always a feast. There was a certain amount of satisfactory anticipation in just waiting to be served. On this particular morning I took no heed of my mother's command. For some reason she paid no attention to my inattention either. By noon she had retired for a rest while my father read the newspaper in the sitting room—a room, I might add, that was rarely used by us children.

My brother and I were outside at the five-barred gate which led into the farmyard. He was sitting on the pillar, and I decided to sit on the top rung of the gate. Unfortunately for me there was a rusty broken rung just below. This caught in my trousers, and the ripping cloth sent shudders through me that in later life would have induced a heart attack. What was I to do? Surely my life was nearing an end! My mother would simply end it for me.

I sneaked into the kitchen, first making sure the way was clear. My grandmother was there, readying one of her cakes for the oven. At this moment she was my only refuge in life. I told her what had happened. "Go now and take it off," she said calmly and with a twinkle in her eye, "and I will fold it for you and hang it up. Later on, I will mend it when your mother is doing the shopping, and I'll bet she won't notice." The crisis was over! Thank God for grandmothers who can sew! The trousers were restored to normalcy and it must have been several months later that my mother remarked that my trousers looked as if it might have had a tear in it—to which my grandmother replied, "Mmm." Did my mother know? Had Nan told her about my dilemma? I never found out. But Nan was no telltale!

In the era in which we live I often feel sad for children who are separated by long distances from their grandparents. My grandmother was the light of my life in my early years. We now live in times when debates take place as to the "rights of grandparents," and whenever I hear this debate, I am saddened that we have reached this stage in the world in which we live.

In my own life, I have no doubt my grandmother played a very important role in my Catholic formation. She taught me many things. When I visited the Holy Land—a long time after Nan had been called from this world—I remembered my grandmother by the Lake of Galilee. She was a great storyteller and her imparting of the story of the miraculous draft of fish left nothing further to imagine. She had it all for the young mind, including the look on Peter's face! She told me too about the Valley of Josaphat and how God would line people up at the last day, and separate the good from the wicked. "And you and I will be smiling," she said, "because God will have us right by Himself."

Today the secular has invented its own stories, but mostly they are tales without God. And as far as I am concerned, I had the better part. My grandmother's stories would help me throughout a lifetime. And her tales were founded on revealed truth. Nan accepted her faith as it had been passed on to her. She gave it to her children, and she shared it also with her grandchildren, creating memories for them that would enhance their journey through life.

Nan was a believer. We lived two and one half miles from church. I can never remember her missing Mass until the latter days of her life. If the buggy wasn't going, she walked. Once a month she faithfully went to confession. Occasionally I walked with her She would don her black overcoat and carry her umbrella, and I had the sure knowledge that she would be back in a little less than two hours. Even before my own first confession I knew that she was "going to confession" and that somehow or other it was a meeting with a forgiving God. I knew it was important to her to go, although I couldn't conceive in any way, shape, or form how Nan could commit a sin!

Chapter Three:
Faith Steeped in History

I was six years old when the long shadow of the future cast itself back toward me. A close relative of my mother—John O'Neill—was ordained to the priesthood at Maynooth Seminary. His first Mass was celebrated in the parish church in his native Killala. I well remember, even though I was barely five years old, the journey by horse and buggy to Killala Church that morning long ago to be with my family at Father John's first Mass.

Killala is one of the oldest towns in Mayo. It stands on the north Mayo coast. From my youth I remember that it had wonderful, warmhearted people who were always concerned about their neighbors. It was, and still is, a historic town. There is something aged about Killala, and perhaps something changeless. The town of my childhood has not changed; only the names are different, and the stores are either closed down or have been taken over by successors who ply different trades. The population was always small and still is, consisting of probably less than one thousand people. Perhaps it's the round tower that makes Killala seem aged, or it may be the spire of the Protestant cathedral reaching into the sky. The tower is the oldest building in town and has seen the variations of history down through the centuries since it was first erected, probably in the sixth century.

There is a tradition that it was from Killala that Saint Patrick made his escape from slavery under an Irish landowner to return to France. The story goes that the sailors who were taking a cargo of greyhounds to the continent, first refused to take Patrick on board. Patrick had been herding sheep far away in County Antrim when he made his escape westward and arrived in Killala as the ship was leaving. They left without him but got only a short distance out to sea when a mighty storm broke and they had to return to port. When they departed again, they took Patrick with them, thus concluding his first sojourn in Ireland.

That there is some veracity to the story may lie in the fact that Patrick relates in his memoirs that after he had been ordained priest he "heard the voices of the children of Fohill calling him to return and bring Christ to them." To this day, there is a place named Fohill just across the bay from the town of Killala! And we are sure that Patrick returned to Mayo after he had landed in Ireland on his missionary commitment. A holy well named for his faithful helper Saint Cumeen still exists some miles outside the town.

Killala also boasts one of the finest specimens of round towers in Ireland. I remember looking at the tower as a child and wondering how one might climb to the top—an impossible feat, of course! The builders had made sure of this. The impossibility of climbing was the very purpose of the tower's being.

Round towers are a peculiarity to Ireland. It is believed they originated with the Viking invasions in the ninth or tenth century. History archivists can show that where there is a round tower today, there was a monastery a thousand years ago. The Vikings were ruthless in their assaults on the towns, carrying away the pretty women as well as whatever precious articles they could find. These were times when monasteries flourished. Around Killala today lie the ruins of at least three such conserves, silently testifying to the faith of other times. It is thought that the monks built the round towers. There is no entrance above ground. They could only be reached by tunnel from underneath. With the first sight of a Viking ship the monks dragged their church vessels of silver and gold to the top of the round tower, pulling themselves and their precious cargo to the top by ropes. They came back down when the danger had passed and the ships were seen sailing away.

I make reference to the Killala round tower, because, even to this day, it creates within my mind images of other days and other times. Was God

Well preserved Round Tower, erected c.800 A.D.

foremost in the minds of the people of those early times? You can stand miles away from Killala on a sunny day and see the round tower, still acting like the sentinel it once was, hovering over the local population. Thousands of persons have come and gone, have looked at the ancient monument, have passed on their way, but this aged sentinel still keeps guard. It is fitting that beneath it, within a couple of hundred yards on either side, stand the Catholic and Protestant churches of the town. The round tower witnessed the arrival of the Viking ships in the ninth century, and nine centuries later it would overlook the arrival of a small French fleet into Killala bay as the 1798 rebellion got under way, trying to establish an Irish Republic. From the top of it too, surely can be seen the remains of the medieval monasteries at Rathfran and Moyne. Those monasteries would have been built along with the tower when it first stood guard over the countryside and the ocean. The monks would have prayed and worked within its sights in times when Christianity was not divided. Many of them would have surrendered their lives for their Catholicity when in the middle of the seventeenth century Oliver Cromwell put the people to the sword because of their beliefs, increasing the numbers of the martyrs, and destroyed the monasteries.

A short distance toward Ballina and along the river Moy, stand the remains of the Franciscan abbey of Rosserk. This ruin is regarded as the best preserved ancient monastery in the west of Ireland. Extraordinarily this third-order Franciscan development was established to facilitate the coming together of married people who sought out monastic life without celibacy. I mention these facts because, perhaps despite the inattention of its native inhabitants, the little town of Killala is surrounded by monastic enterprises of other centuries, and I often wonder what response has been given by God to the prayers of the monks, many of whom suffered martyrdom for their beliefs. Much of their blood was shed by Cromwell and his ilk.

The early writer Tertullian once wrote that "the blood of martyrs is the seed of Christianity." I wonder if that seed still sprouts along the shores of the Atlantic in north Mayo. Are the sacrifices of the martyrs still paying dividends around my own native place?

Indeed, on the day my mother was buried, I found solace in looking across the inlet at the tower. It represented everything she had stood for in her life. It had been built to protect and defend the monks who brought Christ to the people and raised their minds and hearts in prayer as a lifetime commitment. It had withstood the ravages of time and tyrants. My mother loved her Christian faith and the Church that had preserved it for her. Beside my father she would sleep in peace beneath the tower's surveilling outlook and in a cemetery once hallowed by Franciscan dedication to the teaching of Jesus.

In more recent times it was the 1798 rebellion that made Killala famous. The Irish had been organizing under their leader Wolfe Tone, a northern Irishman and a Protestant. Tone saw the futility of a religiously divided Ireland. Like the American colonists he also saw that the country would never progress under the influence of British rule. He had spent some years in France, and his arrival back home also heralded republican ideas and an effort to unite the peoples of north and south into one body.

Tone was already dead when the French fleet arrived. He had been incarcerated for his rebellious ideas and died in prison. In my school days, there was a strong conviction that he had been murdered within the prison walls. Before his untimely death he had sought help from the French government. The help arrived in Killala Bay on August 21, 1798—and it arrived in the wrong place. Poverty-stricken Mayo had little means of supporting an uprising. The volunteers were in the north of Ireland, and the French intended to arrive at Derry. They made a mistake in their calculations and landed at Killala, more than a hundred miles away. General Humbert was their leader.

The landing place was Kilcummin on the shores of Killala Bay, six or seven miles distant from the town itself. My father taught close by for twenty-five years after he had left Innishkea. I was to become very familiar with Banagher and Kilcummin and the people so beloved of my father.

Joined by a small group of insurgents with pikes, the invaders advanced on and captured Killala. British troops, we are told, put up stiff opposition around Palmerstown and the narrow straits near Cortoon—places a couple of miles from Killala town—but failed to hold back the invaders. The landing French then headed for a friendly Ballina, six miles up the road. It was well into the night when they reached Ballina. The people of the town were so delighted that they came out with lighted torches to welcome the invaders and show them the way. The way of the French through Ballina is remembered to this day with a road named in Gaelic *Boher na sup* ("the road of the lights"). The surprised British retreated to Castlebar to make a stand. And here they lost again. They were totally routed, and from the battle that took place comes the slogan "the races of Castlebar," indicating the speed of the British retreat and their total defeat.

Success was not to last long, however. General Humbert then led his forces to Ballinamuck—toward the center of the country—where they were soundly thrashed by Lord Cornwallis and his army. Cornwallis had just returned from a disgraceful defeat in the colonies (the United States), and in Ireland he found the recipe for his troubles and the saving of his reputation when he came up against the small French force and the undisciplined Irish insurgents fighting with pikes and with little or no other ammunition. General Humbert and the defeated French forces were sent back to France. The Irish insurgents were not so fortunate. They were hanged by the hundreds. The place name "Gallows Hill" has attached itself to many localities in Mayo, a reminder of past agonies and a time when "might was right."

Among those whose life was taken on a gallows tree in Castlebar was a priest who had little or nothing to do with the invasion. His house happened to be on the French route, and his accusers charged him with aiding and abetting the enemy. A French officer had gone there for information on the direction of the road. Patrick Flanagan, in his relatively recent novel *The Year of the French*, illustrates how easy it was for innocent civilians to find themselves hanging from a gallows tree.

This was how sleepy little Killala, with its kind and charitable people, had entered forever into the pages of Irish history and Irish gallantry. I may add that what gives me great pleasure when I think of Killala is the round tower and the numerous remains of monasteries that once flourished there. I pray that the sacrifices and prayers of those martyred monks will be efficacious for all who live or will ever live in the region.

There was great joy when my cousin John O'Neill was ordained. The Catholic Church was going through a golden era at that time. It was the prayer of almost every mother that her son might be a priest. It has been alleged in modern times that frequently the "vocation" to priesthood belonged to the mother. There were indeed privileges attached to being a member of the clergy. For one thing, they were ordained after a long and comprehensive education. They were highly respected by the people. Most of those they served had no further education than primary school.

However, when all the arguments are weighed, it is my conclusion that Ireland abounded in priests because of the deep faith of its people. And should a mother not wield an influence on the future faith commitment of her son? In Mayo especially, many young men joined in Saint Patrick's dream to "come and bring Christ" to the children all around. His dream and his call certainly affected my own life.

Father John's Mass in Killala parish church and the celebration surrounding it planted within me my own dream of priesthood.

Chapter Four:
The School Inspector

We lived two miles from our parish school. My father's school was five miles away in another direction. He rode his bicycle to work every day of his life.

Many things have changed in north Mayo since my childhood. But one constant is the weather. If you go back and live in that part of Ireland, you will find that the countryside is frequently harassed by Atlantic storms. We had a very tall chimney on our home, its purpose being to create the proper kind of draught that would take out all the smoke. (That it never worked is another story.) I remember the howling in the chimney of a winter's night, sounds that were perhaps even angrier than the raging sea when the mighty windstorms ruffled its waters. There was many a night that my father worried that the entire chimney might come down on us. If it did, it would take the roof with it into our kitchen.

The weather of Ireland leaves much to be desired. The weather in the west of the country may be worst of all. It was through this kind of weather that my father cycled through twenty-five winters, sometimes battling the high winds and rain that made his journey a misery, sometimes being careful to keep his bicycle upright on the solidly frozen roads. And when he got to journey's end, he knew that in the afternoon the same task awaited him as soon as school was out. Extraordinarily, one of his pupils recently related her constant image of him pedaling his bicycle into the wind and rain, head down, determined to defy the storm.

In the morning he would hurry along in the face of wind and weather, since he had to open his school on time. Not infrequently an "inspector" awaited his arrival, his car sitting at the school entryway. The inspector system had been handed down from the days of British ascendancy. In many ways it was a demeaning system. It conveyed the notion that a teacher could not be trusted. Overseers were appointed to visit the schools, examine the children on their knowledge, go through the roll books, and establish the competency of the teacher.

These individuals usually portrayed themselves as unfriendly and the enemy of the teacher. Each teacher was "examined" in this way on a regular basis, every three years or so. In between, the inspector could arrive at any time he chose, even be sitting outside in his car before the school opened in the morning. The heinous system gave rise to inspectors' nicknames such as "six-months Pete" arising from their threats to teachers following a school visit. ("Improve in six months, or you are out!") I was to find out all about this in later life in my short time as a teacher with the Marist Brothers. My experience with school inspectors is not a cherished memory.

One of the requisites for the teacher was that each day's program was to be set forth in writing. This was a humongous task in a school where a teacher had more than one class. In my father's case, he taught at least three classes in the course of any given day, with perhaps ten to twelve children in each class.

Since I did not attend my father's school, I can give no account of any examinations either by the inspector of the teacher or children. Kilfian School was much closer than the school in Banagher—just about two miles from our home as against the five miles to Banagher. In common with all the other pupils, we walked those two miles every morning on the way to school and every afternoon when school ended.

An incident that took place in our school is still quite vivid, remaining in my memories for all those years since I was just about six years old. An inspector arrived one day when I was in first class. He looked at the class and whispered something to the teacher. I was picked out and taken to the front of the classroom. Then, he seated himself on a chair like Pontius Pilate and proceeded to speak to me in the Irish language.

These were the times when it was requisite that each school was compelled to teach the Irish language to the pupils. I have a feeling to this day that I was picked on. The inspector knew who I was and wanted to see for himself, in another school, how fluent my father's children were in Irish. It was well known that my father had a great love for the Irish language, and he had taken part in the founding of a school for the teaching of the native tongue. We spoke the Irish language at certain mealtimes in our home, and even at that young age I could comprehend the language very well. It was possible too that the inspector believed my father had been on the wrong side during the Civil War. I was the son of a "blueshirt"!

The situation in which I found myself that day was farcical, and that is being charitable. The conversation was imaginary, only the inspector did not say so. In Irish he said to this child of six, "Look at the mouse." I knew exactly what he was saying, and I looked for the mouse, but there was no mouse. However, I felt like a mouse must surely feel in the sights of a mighty cat. Here I was, standing before this big monster sitting in a chair, a frightened child of six, trying to make sense of the situation, with the entire school looking on! Although I understood very well what he was saying, none of it made any sense, and I was not about to answer. I did what any child would do: I remained silent. I saw no mouse. I was not prepared to say what the mouse looked like since he wasn't there, nor was I prepared to discuss his color for the same reason. Even at six, were I to discuss anything, it would be the folly of the "monster" who was quizzing me. I never knew how the matter ended for the teacher, but since she was a very good teacher and her reputation went untarnished, I have always believed the inspector was, in modern terminology, "discriminating" against me—or rather my father.

Normally we arrived home from school before my father. We had to walk two miles, and he had to cycle five, which might have evened up the time the journeys took. But on the way home my father took time to chat with everyone he met along the way, and since he was well known along the five-mile route, he had a myriad of friends who took great pleasure in chatting with him. And at home the conversation with my mother at dinner was frequently related to the "news" he had gleaned on his way.

My father was both a teacher and a farmer. Farming calls for work in the fields, and I have memories of my father coming home from school in the summertime, eating his dinner, and than going out to work in the fields, especially in hay-saving season. He would spend many hours at this laborious work, and looking back I am always amazed at his energies that allowed him not only to do a five-mile journey each way every day on his bicycle, uphill and down, perform a day's teaching, and afterward be able to attend to manual labor sometimes until the sun dropped below the horizon. Will his like and the generation that bred him ever pass this way again?

Chapter Five:
God Reigns!

There was a picture of the Sacred Heart on the center wall of our kitchen. The kitchen was not too large, but not only was it the kitchen, it also constituted the living room of our home. We gathered there as a family, ate all our meals there, played there as children, and later sat around the open kitchen fire at nighttime as the adults discussed world events. Whenever we returned to the kitchen from outside, the Sacred Heart always seemed to be looking down on us. It was difficult to really forget the presence of God.

In front of the Sacred Heart picture a lamp was always lit in the daytime. This little kerosene lamp stood on a stand and was tended to every day by my grandmother after she moved in with us. Since my grandmother was an early riser, she lit the lamp in the morning—after first replacing the oil if that was necessary—and last thing at night she took down the little lamp with the red globe and quenched it before retiring for the night. It was not judged safe to have a light burning in the house while the family slept. The lighted lamp was to serve as a reminder of God's presence in our family.

Each evening we prayed the rosary as a family. It was toward the picture of the Sacred Heart we faced, a proof that His picture represented His presence in the house. Just as we did around the dinner table, we had our own places for the rosary. Mine was by the fireside, nice and comfortable of a winter's evening. Each person knelt and leaned against the back of a chair. Younger children were sent to bed long before the rosary. I remember how grown up I felt when finally the day came that I was allowed to stay up for the rosary.

My father would announce the mysteries and lead us in prayer. When the rosary was finished, my mother took over with what were called the "trimmings." These were additional prayers that were recited at the end of the rosary. The very first was always the Litany of Our Lady. My mother never used a book to recite this litany. But she never had a problem remembering the various titles of Our Lady. This is a feat of memory I have never been able to master. But up to her dying day my mother never had any hesitation in reciting the litany without help. When the litany was over, my mother would add additional prayers—for someone who was ill or for one of my sisters at school who faced an examination. On the first Friday of every month she would recite the Prayer of Consecration of the Human Race to the Sacred Heart. In reflective moments I can still hear her reciting that prayer with the words that always remained in my memory: "We are thine, and thine we wish to be." In one way or other those words came home to me even in childhood! "We are thine." I was reminded I belonged to God. "Thine we wish to be." A desire for God should pervade the heart of every follower of Jesus. When World War Two broke out in 1939 my mother added a long prayer for peace that was also addressed to the Sacred Heart. This prayer was recited at every family rosary until the war ended six years later.

Until I was about the age of six, my mother always tucked me into bed. This was a wonderful time of day for me. Mother would say my night prayers with me, night after night, for what seems to me many years. She had a wonderful memory, and every night at bedtime she repeated the same prayers in exactly the same order, until she came to the final prayer: "Father, into your hands I commend my spirit, Lord Jesus, receive my soul. Amen." Finally I knew them all by heart. Then came the time when she told me to "say your prayers and go to bed." All good things must come to an end! But I still say those prayers last thing at night, seven decades later. There is no replacing a mother's love or the effect her faith has on her children.

But my mother was a teacher, not only by word but also by example. We children walked to school, and we took our time walking home.

Frequently, we would meet my mother, on what could be any day of the week, cycling to church. She was a lover of the blessed sacrament, and whenever time allowed, she would take her bicycle and cycle the two miles to church to make a visit to the blessed sacrament. Since we dallied along the way coming home, it was not unusual for her to pass us out again before we got home.

She did her shopping on Saturdays. There was a bus service that ran about a half mile from our house. She would take the bus to town and get all her groceries for the week. Frequently one of us children would accompany her. It was a great opportunity indeed, because it meant not only an afternoon in the big town but also more than one treat to candies and all the good things that being with my mother on such an occasion involved. Sometimes she would take time to have a meal in a restaurant. Eating in such an establishment was in itself something wonderful for a youngster. But there was always one custom she never forgot. She would always go to make a visit in the cathedral. First she would kneel before the main altar, then she would move to the statue of Our Lady and then to Saint Joseph and sometimes another statue. To me as a child, her visits seemed interminable, but as I grew older, I came to realize she most likely spent no more than twenty minutes in the church. More important, as a child I came to understand that something drew her to the church. That special "something" was her understanding of the Eucharistic Presence of the Lord.

Many years later, after my father's death, my mother moved to Dublin to live with my sister. Her devotion to prayer never subsided. It might even have grown stronger. She rarely went to less than two masses on Sunday in Dublin. She also found a church that held a perpetual novena to Our Lady, Help of Christians, every Saturday. It didn't matter that this church was miles away. It didn't matter that it took her several hours to get there and back. After lunch on Saturdays she took a bus downtown, transferred to another bus, and walked the last quarter of mile or so to the church to catch the novena. This she did Saturday after Saturday until her health failed and she could no longer leave the house. And during the years of her failing health, she liked nothing better than to sit with us and recite the rosary before we went to bed. It could never be said that her commitment had weakened in her older years.

You will recall we lived on a farm. Those were times when every farmer kept a couple of milch cows. My father always stocked from five to eight. Those cows kept us supplied with fresh milk every day and I well remember that learning to milk a cow was an accomplishment almost as exciting as learning to ride a bicycle. Naturally, seven or eight cows gave us more milk than we needed for daily use. My mother would skim the cream from the extra milk and keep it in a large crock to be churned later on. The churning took place about every two weeks when the cream was poured into the churn—a round, barreled wooden instrument with a handle on the outside. When turned with a circular movement this handle helped move the cream about within the churn, and in fifteen minutes or less the cream began to form itself into butter. The butter milk that remained was then drained off and my mother would make the butter into rolls or patties for use by the family. I remember the churning for two reasons. There was a custom that if someone happened to visit the home while the churning was taking place they would utter a prayer, "God bless the work." Then the visitor would immediately take a turn twisting the handle for a minute or two before taking a seat. With the arrival of the butter in the churn my mother would always take a pinch of salt and drop it into the newly made butter while making the sign of the cross three times as she released the salt from her fingers. This was to acknowledge that the new butter was a blessing of God. Unfortunately, butter making has disappeared to a large extent in modern Ireland and with it the beautiful religious reminders of God's reign.

My father's devotion, of course, was complementary to that of my mother. He too loved the rosary and always carried it on his person. He had a great love for the Passion of the Lord, and on many an occasion he arrived at church a little early to give himself a chance of making the stations. This was a practice of his particularly during Lent.

His wake was attended by many of the people he had taught. One of them told me that it was not unusual for my father to arrive at his school in the morning on his bicycle, rosary in hand. He had been praying as he cycled along. One Saturday morning when I was suffering from a child's headache, my father came to my bedside and told me to recite the prayer to Our Lady "O Mary, conceived without sin, pray for us who have recourse to thee." My headache did indeed go away, but the prayer has been recited in my life many times since. It was the beginning of a frequent daily invocation of the Mother of God.

During my time at Mary's Shrine in Orlando, many moons further on, I made the rosary a mission of the Shrine. I took a few minutes at every Sunday Mass to reflect on the power of the rosary—a power, I may say, that has always directed my life. The rosary ring has come into its own in modern times. Supposedly the ring came from the penal days in Ireland when possession of any Catholic symbol was grounds for a sentence of prison or perhaps even death. But in these times of ours, with so much hustle and bustle, the rosary ring serves a wonderful purpose. How often I have been stuck in traffic and occupied my time fruitfully by using the ring to pray the rosary. And I want to tell you that whenever I drive, even a moderate journey, the rosary ring is always in my fingers. On a hundred-mile journey I am likely to pray the entire twenty decades of the rosary.

In all my years of priesthood I cannot recall any family that prays the rosary on a daily basis, although I have met a few who have prayed it together now and again. So frequently we hear the arguments about prayer in our public schools. The question that arises in my own mind is, what about prayer at home? There are no restrictions there, no civil liberties to be interfered with, and no civil liberties to interfere with us! It seems to me that for the most part prayer may have been downgraded in the home, and society is the worse for it. After all, the family is the first unit of society, and for followers of Jesus it should also be the holiest unit.

Looking back, in our home there was prayer. Coupled with it there was discipline. Every child knew the limits. And let me say they were confined limits. Prayer and discipline are part of the learning process of growing up. Through them we learn lessons about ourselves, how to respect ourselves, and how to care for the feelings of those around us. Discipline is a virtue that governs our everyday actions right through life, as well as our relationships with each other. The media of my Irish homeland in modern times has certainly been antichurch and possibly at times anti-God. Writers have proclaimed time and time again "the slavery" to which the Church has subjected the Irish people.

I must say I never felt that slavery! But I do recall a murder case in the middle of the country when I was a youngster. Murder was so unusual at that time that every moment of the trial was reported, taking up several pages of the daily national papers. Today, there is probably a murder every day in Ireland—maybe even more. And the report gets three lines in the daily press. How times have changed! Ah, but the numbers of people attending Mass in Ireland have dropped in recent times, religious orders who teach have all but disappeared, in general the influence of the Church has waned—and the nation is the worse off for the diminished awareness of the presence of God. (In recent times, Church scandals have taken their toll in Ireland, indefensibly so, but it is always important to remember that faith is not placed in human beings but in the Son of God Himself. His is the only perfection.)

In the United States, it seems to me, the influence of the Church has been deteriorating for decades. If as Catholics we wish to make an imprint on society, we must stand for our beliefs. Righteousness comes from our relationship with God. In the past fifty years we have dropped prayer from family life (our own fault), we have in great measure given up on discipline (our own fault), and we have allowed school systems to install a new sexual morality that is no morality at all. Worse still, we have consistently elected representatives to government who do not share our beliefs or values. Loyalty to party takes precedence over loyalty to Jesus, the Lord. The separation of church and state has invaded our homes as well as our personal lives. Public prayer is accepted as being all right in church. Private prayer is seen to be useful when we face a problem that seems insoluble, and otherwise to be neglected. These are the philosophies pushing themselves in our modern world.

I will always remember our family rosary, the Sacred Heart picture on the kitchen wall, the little burning red lamp that reminded us as children that God was always present, and my mother's calm recital of the consecration with the words "we are thine, and thine we wish to be." Through those home prayer routines I believe my faith was deeply implanted, and my future life as God's servant in the priesthood was put firmly on course.

I remember too the promise of Jesus: "I am with you always." Sincere followers of Jesus can make a difference. If we walk with God, Sodom and Gomorrah will be overcome. There won't be need to build another ark.

Chapter Six:
A Meeting on the Bridge

〜

wo miles from our home there was a bridge. It was a landmark bridge. It stood, (and still stands) strategically between a river and the rest of the mainland. The river is the Owenmore. It enters the sea near Killala, having meandered for fifty miles or so through the boglands and fields of northwest Mayo. To get to Killala or parts beyond, from the shore side of the river, one must first cross the Owenmore, known by different names in various localities. French troops under General Humbert crossed this bridge—then a wooden structure—after the French landed in Killala Bay in August 1798. As it approaches the sea a few miles from Killala, it is also known as the Palmerstown River, a name taken from the locality through which it flows.

Palmerstown of course comes from the generic name, *Palmers*, given to British settlers on Irish lands. Britain colonized Ireland over a period of hundreds of years. Before the arrival of the British the Irish had been occupying and working their land for centuries. They owned the land. It was theirs by right. But Britain rewarded its soldier "adventurers" with large tracts of land in Ireland. The only way the land could become available was to take it from the rightful owners, leaving them by the roadside or imposing intolerable taxes on property leased back. In many situations the native Irish left, having lost their property. But in many instances they remained behind and became tenant farmers, paying "rents" to their new owners for what was once theirs.

Some of the new landlords were compassionate and caring for their tenants. Many were not. Exorbitant rents were charged frequently, and when the tenant could not pay, the entire family was evicted. The fact that there was nowhere for them to go or any further means of subsistence was of no importance to the landlord or the government. Worse still, a tenant who might appear to be doing well would have the rent raised for no reason. Bailiffs were sent around to collect the rent or to bring about an eviction. The bailiff frequently represented a landlord living in London or some other part of Britain. Laws were passed taxing improvements—for example, extra windows in a home. The more windows, the higher the taxation. Life for the tenant farmer had become a nightmare by the middle of the nineteenth century.

The desperate situation caused the formation of the Land League by a Mayoman, Michael Davitt, who was born in Straide, not a great distance from Killala. Davitt knew all about eviction, his own family having lost their holdings, forcing them to move to England. Years later Davitt returned to the place of his birth but not before spending time in an English jail for his philosophies. The story of the jail sentence is a strange one, in that Davitt had lost an arm as a youngster working in an English factory. He was found guilty of agreeing to carry a bag of guns from a London railway station and get them to Ireland, an unusual task for a one-armed man. Be that as it may, his time in prison might have been time well spent as it allowed Davit to consolidate his ideas and strengthen his aspirations to return to Ireland.

He eventually did come back and found conditions even worse than before his family had left. The tyranny of the "landed gentry" bothered him, and he decided to throw his hat in the political arena. On his return, he advised his followers not to work unless they were paid a fair wage, even when faced with eviction. The first real trial of Davitt's theory came in the fall of 1880 with a Captain Boycott who managed large acreage in south Mayo. The owner, the Earl of Erne, lived in England. "Fair rent," "fixity of tenure" for farmers holding property, and "fair wages" were at that time among the political aspirations of the Irish politician Charles Stuart Parnell, and he was ably supported in the west of Ireland by Michael Davitt. Boycott had a strong sense of allegiance to his employer living far away in England, and when he refused to listen to the exhortations of

Davitt or Parnell, tenants and workers refused to have anything to do with harvesting his crops. Soldiers were employed as harvesters with disastrous results. From the situation a new word was given to the English language: to *boycott* would mean "to ignore," "not to render help," "to ostracize."

Here I would observe that the people of Mayo were the first to stand and give challenge to the racketeering landlords who shamelessly abused their positions of power over their Irish tenants. The Land League established by Davitt proved a great success, bringing about vast change in the administration of Irish land holdings. It beggars belief for modern times that on April 20, 1879, an estimated fifteen to twenty thousand persons turned out for a meeting of tenant farmers at Irishtown (near Claremorris), County Mayo. That's almost as many people as now travel by automated transportation to the Connacht Football Final in Castlebar! How did all those people get together? What sacrifices did they make to achieve their goals? How long did it take for them to make their way home? Indeed, as a native of Mayo I am proud of the fact that the Irish Land League was itself founded in the Imperial Hotel in Castlebar, on October 21, 1879. The "races of Castlebar" had taken place a century before but the historic founding of the Land League evidenced that the people of Mayo were still prepared to stand for their rights.

If there was a place known as Palmerstown, and a bridge by the same name, it can easily be deduced there were "landlords" with tenant farmers in the area. Monasteries had once flourished here under the surveillance of the round tower previously mentioned. Now times had changed. Not only were the monasteries destroyed, their golden days gone for ever, but now new owners were on the land, and as far as the people were concerned, the religion they practiced was not that of Saint Patrick. Indeed, the stones of the monasteries had been used to help build some of the pretentious mansions of the new occupants! And the once-proud native was now a tenant, paying a rent and submitting to a different culture. All that remained as a reminder of better times were the ruins of the monasteries that had been destroyed by the Cromwellians way back in the middle of the seventeenth century.

We don't need to enter here into the history of the landlords around Killala. In time many of them became "more Irish than the Irish themselves."

Others thrived on their ascendancy. The feared name of one, a lady named Miss Gardiner (was her first name ever known to anyone?), still lives in the lore of the area. So bad was she and so many evictions did she bring about that storytellers record that at her death her coffin would not adjust itself to the prepared grave, and she was buried in an upright position! That lore, of course, merely reflects her standing with the local people.

Palmerstown Bridge, once a gathering spot on Sunday afternoons.

The locals had no choice other than to work for their landlords. There are horror stories of the work these people had to do and the long hours they put in with very little recompense. Many, in the course of their work, became very submissive. They learned the hard way to show respect for their employers. Whenever the landlord passed by, on horseback or in his carriage, he was to be saluted with the doffing of the cap if a man, or a bow if a woman. This kind of servitude became so ingrained in the life of many natives that in time it became a natural reaction. The peasant had to acknowledge with humility the superiority and greater dignity of the landowner.

One of the remarkable facts of Irish history is that when the 1916 rebellion was successfully concluded with the treaty of 1921, and most of the island of Ireland at last governed its own people, the landlords were not removed and were allowed to retain the property in their possession. Quite a few were given large sums of money by the new Irish government to move to other parts. Many of them, who have never set foot in Ireland, are still being paid "ground rent" for the use of their land or buildings. Occasionally an advertisement for sale of a home will appear in a newspaper, stating that the property is a "freehold." This statement evaluates the property, because it indicates no ground rent has to be paid.

The leaders of the rebellion were not the vengeful kind. For many reasons they did not wish to become embroiled in a new and unwinnable war over property rights. They decided to leave well enough alone. I recall seeing, on a wall outside one landlord's estate, a slogan painted in easily readable letters: "The road for the fox and the land for the people." When all is said and done, the Irish fight was not only about religion or a particular hatred for the conqueror but also a battle to regain lost lands. And when the battle was over, "Planters"—once a sign of British dominance over the island—still held many of the properties allotted to their forebears as a reward for their involvement in British adventurism!

My father came from a family of rebels. In Mayo my father had sought safety from the same kind of criminality being imposed on him as had happened with his younger brother. He remembered the fate of his brother, who had died without ever speaking to anyone again after the torturing he had received. The martyred Patrick was close to his heart.

One day, it so happened that as my father cycled over "the bridge," a horse-drawn carriage of the gentry was coming the other way. It is customary in Ireland to greet those one meets on the road. Those were days when almost all travel was on foot, by horse, or bicycle. My father bade "good-day" to the people in the passing carriage. That was all he did. It was a courtesy he would extend to any other fellow traveler.

There were quite a few people on the bridge that Sunday afternoon. It was a favorite meeting place for the locals from as far away as seven or ten miles. They would gather to chat about the week's happenings (there were no radios in Ireland in those days) or entertain each other playing roadside games. Now and again, someone might take a boat down to the river and allow the venturesome ones to row with them over the waters. In my own youth, I joined in the games and watched the boatman.

On this occasion, the carriage was on its way over the bridge. Those on the bridge stood as if at attention. The men doffed their caps. The few women bowed. The carriage moved past. This was fifteen years after Irish independence. My father could not contain himself. He dismounted from his bicycle and signaled to the men that he wanted to say something. He might have been an outsider from Cork, but he was also "Master Harte." In those days the local schoolmaster always got attention.

The "economic war," a trade war between Britain and Ireland, was raging at the time. When the first DeValera government was elected, it decided to go back on the articles of the treaty signed in 1921 and refused to pay annuities to Britain for land held in Ireland. The resultant dispute, which lasted five years from 1932 to 1937 or thereabouts, led to Britain imposing tariffs on Irish meat products, whereupon the Irish government refused to export any meat to Britain. Naturally the farming community suffered severely, and the small farmers of the west of Ireland were reduced to sheer poverty with no market for their farm animals. An inflamed hostility to Britain at that time was a natural outcome of the dispute.

So on the bridge that day the men listened to what my father had to say. He reminded them of how they had acknowledged the passing carriage. "We have paid a price," he said, "for our freedom. We have our own government now. We are all equal. Why do you doff your caps to these people?" He pointed to the carriage moving away some two hundred yards. "You wouldn't doff your caps to me, and I wouldn't expect it," he said. "And there is no need for you to show slavish attention to anyone." He stood for a while, talking over the incident with a few men who wanted further discussion. Then he remounted his bicycle and continued on his way home.

It was not the only time he discussed with me—even in my very young years— his impatience with those who found it difficult to rid their being of the servitude instilled by the tyrant. The fate of his brother Patrick was always to the fore in his memories. But there was also another lesson. God made us to love and respect each other. That respect is a two-way street.

We don't allow ourselves to live lives of servitude. The example of Jesus is best. "I will not call you servants but friends," and this charitable theme should govern all human relations.

He did not make converts of all on the bridge that day. The word got back to the landlord. One of his workers present on the bridge would later be appointed to oversee the distribution of bogland for local farmers. In those days the bog was important. It provided the source for winter heat. The turf had to be cut and spread until it was dry. Then it had to be hauled from the bog. Getting into the bog could be a problem. Before machinery arrived in much later years the donkey was well known as the best animal to traverse boglands. Somehow or other the donkey managed to extract himself from the soft terrain and keep on going. And so the animal was used to bring the harvested turf out to be stacked roadside where the owner could easily load it on to a larger carrier. But in my father's case the measure of bog allotted to him was as far into the bog as it could have been. Sometimes even the tireless donkey could find the going underfoot difficult or impossible. When the turf was ready to be moved came the big challenge. Getting out the turf would always constitute a problem. And my father would often remark that he paid dearly for his "discussion on the bridge."

History repeats itself! In my own life I have often paid the price for standing for what is right. And weaker individuals will always be vengeful in their own way. But the truth spoken fearlessly always brings its own reward. My father came from a fearless breed and was never one to agree with wrong when he knew what was right. He believed too in his own dignity, a belief that was passed on to his children.

Chapter Seven:
A Parish Mission and a Picture

Example, they say, is better than precept. The example I am about to narrate has remained in my memory all my life. There was a "mission" in our home parish of Kilfian. I was probably no older than six or seven. The mission was a special time for the parishioners. They were expected to attend the mission, listen to special talks by the priests who had come to preside over the occasion, go to confession some time during the week, and generally make it a week of prayer, reflection, and repentance.

In those days in Ireland electricity had not yet come to rural areas. There was a morning session of the mission and an evening session which was better attended. But since everything had to be over before the fading daylight (electricity had not yet reached country areas in the west at that time), the evening session would take place around four o'clock on a springtime evening. In those less than wealthy days, local farmers, most of whom owned very small acreage, would simply end their day's work early in order to attend the mission. These were times of wonderful faith in Ireland.

Most parish missions were given by the Redemptorist Order. To me, as a child, a Redemptorist priest looked formidable. He wore a long cassock that seemed to differ from that of the parish priest. Tucked into a belt around his waist was a large crucifix, and a mammoth set of rosary beads hung from the crucifix. The Redemptorist looked the epitome of religion, and there seemed something about him that made heaven a difficult place to reach. To my child's mind the Redemptorist was saying the only way to God was through austerity and perhaps suffering, and heaven was a hard destination at which to arrive! At my young age I didn't find the teaching, as I saw it, very attractive. Redemptorists have changed since my childhood. Or perhaps my understanding of them changed with maturity. There is nothing about them now that is discouraging. They are a friendly group of men—as they always were—doing their best to fulfill their vocation in a world that needs them very much, promoting Christ's kingdom to the best of their ability.

Two Redemptorists served at each mission. One was always gentle and kind and beloved by the people. The other preached "fire and brimstone" and everlasting punishment and came across as harsh. Naturally, when it came to confession time, the gentler man had far more penitents. That did not bother the brimstone priest. When confessions were taking place, he would leave his confessional, come out into the church, and usher to his own place many who had no desire to confess to him. As I look back, he had to do this. The practice of his order called for what was happening, a sort of charade in a way, and it was important to help out his companion. Now I realize that in the next mission the tables might be turned. He might be the gentle one, and the other might be preaching hell and brimstone.

Whenever a mission was taking place, traders of religious articles would set up tents outside the church. For them it was an occasion for profit, but it was also a practice that was approved by the parish priest. A rural people with limited transportation available to them did not have the opportunity of getting to town often, and furthermore religious articles shops were few in number. In Catholic tradition it has always been customary to place reminders of our faith within our homes. Much later in life I would remember the mission, and the memory would influence me to institute a religious articles store at the Shrine in Orlando. And from this place, religious artifacts—reminders of the God of love—would find their way to persons and homes throughout the entire United States and beyond.

My mother bought a picture of her favorite devotion—"Our Lady of Perpetual Help"—a devotion that was also promoted by the Redemptorist fathers. At one of his mission talks the priest had narrated the history of the picture, how it came to be, and what it represented. The loose sandal on the foot of the divine Child as he looks upward at an angel bearing a cross indicates the fear that filled His heart as He saw the representation before Him, a presentiment of His future agony and death. Mother placed that picture over my bed. It hung there for many years, long after I left home.

Extraordinarily, after my ordination, when I arrived at my first assignment—feeling, I must confess, no great excitement about the appointment—one of the priests who would be working with me looked into the tiny bedroom I would occupy and remarked that there was no religious object anywhere in the room. He went off and returned with a picture of Our Lady of Perpetual Help, smaller in size but otherwise an exact replica of the one that hung over my bed in childhood days! It seemed to me at the time Our Lady was saying, "Welcome home. I'm glad you are here."

That picture is still with me in my bedroom to this day. And every night before retiring I thank her for her motherly love. I am also reminded of my calling to promote the kingdom of her divine Son. Her picture at my bedside has endured for half a century now and, together with the one purchased by my mother, has assured me of the protection of the Mother of God for almost all of my life. And just as with the Lord Himself, we must all face the cross at some time or other, but we live with the certain knowledge of "all things working together unto good."

Another aspect of the parish mission and the times comes to mind too. In the mid-thirties, the Ireland that had struggled for freedom from foreign interference had just come through what was termed "the economic war," the trade war with Britain. Ireland exported meat for many years to its neighbor. Britain was the only market. Disagreement between the governments, already mentioned, resulted in an embargo being placed by the government of the Republic on all Irish meats, dead or alive, to Britain. We will not comment here on the wisdom or otherwise of the government's decision at the time. But the resultant poverty to smaller farmers because of this decision was widespread. There was a shortage of money and in many cases an inability to procure the necessities of life.

Long before the British departure an impoverished people took refuge in drowning their sorrows with an illegal "down on the farm" alcohol that was called "poteen," the equivalent of the American "moonshine." In the

Ireland of the thirties there was plenty of reason in the west of the country to forget the cruel realties of life by turning to the beverage that came from the "poteen still" (pronounced "putcheen still").

The Redemptorists addressed this problem, and following a fiery sermon the priest invited those who produced poteen to bring their stills to the churchyard on a particular afternoon, no questions asked, and take part in a communal destruction of what he called an occasion of sin. There is no way I could see this happening in modern times. But in those days the summons of the missioner was respected, and his appeal was successful. There was no follow-up by the police, no further discussion at any level, and temperance reigned long after the missionaries had departed. That is not to say the making of poteen had stopped entirely, but the problems it caused were greatly diminished. Can anyone imagine a priest making this sort of call from his pulpit in the modern-day world?

Many years later one humorous individual told me his father had not made poteen but did drink it. So on that Sunday he went to the church just to find out who the suppliers were, since he felt some of them would be back in the market soon. And he told me with a grin on his face that his father was dismayed to see such wonderful instruments of merriment being destroyed!

Chapter Eight:
Supernatural Crisis and the Joy of the Lord

ℳiss Clarke was the teacher who prepared us to make our first confession and receive our first Holy Communion. She remained Miss Clarke until the end of her days. Hard to believe that in that era of Irish life, a female teacher who married had to give up her teaching career immediately. Miss Clarke never married and was a gentle soul who rarely used any kind of punitive methods and left warm memories with her students long after they had departed her classes.

On one occasion while in kindergarten, I had refused to eat my breakfast in a childhood contest of wills with my mother. My mother won of course! You didn't get the upper hand on my mother at that age, and probably not at any age. I was packed off to school without any breakfast, but what I didn't know was that my mother had sent a note to Miss Clarke informing her of the situation and asking her to look out for me. In no time Miss Clarke had cajoled me into eating the breakfast my mother had sent with my older sisters. It was a learning experience for a young boy: Do what mother says. Hunger strikes don't work!

In preparing my companions and me for our first Holy Communion, Miss Clarke had a good helper in my mother. Mother had a keen awareness of sin—or so it seemed to me. She wanted to make sure that my first confession would cover all the bases. For quite a few years after my first confession, when she sent me to confession, she also examined my conscience for me, pointing out, mostly, my "disobediences" and perhaps the times I had been angry or contrary. In those days I did indeed have a hot temper as well as a mind of my own. (Whatever happened to those traits?) Like most children it was not always easy for me to agree with my parents' wishes!

For my first confession Miss Clarke had outlined the procedure very well. She made sure we knew the formula: "Bless me, Father, for I have sinned." And she went over the Act of Contrition with us so often that it would be virtually impossible not to know it. My mother did the same thing at home, as well as going over the "possible sins" and some that she said needed to be confessed! I was well prepared when the day came. I knew as much about sin as any theologian, and I was barely six.

We went to the church, and the parish priest arrived. There was a communion rail across the front, as was the case in all churches before the Second Vatican Council. Father Davis, our parish priest, a kindly man who always seemed to wear a heavy black overcoat, sat with his back to the communion rail, but in plain view of all within the church. Most likely this was to help the young penitent who would not have to face the priest in a dark confessional.

One by one my young companions went to make their very first confession. I watched carefully as each knelt at the rail. Now and again the priest would turn his head and say something. Then he would make the sign of the cross, and I knew he was giving absolution, because that is what Miss Clarke and my mother had said. From where I waited, the priest didn't seem to be anyone to be afraid of, and when my turn came, I went forward and knelt at the railing. Now it was my turn to confess my sins.

Suddenly I found I was not ready for this ordeal at all! I might know what to say, I might recognize sin in my life, and I might be prepared to accept my penance. Ah! But nobody had really explained what the presence of an old priest and having to confess to him would do to one's psyche! From a distance the priest had looked tame enough. But when you can hear him breathe, can hear him speak as he bids you tell your sins, everything changes. He could have been my father. Indeed, I think I would have rather confessed to my father! This priest was right here beside me!

My mother had helped me examine my conscience, and I knew what to say. But for some reason I couldn't say it. Like King Belshazzar in the Book of Daniel who saw the wrist and fingers writing on the wall of his palace, this child's "face blanched, his thoughts terrified him, his hip joints shook and his knees knocked." The "list" of sins simply fled from my memory. There was nothing to tell at this time, and nobody, not even Saint Michael himself, could have helped me out of this dilemma! The preparation was about telling sins, not about forgetting sins! My memory was gone. My mind whirled faster than any racing-car engine. I was a drowning person grasping at a straw for survival—except there wasn't even a straw!

A serious decision had to be made, and it had to be made now. Somewhere in the recesses of my mind there were "sins" to confess. But I couldn't remember a thing. It was a crisis of supernatural proportions that only the supernatural could resolve! But where was the supernatural now?

The priest waited. "Well, my son," he said, "what sins do you have to confess?"

My heart fluttered. My tongue was twisted like a rope on the riggings of a sinking ship! No sound was coming! The priest waited. At last I was able to speak, and sounds came. I simply said "Father, I have no sins."

The priest made no gesture of impatience. He said something to the effect that I was a "good boy," gave me a blessing, and let me go. The ordeal was over. Nobody but the priest ever knew what I confessed, or didn't confess! Looking back, it was the best confession of my life! ,

There have since been times when, on leaving the confessional, I have not been satisfied with the content of my confession or the manner in which I confessed. But my first confession was truly worthy! What I had forgotten was surely unimportant!

The preparations went on apace for my first communion. I had good teachers. At school Miss Clarke instilled the teaching of the "real Presence" into my young mind. At home my mother cooperated with her, going over and over again the teachings of the Church in regard to this most important sacrament. Now and again my father lent a hand too, asking questions or teaching me a prayer. When the big day came, I was really ready.

I don't remember the date, but I know it was a Saturday in June. I was a precocious child, barely six years old yet. The day came wet. My mother got me ready. There was no particular recognition of the importance of the occasion apart from the preparatory work. First Communion was just that—a great day in the life of a child, but remarkable only in its spiritual aspects. Besides, an economically poor country did not lend itself to costly celebrations. My mother took me to church on this wet Saturday morning on the back carrier of her bicycle.

I had to fast from midnight the previous night. Mass was at nine in the morning. It was a two-mile ride, and I had no idea of the hardship on my mother as the rains came down on both of us. But my mother was combatting it all efficiently and without complaint.

Father Davis said the Mass quietly, and when the time came, we advanced to the altar, aided by Miss Clarke, to receive for the first time the body of the Lord. In my soul I felt this sacrament was connected somehow with priesthood. I am sure I understood that when the host was placed on my tongue, a wondrous happening was taking place: I was meeting Jesus in person. Twenty-five years later as I lay prostrate before the altar of All Hallows Seminary during my ordination ceremony, I would remember this first coming of Jesus to my soul. That coming would be repeated again and again throughout my life. The admonition of Jesus, "Do this in memory of me," would be honored time and again—and eventually every day. The power of the Lord would guide me throughout my life. He would keep His promise: "I am with you always." Not only that, but I would enable Him to come to the souls of countless others.

I cannot remember what Father Davis said to us that day, but I recall coming out of church into the dampness of the morning. My mother took me across the road from the church to a deserted old house where she provided a sandwich she had prepared, and then she started the dreary, wet, and windy two-mile journey home with her first-communicant son firmly holding on as she pedaled into the hostile elements. My first communion celebrations were over when we left the church. There was still an amount of maturation ahead of me!

I suppose I remember the following incident because it was Eucharist related. For whatever reason, it has stayed with me down through the years. One Sunday morning, having gone forward to the communion rails to receive the body of the Lord, my brother and I somehow or other became separated from my father. In those days the women went to the pews on one side of the church and the men on the other. Young boys normally accompanied their father. At communion time we became separated from my father, and the two of us went into another pew. It was no earthshaking crisis. It would be difficult to get lost in Kilfian Church, and besides, everybody knew everybody else.

After communion, instead of focusing on the Lord and the prayers from the altar, my brother and I entered into a deep conversation. I have no idea what it was all about, but at the age of eight or nine I know it had to be a sophisticated discussion! Mass ended, and all was well. My father was a few pews behind us, and we found him easily as the congregation exited. The morning was very normal, nothing was said, the usual worthy Sunday breakfast. But just before dinnertime, as we gathered around the table, my father surprised us with a statement. "I want to talk to you boys." He then went on to state his dissatisfaction with the behavior he had witnessed from us in church that morning. He had seen everything, he said, and he was ashamed. "You have disgraced your mother and me."

Believe me, as he spoke, he was getting our attention! My mother was the normal disciplinarian of the family. She was, so to speak, the circuit court. Occasionally, when we seemed to be giving a negative response, she would appeal to my father, the supreme court. On the occasion this happened, everybody knew the game was over! The supreme court not only backed my mother but could enforce even heavier penalties. Not that my father ever used physical punishment, but somehow when he assumed his judicial status, he came across as someone to whom one should pay attention!

My father continued to remind us of the sacredness of what went on at the altar. "And," he said, "you are being watched by all around you." Now this was something that had never occurred to me. People would watch a kid like me! Behavior in public, my father said, told a story, and the story we had imparted was not one of which to be proud. "The Harte boys were little miscreants—and where were their parents anyway?" It most likely was the last time I ever misbehaved in church! I am reminded of the episode every time I come across the saying of Jesus: "By their deeds you shall know them." We Christians really are Christ's light to the world.

But as time went on my father had reason to be proud. There was a little magazine called *The Messenger of the Sacred Heart* that came into our home on a monthly basis. I am happy to relate that little publication by the Jesuit Fathers is still going strong and every time I come across it I think of "Young Crusaders' Corner." This particular feature no longer graces the magazine, but at the time it influenced me greatly. A "Young Crusader" was someone who committed to frequent reception of the Blessed Sacrament, and having enrolled as a member was the recipient of a badge in the form of a little cross with a symbol of the Eucharist in the middle. I was proud of my badge and wore it every day. Not only that, but I did everything I could to fulfill my promise of frequent communion. And somewhere in an old issue my name appears as the winner of an essay that related, as best my memory serves, to the Blessed Sacrament. That was indeed a long time ago! Was God preparing me for my future ministry? I think He was!

Chapter Nine:
First Experience of Death

꧁

S ooner or later in life a young person must come face to face with death. In the Ireland of the nineteen thirties no effort was made to sweep the sad reality under the carpet irrespective of age, except perhaps in the very early years of infancy. There were no funeral homes and few hospitals. Most people died at home. And even if they didn't, they were waked at home. The wake provided an opportunity for the neighborhood to pay its last respects for the departed. And there was another objective as well: to bring comfort and solace to the grieving relatives.

The wake went on all night. In fact, the term *wake* meant that it was a nighttime affair, and those who attended the wake had planned for a sleepless night. Indeed, people could arrive at a wake at any time of the night until early morning. The idea was beautifully charitable. It allowed the grievers to be with people, to take some rest, and to shed their tears with good neighbors. Naturally alcohol was provided for the participants, sometimes leading to abuses and a bad name for the Irish wake. But despite this the custom itself was founded in Christian ethics and rendered wonderful solace to many a grieving family.

Normally the dead person was laid out either in a coffin or on a bed. "Going to the corpse house" was a familiar expression when someone in the neighborhood died. The term *corpse* was a mystery to me until my grandmother told me a corpse was the remains of a person who had died. She explained that the person's soul had left the body, and all that was now left was the corpse, a body without a soul. But I would be past my tenth birthday before I would see a corpse for myself.

On Saturdays my parents sent me for piano lessons in Ballina. The town was ten miles away. I took the bus which passed less than half a mile from our home. Sometimes I would walk further along from the normal stoppage place to the bridge, if time allowed. For one thing the fare from the bridge was cheaper, and there was the possibility of having the extra penny or two to spend on chocolate.

In many ways it was a picturesque bridge. It had eleven arches, and the serene waters flowing underneath when the tide was out seemed to give promise of an equally peaceful day. Just a few hundred yards from the bridge was an old mill with its large mill wheel now quiet, a reminder that time marches on, that nothing ever remains the same, that people of yesteryear somehow or other disappear, and so do their habits and customs. The land sloped up from the bridge, and since wealthy farmers owned that property and grazed it with a herd of deer, there was always the possibility of seeing the deer nearby.

More often than not there were several persons awaiting the arrival of the bus at the bridge. A couple of them I remember well. One was William Coultry. He would always talk to me, sometimes about the deer, the weather, or perhaps the most recent events of the war that was now going on in Europe. But he seemed to know a lot about deer, and it was always interesting to hear him tell his stories or give his description of the particular animal and where it might have originated. William was at the bridge just about every Saturday morning. He was a large and robust man, with a charming disposition, a watch chain hanging from his waistcoat, and an air about him that said he was more than satisfied with his lot in life. Now and then he would check his watch and announce that the bus would be here at any minute.

Then one Saturday morning William was missing. He was sick, someone said. Someone else thought he had caught a cold. But on many successive Saturdays he was still missing, and then came the word that he had died. The news saddened me. I knew I wouldn't see William anymore, there wouldn't be any further interesting discussions on the deer and nobody to check how soon the bus would arrive.

His remains were removed from his home on a Sunday afternoon, to be brought to the parish church in Killala. In Ireland the coffin is usually placed overnight in the parish church, placing the dead body one last few hours in the presence of the Lord. Even though he lived about two miles away, in the parlance of the time "it was a funeral for us." There was a custom of attending funerals of those near or far who at one time or another had gone out of their way to attend one's own family funeral or who might have grown close to the family in one way or other. Attending the funeral was regarded as a very special mark of respect to the family, especially if the attendee had to make a special effort to get there from a distance.

My father cycled to the home and I accompanied him on my own bicycle. "You knew William," he said to me. "Why don't you come with me to the corpse house?" There seemed to be an air of gravity as we entered the room where the remains were laid out on a bed. I am sure that it was somewhat of a shock to my ten-year-old system. The last time I saw William, he was laughing and talking with me on Palmerstown Bridge. Now here he was, lying pallid and motionless on a white sheet, in a brown Franciscan robe, with his eyes closed as if asleep. I knew I was watching "the sleep of death." Even though he looked like the man I had known, there seemed to be something missing. I was learning about a "corpse." It was not a pleasant experience but a fact of life that had to be faced sooner or later. Nobody lives forever. To die was part of life, a reality to be met and faced down.

The custom in Ireland until recent times was that the dead person was always dressed in the brown habit of the Franciscan order. This was as a result of the influence of the Franciscans who had given much time and energy, as well as an amount of their own blood, in serving their people throughout the penal times when Catholicism was banned and a price put on the head of any priest who could be identified to the forces of the British Crown.

Just before the remains were placed in the coffin, it was customary to recite the rosary for the dead person. My father was always called upon if he was present, and because of his work as a teacher and the many people he came in contact with, he was present at many local funerals. On this occasion he recited the five Sorrowful Mysteries as well as the Litany of Our Lady. There was a great message of hope in all of this. William had gone to God. We prayed that his journey would take him there quickly. My young mind was able to put it all together. The steady murmur of the recitation and responses of the people seemed consoling and assuring. After the rosary, all were then ushered from the room with only the relatives remaining within to kiss their good-byes on the body of the departed soul and see it placed in the coffin. The funeral cortège then started out for the church.

That night as I lay in bed, I continued to think of the dead man for some time before falling asleep. When sleep finally came I had come to grips with my first experience of death. I had witnessed the grief of the relatives, and I understood it. This good man's time on earth was completed. I wouldn't meet him on the bridge again. He wouldn't be talking to me about the deer or plotting the arrival of the bus. He was gone to God. There was a finality about death that somehow or other had to be confronted. There would be other deaths and other funerals, but somehow none of them would affect me as that first one. I had learned our time on earth was a temporary lease. Death had come to my friend William as it would come to all of us sooner or later. The comforting murmuring of the rosary at the wake left me in no doubt that the God of love who created us and died for us would also take us to Himself. I remembered too the grief of my mother when our little Aidan died so many years ago. Now I completely understood.

Chapter Ten:
A First Answer to Personal Prayer

In my life there came a time when I realized God listens to prayers. I am sure that realization comes to all of us sooner or later. But growing up, as I did, in a prayerful and believing environment, with the picture of the Sacred Heart looking down on us in our kitchen, I quickly realized the goodness of an all-loving God. I remember the day and the occasion that my own special prayer was answered.

My mother was preparing to go to town to do the shopping. She usually did her grocery shopping on a Saturday and took one of us with her. But it was not a Saturday, and nobody else was to accompany her this time. For some strange reason I wanted the impossible—or at least I realized my request was tantamount to the impossible. I wanted a football! A nice Gaelic football would enable me to imitate the great and famed Mayo players of the time. I decided to ask anyway. Footballs were made solely of leather at that time, entirely different from the footballs of modern times. In a rainy climate such as Ireland the stitching of the leather was liable to separate in multiple places, and the leather itself would deteriorate in a short time. The life of a football was brief, and furthermore footballs were an expensive item.

A football! My mother was totally uninterested. She was not the kind of mother who toyed around with her children's requests. It was a bad investment! When my mother said no, she meant *no*. "What happened to your last football?" she asked. Further argument was useless!

But my mind was made up too. I wanted a football. In my mind's eye I could visualize myself kicking that football in the field, jumping high to catch it in the air, running with it, doing everything I had heard in radio broadcasts. I looked at the Sacred Heart picture. The face of the Lord seemed to be smiling down at me. I wanted to talk to Him, but I knew I just couldn't do that in the kitchen with everybody around. I decided to go upstairs to my bedroom. I knelt by my bed and I prayed the prayer I had read about in the *Messenger of the Sacred Heart*: "O Sacred Heart of Jesus, I place my trust in thee." I must have prayed for a couple of minutes or so, repeating the prayer and adding the Our Father. Then I resignedly rose from my knees and made my way back downstairs to the kitchen.

My aunt, my mother's only sister, had stopped by. She was seated on a chair in the middle of the kitchen. This aunt, known as "Baby," was in many ways like my grandmother. She had a contagious sense of humor, and by the time I reached the bottom step and entered the kitchen, there was laughter all around. My aunt wanted my mother to sing a song. There was nothing unusual about this. In my young days in our home anytime was a time for singing! At first my mother protested that she had to get ready for town, but on insistence from my aunt, she began to sing "The Old Bog Road." Mother had a beautiful voice, and when she sang, everybody listened and joined in at the appropriate time. "The Old Bog Road" is a sad song of an emigrant who leaves for New York and never comes home, not even to his mother's funeral because he can't afford it.

My thoughts, however, were much closer to home than New York. My thoughts were on that football! Quietly I asked again, and with the same resolution as before my mother said, "No, son."

My aunt, however, on hearing my request appealed to my mother on my behalf: "Ah, God help us, get him the football. Sure he's only a child, and it will keep him out of your way too." My mother melted. She agreed to buy the football. That evening I was the proud possessor of a brand-new football!

But I knew that something wonderful had happened that day! My prayers had been answered. What seemed impossible had become a possibility—and then a reality! And all because I had prayed to the Sacred Heart. It was a thrill to know that God was so close to me as to hear my prayer and then grant it so quickly.

The Sacred Heart entered my life seriously that day and never left. The football was the first recognizable answer to prayer. It would be followed by innumerable other responses. Every day of my life I include the Litany of the Sacred Heart among my morning prayers. Indeed, I now realize that many of our "aspiration" prayers such as the one I offered for the football are simply shortened forms of the Psalms of David. The Psalms are filled with notions of trust, as for example in the well-known twenty-second—"But you, O Lord, be not far from me; O my help, hasten to aid me"—or the inferences of the thirty-first: "You are my rock and my fortress; for your name's sake you will lead and guide me."

The Psalms can be prophetic too! Generations before Christ came among us, the psalmist declared "But the plan of the Lord stands forever; the design of his heart through all generations" (Psalm 33:11) God had destined from all eternity to send His Divine Son among us.

In my mature years, I am happy to recite the psalms of my breviary every day. Their content expresses the desires of my soul. I no longer make the sort of "demand" on God I made in my young years. To be with God is the only objective of my life. With confidence I can now pray with the psalmist "keep me as the apple of your eye, hide me in the shadow of your wings" (17:8). Or the other beautiful sentiment so well expressed in Psalm 27:4: "One thing I have asked of the Lord, this I desire, to be seated in the House of the Lord all the days of my life." As we mature in years, we realize more and more that the only answer to prayer that matters is reflected in the aspirations of the psalmist. God the Father knows our needs. But His greatest desire is that we constantly seek to belong to His Kingdom and to help in establishing it.

Chapter Eleven:
Christian Hospitality

The west of Ireland was a depressed area for a long time after Irish independence had been achieved. Way back in 1641 the loathed English army commander Oliver Cromwell had ordered the evicted farmers of Ulster "to Hell or to Connacht." Vast tracts of land in the west of Ireland, that part known as Connacht in which our family lived, were simply bog, unfit for any kind of farming operations other than extracting peat. And the arable lands were awarded to British gentry.

In the centuries following, poverty reigned in the area. The Great Famine of the mid-1800s decimated the population either by death or emigration. In my childhood days, the remnants of the "workhouse" stood here and there as a reminder of a horrific history. The workhouse was a sort of shelter built by the British government, following the famine, for those who were homeless and with little hope for future self-preservation. The idea seemed good, but it was to prove a great failure. Pride took preeminence over hunger, and people refused the opportunity in droves.

The name *workhouse* came from the price the occupants had to pay for a meager subsistence. There would be an obligation to carry out certain tasks, whether roadside work, digging ditches, or simply scrubbing and cleaning the new abode. What the government overlooked was the stigma attached to belonging to such an institution, and the majority of the impoverished citizens chose to take their chances begging from their more fortunate neighbors and sleeping under the stars. These were Ireland's first truly "homeless" people.

The Killala workhouse, that grim reminder of hungry times and a laissez-faire government, in my growing years stood on the Ballina road as one exited the town. It is now long since gone, replaced with comfortable homes and a contented population. The Ireland of my childhood, itself not very well-off, had also to care for the less fortunate descendants of bitter earlier times. The Irish government was young and not monetarily enhanced at that time, and so the task of caring for the less fortunate fell solidly into the hands of the population itself. And the example of charity taught a lesson for a lifetime.

First there were the "traveling families" who at that time lived in canvas tents by the roadside. The tent was about four feet tall, allowing the inhabitant to either sit or lie down beneath its cover. The travelers would arrive with a horse-drawn pony and cart. Some of the more fortunate might occasionally travel in what looked to my young eyes like a fancy caravan. It certainly was a step up from the canvas tent, but even in my young years I realized the hardships involved in either form of living without sanitation or the requisites of life that we so often take for granted.

There was a roadside spot close to my grandmother's home that was popular to the traveling people. Here they would pitch their tent for several weeks at a time, allowing me as a child to become familiar with their way of living. I often wondered about them on a winter's night, with the rains pouring down and icicles forming before daylight. How did they keep themselves dry and warm? Life, I learned, was harsh on some.

In those days those families continued to dress mostly in the old Irish way. The women wore long flowing dresses and kept warm with a woolen shawl thrown around their shoulders. Their men worked at odd jobs for the farmers, and in the days before plastic utensils, they were right good at mending leaks, especially in kitchen equipment such as water buckets or cans. The women, on the other hand, went from home to home collecting charitable donations that consisted mostly of foodstuffs. There was little loose change in the west of Ireland of those days.

My parents always welcomed those visitors. If a traveling lady came at mealtime, she shared in the meal. If she came at another time, she was always welcomed, offered a chair, and first given something to drink.

There would be a conversation about family and health, and of course neighborhood news would find further ears in which to homestead. Traveling people had a lot of news! An old Irish proverb states that "the traveler has stories to tell!" And certainly, before departing, the visitor would be offered a substantial sandwich, and the parting gift could be a portion of meat or vegetables to be put in her basket. There was never any inkling of the visitor being a "nuisance" or a refusal to be charitable.

Then there was a lady who lived shoreside in Killala in a quaint little home. Not by the farthest stretch of the imagination could this lady be called a mendicant. She possessed her own nobility, was well known in the surrounding area, and indeed had a charm that somehow won the hearts of those who knew her. She owned a donkey and cart and occasionally made forays into the countryside where she picked up from her friends enough vegetables and other necessities of life. She too dressed in a black (always black) woolen shawl.

She and my grandmother were great friends, and since my grandmother had a little garden with apple trees and other fruits, this lady came often to visit her and stayed chatting and laughing with her for hours on end. When I saw her coming I knew that Nan was going to be unavailable for a couple of hours at least! Of course by the time she left she had also been served a good meal and was ready for the road.

She had her donkey for sale on one of her visits, and my father promptly bought it. In those days, donkeys in Ireland were used for many purposes: to pull a cart, to work in the bog, and also simply to get from one place to another. The donkey was a complaisant animal that for his work got as much abuse as feeding stuff.

I remember this particular donkey very well. My brother Enda, who was a few years older than me, found this donkey had a will of his own! Shortly after the purchase my mother sent us to Killala for some household provisions. We took the donkey and cart. This was the donkey's first trip to what had been his home ground. Nobody, it appeared, had informed him he now had a new owner. So, despite my brother's best attention and pulling of the reins, the donkey insisted on pulling into as many homes on the way as he had been accustomed to do previously. The donkey wanted to visit his old friends!

While on the subject of donkeys and donkey transportation, there was an old neighbor (perhaps not so old, but I thought he was) who lived a mile or so from us. He had a small bogland piece of property about three miles to the other side of our home. His name was Pauric, and frequently throughout the week he would journey the three miles on the back of his donkey. Why do I remember him? Because Pauric gave total free rein to the donkey. There was no harness of any kind, and Pauric sat on his donkey facing backward, watching the surroundings he had passed and the road he had traveled. He was totally satisfied that the donkey could take care of oncoming traffic (of which there was very little) and lead him to his destination. The donkey did just that for many a year, and the image of Pauric riding backward is still imbedded in my memory and must surely be remembered by many neighbors. Pauric, of course, never sought any kind of assistance, but his image comes up whenever I think of donkeys and their use in those times. And I wonder how a modern Irish policeman would deal with him allowing his donkey to be the sole guide.

There was one real mendicant who visited our home once a year, and that was all. Like Melchizedek in the Old Testament, no one knew whence he came or where he went. His name was Joe Keogh. There was nothing to remember about his mode of dress—except everything! The jacket he wore bore the dust and dirt of many a road and of a long time wearing. It certainly never saw the inside of a dry cleaner's establishment. I never saw him in an overcoat, but perhaps it was as a result of the time of year his visit to our home occurred.

Joe would arrive at any time of day, mostly before dusk. Over his shoulder was thrown an old sack that contained all his belongings and his necessities of life as well. Let it be said that Joe's necessities were very meager! Where he slept was known to none, and the details of his personal history remained a secret. There was a rumor around that Joe came from good stock, that once upon a time he was a member of the teaching profession on the east coast of Ireland, and that he had suffered a nervous breakdown and taken to the highways with sack on back. There was no verifying the rumor, and to this day I have never met anyone who could give me any information about Joe Keogh.

Joe might have been none too clean, his clothes might have been ragged and dirty, but when he arrived in our kitchen he was treated as the human being and creature of God he was. Indeed, if we youngsters were playing outside we always abandoned our games to go see Joe. He would be seated on a kitchen chair, his knapsack beside him on the floor giving away no secrets as to what was inside. Both my parents would chat with him, extracting whatever information he was prepared to give. As I recall, most of the time he spoke about his health or someone who was ill he had come across on his travels.

He surely enjoyed the good meal always given him and when he had finished he would get up from his chair, thank my parents, and—without asking for any further charity—prepare to leave. He did of course always receive something extra to put in his sack for the journey ahead, wherever that might take him. Joe must be dead for many a year now, but I have no doubt he was beloved by God and is now sharing the joys of eternity without having to worry about where or how he will survive the next day.

Hospitality is a major among the Christian virtues, and without any specific instruction but rather the force of example, I had the virtue instilled in me as I grew up. Indeed, there is a sad tale to tell here too. My mother's aunt, Celia, sister of my grandfather John O'Neill, was taken from this world as a result of an act of charity. On a cold and wintry night with temperatures well below freezing, she extended the hospitality of her home to a poor beggar-woman who had no place in which to shelter. The lady was a carrier of a very contagious fever which was caught by my great aunt, causing her death in a very short time. I visit her grave every year when I return to Ireland. It is quite close to where my parents and grandparents lie. They are all together now in the kingdom of the Lord where they are surely rewarded as He Himself promised: "As often as you do it to one of these my least brethren, you do it to me."

Chapter Twelve:
A Year to Remember

ℳ ost likely there is a year in everybody's life that begins to tie memories to dates. For me the year was 1939. I have many great memories of childhood days prior to that year, though I cannot tie them down. But 1939 is different!

We lived about forty miles from Knock Shrine. Our Lady had appeared there in 1879. Twelve people witnessed the apparition. It took place at a gable end of the church. The evening was wet. The apparition lasted for several hours as a group of people knelt in the pouring rain. The parish priest was sent for, but he refused to come. The Mother of God was reported to have been seen with Saint Joseph and Saint John the evangelist. A lamb was lying in front of the three.

Efforts were made to disprove the actuality of the happening, but all to no avail. There was no variation in the accounts of the twelve persons. In a short time, the locals began to make special pilgrimages to Knock. Seemingly inexplicable cures were reported. Before long Knock had become a place of pilgrimage not only for Mayo but for all of Ireland.

There was no message, and the Mother of God did not speak. The happening was taken as a celestial sign of affirmation for the poor people of the west of Ireland who at that time were still suffering the effects of the recent terrible famine of 1846–47 and the general state of poverty throughout the region. But the people of Mayo had always remained faithful to Christ. In time, the apparition came to be seen as an act of divine providence blessing the people for their fidelity.

My mother was a great believer in the apparition. All throughout her life she loved to visit Knock and join the thousands making the official pilgrimage. Although 1939 was not my first year in Knock, it is the first dated year I remember. Every year on the Feast of Our Lady's Assumption there was an all-night vigil. In 1939, my parents decided to make the vigil. I was nine years old.

I asked to be taken too. My parents surprisingly agreed, having first reminded me that staying up all night was not an attractive proposition. Older members of our family also came along. We arrived around nine o'clock in the evening.

One of my recollections from the drive into Knock was that along the way, as we came within a few miles, we passed people walking toward the shrine. It was customary in that time to do a pilgrimage on foot for greater efficacy, and many of the pilgrims, we were told, had walked over forty miles to get to their destination. I clearly remember women in the church that night wearing their Connemara shawls and praying their rosary. It was a wonderful reminder of our ultimate goal—to be with God!

The pilgrimage called for fifteen decades of the rosary to be recited walking around the church, then the Stations of the Cross either within the church or on the grounds outside. The regulation was completed by a visit to the Blessed Sacrament. For some reason, Irish pilgrimages always seem to call for lots and lots of personal repeated prayer.

There were some formal devotions too that I cannot recall. But I clearly remember having a sort of picnic in the hired hackney car around midnight. And as night went on and the climate within the church grew warmer from the crowds piling in from the cold night air, I found that keeping my eyes open was quite a challenge. Since it wasn't necessary to pray all the time, my father took me for a couple of walks around the grounds. As the seemingly never-ending night dragged on, announcements were made over a bullhorn that Mass would be celebrated at the gable end at dawn. The opening chapter of this book has recounted the rest of the story.

To this day, very few people know what I prayed for on that Assumption morning of 1939. I certainly did not tell my father, and he would have been amazed had he known. It was the prayer of a child who had not yet come to realize what sacrifices might be entailed for the request to be granted. But twenty-two years later Our Lady gave her positive answer when I was ordained in Dublin at the age of thirty-one.

Looking back, I am sure I always wanted to be a priest. I prayed for it every night when I went to bed. I had my own formula of prayers. Before going to sleep I made sure to recite seven Our Fathers, seven Hail Marys, and seven Glory be to the Fathers. I recited the aspiration to the Sacred Heart, "O Sacred Heart of Jesus, I place my trust in thee." I have no recollection when this practice stopped, but I know I was doing it until I left home for secondary school.

As I reflect on it all, I am convinced those prayers were really answered. Even more so, I believe the prayers offered in my childhood were efficacious throughout the rest of my life. Children should be encouraged to pray, for whatever they want. And even for family intentions too. Too soon innocence is left behind, when prayer becomes more difficult. But the prayer offered in childhood innocence is heard by the God of love, to whom there only exists the eternal *Now*. God is still hearing my childhood prayer eight decades later! In my retirement, as I review this early part of my life, I am contented that the priesthood is what God wanted to give me. Any other way of life would have been unthinkable.

The year I made my request at Knock Shrine was also the year when my native Mayo lost to Kerry after a replay in the all-Ireland football championship. The drawn game took place the Sunday previous to our pilgrimage to Knock Shrine. There were high hopes for Mayo that Sunday. They had beaten Galway, the All-Ireland champions, in a rousing Connacht final.

The game was broadcast over the radio. The broadcaster was Michael O'Hehir. This genius of broadcast Gaelic games was in the very beginning of his career. He knew every player, and with the raising and lowering of his voice he could bring his listeners into the stands of Croke Park. He could increase the heartbeat with an inflection, but there was reason for him to raise his voice that day! It was torrid football, with scoring at a premium. With time almost up, Mayo was awarded a free in front of the Kerry posts. The score was tied at this time. Tommy Hoban, the Mayo magician of free taking, would take the kick.

O'Hehir's voice began to rise to his famed crescendo as the ball was placed. But wait! The referee had changed his mind. It was later alleged that a Kerry official had remonstrated with him on the field beforehand. He picked up the ball and restarted the game, throwing the ball between the players and almost immediately blew the final whistle. The score remained four points apiece.

The replay took place on the second Sunday in September. Mayo was trounced. It would be nine years again before a Mayo team would appear in Croke Park, when I was well into my teen years. Then too a referee's decision ended in a Mayo defeat. The final whistle was blown four minutes too soon in the final of 1948 with Mayo in possession on the opponents' twenty-yard line backed by gale-force winds.

Only twice would Mayo win glory from then on—in 1950 and '51. I am grateful to have seen those days and that wonderful football team. They were a team apart. They represented the style of Mayo football, but unlike many other Mayo football teams, they also had power and a prideful commitment. Too often in the intervening years Mayo teams have been beaten by inferior opposition, mostly because of lack of self-belief.

Mayo people are softhearted. They play football as "only a game." Their philosophy shows itself time and time again and a recent defeat of a team from Mayo illustrates the point. "The lads will not be happy with their display," said their manager, "and when they talk about it, they will know why they lost." Mayo teams have developed a myriad of ways to lose. It doesn't take too much examination! But apart from the usual "bad luck" that crops up now and again for any team, Mayomen appear to be simply too guileless and far too soft for a game that in modern times is played with much more fervor by their opponents, without exception. The problem may be not only psychological but physical as well. The nature of the men from Mayo does not suit itself to the rigors of kicking, catching, and blocking, and since 1951, it would appear Mayo has never fielded a team with enough self-belief or energy to sustain the major effort it takes to become football champions of Ireland.

Focusing on achieving their goals has to begin for any team long before the game. There has to be a self-belief, not necessarily that "I am a better player" but "together we are a better team." One of the Mayo greats of the early fifties, Eamon Mongey, once explained that in practice he went for every ball with his brain focused on the forthcoming game; he jumped higher and hit harder than perhaps he had to. That didn't bode well for his opponent in practice! But when the big day came Eamon Mongey was rarely beaten to the ball, in the air or on the ground. Team effort got them there two years in a row. Mayo has the players still. One of those years they will realize their potential—but only after they face down their opponents with psychological hostility, à la Mongey!

I often regret that I did not ask for many more national championships for Mayo on the memorable night in Knock! Again, when Mayo failed to win on that Sunday, 13 August 1939, perhaps Our Lady was telling me there were some setbacks to which I would have to become accustomed. Of course there are those who protest that God does not take any interest in football games! Here I like to recall the answer of a fabled Notre Dame coach, Lou Holtz, who was asked the straightforward question: "Surely you don't think God has any interest in football?" "He may not," was the reply, "but His Mother certainly does."

"You have little to pray for," people have remarked to me when they knew I had been praying for Mayo. But it seems to me that any cause for raising one's mind and heart to God is a good one, and if that is caused by football, then so much the better! Does God take sides? Well, He certainly grants the victory to one side or the other. And I have never been able to make peace with the argument that two football teams are left to their own devices in a game where God is uninterested. He is a God of power, a God of involvement. With His lack of interest we would cease to be! Someday He will call the shots for Mayo too—perhaps after Mayomen learn to be more determined about their game, have more self-belief, and get rid of the softness that has cost Mayo supporters many a tear for well more than half a century.

September 1939 has also attached itself in my memory for two simultaneous dates—one world-shattering, the other a sporting occasion. On the first Sunday of September 1939, on coming out from Mass, we heard the word that Britain had declared war on Germany. For six long years horrendous events would take place all around the globe. Nobody knew when or how it would end.

It was the Sunday of the All-Ireland hurling final too. But on the way home from Mass there was little talk of hurling and much conversation speculating on events to come. But that same day a hurling final wrote itself into the annals of Irish sport and I remember it well! Cork played Kilkenny for the championship in a game that was titled the "Thunder and Lightning" final. Suffice it to say it was a crackling game with both teams always in the hunt. But during the game a severe thunderstorm broke out with dangerous lightning. The game continued despite the elements, and Kilkenny eventually won by a point.

My father, always faithful to the ventures of Cork hurling, believed Cork had been outfoxed in the closing moments. A Kilkenny player went down with an injury, the game was momentarily stopped for first aid to be rendered and when it resumed the "injured" player was left unmarked with only moments to go. He had been writhing on the ground for a few minutes and defenders concentrated their attentions elsewhere believing he was no threat. But the ball was flicked to him and in a twinkling he had scored the winning point. Michael O'Hehir, in ringing, excited words, referred to his "miracle" recovery! Don't ask me to name the winners in any other year. I probably would have to guess. But the Kilkenny "Cats" were purring on the first Sunday of September 1939. And World War Two had begun in earnest!

Chapter Thirteen: An Altar Boy!

∽

I n May of 1940 something wonderful happened! I became an altar boy! Like every other happening in my life, divine providence was very much at work.

May devotions were taking place. Those devotions, consisting of the rosary and benediction, were scheduled for around seven o'clock each evening in May. It was the very first day in May. I had come home from school and eaten my dinner when my parents announced they were going to cycle to the church for the May devotions. Then and there I wanted to come, and permission was readily granted. When we arrived at the gate of the church, the curate, Father Gallagher, approached and asked if he might "borrow" me to help serve at the devotions. And so, for the first time, I found myself on the other side of the altar rails! I must have done reasonably well, because Father Gallagher came to my parents after the devotions to ask if he might make me a permanent member of his altar boys. I am not sure who was the more thrilled with the invitation—my parents or myself!

Now there was work to be done. The Mass was in Latin in those days. The server's responses at the beginning of Mass were all in Latin too. My father taught me the Latin responses for the Mass. My mother contacted Mrs. Bourke of the Acres, a renowned seamstress, to ask her to measure me for my altar-boy cassock. Mrs. Bourke came to our home with her measuring tape, took the measurements and promised that in a week the outfit would be ready.

The following Friday she arrived with the finished product. I was suited in the cassock for the admiration of all. Mrs. Bourke had also made the white surplice that went over the cassock. It was an evening to remember! Becoming an altar boy had won for me the high estimation of every member of my family. My parents were unable to hide their pride. Their boy was now serving Mass!

Those days of Mass serving were never to be forgotten. Learning the Latin responses was not easy at the beginning, but my father, well versed in serving Mass himself, made sure I got it all right. My preparatory training was concluded within the church one morning before Mass as my father and I sat under the fourteenth station and he put me through the responses until I had them all perfectly.

The priest offered Mass with his back to the people, since Vatican Two was still years away. In those days the bell was to be rung when the priest placed his hands over the chalice. Kneeling behind the priest, it was not easy for the server to see exactly what was happening, especially in the early days of serving when nerves conquered courage. On many occasions in the beginning I did not ring the bell because I could not see where the priest's hands were.

At breakfast following Mass one morning my father gave me a tip. "Ring the bell," he said, "when you think it should be rung. Then leave it at that. The priest is not going to mind!" What a wise man my father was. I was no longer afraid. I rang when I believed I should ring, and everybody was happy. Soon my confidence had grown, and I had no doubts about when to ring the bell!

There was a special time in the Mass when the altar boy held the priest's chasuble as he elevated the host. (This was discontinued after Vatican Two.) Those were precious moments. When the newly consecrated host was held aloft for all to see, and I was touching the vestment worn by the priest, it seemed to me there was a connection between the host and myself. Christ was on the altar with us, the priest was His visible representative, and here I was with my hand on the priest's vestment as the most sacred moment arrived. I had, in my own estimation, a direct line to the Lord Himself! But uppermost in all my thoughts, I wondered if the day might come when I would be the priest and someone else would be taking the place I was now occupying. And I wondered too how it would come about.

My desire would be fulfilled, but there were still a few turns to be negotiated in the road.

Chapter Fourteen: Holy Week Experiences

⁂

I am quite sure the faith of individuals within a family is enriched by their participation in the liturgies of the Church. The Solemn Liturgy of the days of Holy Week has a special meaning for me, and our family's Holy Week observations have remained with me to the very present moment.

In the late thirties, long before Vatican Two, there was a considerable difference between the Holy Week ceremonies and those of today. Priests of a particular locality gathered in a central church, where a High Mass was offered on Holy Thursday morning. My family never missed that Mass for as far back as I can remember, even though it meant cycling three miles to Killala in all kinds of weather. Because of her age, my grandmother stayed at home and took care of family members not attending the Mass, mostly those not old enough to cycle the journey. However, occasionally someone older might have stayed home. My parents never constrained any of us to attend Mass on a day that was not a holy day of obligation. Personally I looked forward to accompanying my parents for the three-mile bicycle ride, and indeed I was already full of expectation as soon as Palm Sunday arrived.

One Holy Thursday my grandmother called me, in accordance with my own previously expressed wishes, to go to Mass with my parents. I was a "sleepyhead" that morning, and having succumbed to taking a few more minutes, I awakened to find that my parents had already left. Never did anyone get out of bed so quickly as I did when the realization dawned on me. I caught up with my parents well before they arrived at the church.

After Mass, the Blessed Sacrament was always placed on its altar of repose and remained there all through the day. People came to pray as the day progressed. All understood that there was something out of the ordinary about adoration on Holy Thursday. Indeed, my parents would sometimes cycle the three miles back to church again before the day was over. But I was young, I liked to cycle, and my mother would encourage me to go spend time before the Lord even when she or my father was not able to return to church. She would devise an excuse, like a lack of sugar in the house that I needed to pick up at O'Reilly's Stores. And when I was in town would I go into the church and spend a little while with the Lord at the altar of repose? Then she would tell me to pray for the family, for herself, for Grandmother, or for whatever needs about which she felt we needed to remind the Lord. And of course I agreed. Was I not the ambassador for the family? Was not my mother vesting her trust in my ability to pray? It was all so important in my young life. And, I may add, it was all so natural!

Good Friday had been explained to me a long time before. It was the day on which Christ died, the day on which He won our salvation. He gave His life so that we could live forever. In every sense it was a "good" day! And on Good Friday morning the ceremonies took place early in the day. I was always fascinated by the movements of the clergy on the altar, the enacting of the Gospel, and even though the Gospel was sung in Latin, I was always able to distinguish the priest who spoke the part of Jesus, and the others who had less attractive parts.

There was something mysterious about it all, and I knew it was because this service was to commemorate the dying of Christ. Holy Communion was not distributed, and the ceremony ended without fanfare, in a quiet mood. The Blessed Sacrament was no longer present in the church, and there was a feeling of emptiness. Jesus had died for our sins, and He was now in the grave. The liturgical celebration without distribution of Eucharist seemed somewhat strange, but it was meant to imply the barrenness of life without Jesus the Lord.

In our family, the solemnity of Good Friday seemed to last long after the morning ceremony. It was a normal workday, and the operations on the farm continued. My father would be home from school as the day was first of all a bank holiday, and the Easter vacation time for schools had already begun. In the afternoon we might on occasion go to our parish church for the public Stations of the Cross, or make the journey on our own to meditate on the last walk of Christ.

On Holy Saturday morning, Mass would be celebrated early. Little emphasis was placed on the readings surrounding the prophetic readings on the Messiah or the mourning of Jesus, and frequently that part of the liturgy took place in an almost empty church. Even then the liturgy began with the lighting of the Paschal fire and I recall my wonderment about the glowing embers outside as we arrived at the church. The majority of people stayed away until the early readings (in Latin) were over. (What a wonderful change was made by Vatican Two in this regard!) But our family always arrived in time for the main part of the Mass.

Lent officially ended at noon on Holy Saturday, and those who had made Lenten promises were released from their particular penitential resolution. All that remained now was the celebration of the victory of Jesus, and our victory too, on Easter Sunday. If you had given up candies for Lent, noon was a joyous relief! I remember an older sister, candy in hand, sitting watching the clock for almost half an hour until it finally struck twelve! I refer to those memories because of family involvement and the intertwining of religious belief and daily life. Those were days when the formation of our family in Christianity was being established for a lifetime.

To this moment in my life I am always touched by family memories of the Triduum each time the celebration comes around. I think too that the majority of Christians, and certainly the majority of Catholic Christians are struck with a feeling of awe for the Lord of love during those holiest of days. In Orlando, exceptionally large numbers always turned out for the liturgies, and when one considers those days are not Holy Days of Obligation, the attendance was all the more remarkable. The altar of repose always drew good numbers, and no matter when we closed the church, there were always some latecomers testing the doors after the lockup. Good Friday brought its own even larger crowds, and I have been particularly struck by the devotion of our South American Catholics who always seemed to show up in droves for the Good Friday ceremonies. Holy Week at the shrine was certainly a living reminder that the "faith of our fathers" still holds a firm place in the hearts of countless people. It is a time when believers are united in their dedication to Christ the Lord. I may add, that somewhat like my own mother, our South American neighbors carry their own personal devotions with them, as was so evident in their desire to honor the crucifix on that day even outside the ceremonies. They have, of course, a wonderful devotion to Mary, the Mother of God, too, but that is a topic for another occasion in this book. One more point, the benefits of the liturgical changes of Vatican Two are best illustrated in the liturgies of Holy Week.

Chapter Fifteen:
War in Europe

hat was to become World War Two had broken out on the first Sunday of September 1939. On the previous Friday, Nazi troops had invaded Poland. When we emerged from Mass on that Sunday, the news was that the British government had given Hitler an ultimatum: retreat from Poland, or war would be declared on Germany.

Nobody expected Hitler to conform. To all intents and purposes the British statement was a declaration of war. War was in the air everywhere, and the stories of the sufferings caused by the First World War were still on everybody's lips. At church gates and around firesides people gathered to discuss the momentous occasion.

Stories were told from the prophecies of Saint Malachy that had been added to and magnified down through the years. Saint Malachy was an Irish saint, the only canonized Irish saint at that time(!), who reputedly had written prophecies regarding future world events. (Let it be said none of the prophecies bode well for Britain.) That very evening of the declaration of war, an older gentleman who had come to visit our home, a good storyteller himself, dramatically announced that it was "in the prophecy'" that there was to be a naval battle, and only one British ship would survive! The Germans had used poison gas on civil populations toward the end of the First War, and apparently the good Saint Malachy had foretold that too and more! It wasn't just the ships that would be wiped out. Would any of us on these islands survive? It was frightening information for the young mind, but my fears were allayed when my father advised me that "prophecies" made good stories and that I should pay no attention to anything I had heard.

The omens were bad for the British at the time. Truth to tell, Britain had not been ready for this war at all. Neville Chamberlain did not seem to have the ability to direct a war. Hitler was well prepared. Chamberlain's often expressed wish for "peace in our time" was now blowing in the wind. The daily newspapers continuously illustrated in maps where the opposition forces were. My father, who studied the war very closely, taught me at that time how to read a map so that I could decipher the information for myself.

The Maginot Line was presented on every paper every day with arrows hither and thither as to where the armies were. At that time, I did not fully comprehend what the Maginot Line was. My father explained that it consisted of a series of fortifications, but my young mind could not grasp the meaning fully. Was it a series of castles, I wondered? The Allies believed the Maginot Line could not be penetrated. Whatever it was, Hitler had it well studied. The Western Allies somehow or other believed that the fall of Poland was more attributable to the weakness of the Polish army than to any superior power on the part of the Nazis. Hitler would never be able to break the Maginot Line.

They were soon to learn their mistake! It took no length of time for Belgium and Holland to fall. Hitler had gone through the fortifications and around them. Indeed, Holland surrendered in less than two weeks. There was no way that little country could survive the Nazi onslaught. Nazi armies broke through toward the west, forcing the British troops to desert not only their positions but also a large part of their armory. By late May 1940, the aggressors had reached the Flanders town of Dunkirk.

Within a week the initial battle of the war was over. Allied troops were ferried every which way to the friendly confines of the English coast. The survival of the troops was called a miracle at the time. Britain had expected casualties ranging perhaps as high as thirty thousand. In heretofore-unmatched acts of chivalry, owners of yachts, fishing vessels, small boats, or whatever floated risked their lives under Nazi mortar fire to ferry back to the homeland thousands of British troops and their European counterparts. Upward of a half million men were brought to safety in this way—an action that was termed "the miracle of Dunkirk." The greater miracle, however, was that a nation on its knees, with most of its armory captured by the enemy, survived to fight another day. For some reason that can only be speculated on, Hitler stopped the advance. His troops did not follow the fleeing army across the English Channel. In light of the knowledge of later times, God was at work. The forces of evil would not be allowed to prevail.

Those were days of mystery! Would Hitler's armies come to Ireland? Would Hitler try to use a back-door method to invade England from Ireland? Eamon DeValera, then Prime minister of Ireland, sent out signals that Ireland would not be easily intimidated. Ireland would fight to the last man, he said. A land that had known freedom for less than two decades was not going to surrender to any foreigner. Winston Churchill, now prime minister of Britain, had ideas about Ireland too. He wanted Ireland to cede its main ports for use by the British. But the man who was mainly responsible for the partition of Ireland was not likely to be the one listened to. On one particular evening, every family in Ireland that owned a radio, joined by members of neighboring families who had no radio, tuned in to hear DeValera's reply. There was great pride throughout the nation as it listened to the leader of government give a well prepared and logical answer. Ireland, he said, would remain neutral. Irish ports would remain in Irish hands.

The incidences of German planes flying overhead became common. In September 1939, we ran to watch the sight of any airplane in the sky. Until then such a sight was a rarity. After Dunkirk, Nazi planes seemed to be a commonplace, flying here, there, and everywhere over our heads. And indeed the British were there too, despite Ireland's neutrality.

One afternoon in the summer of 1940, what looked to my young mind like a German bomber went through threatening aerobatics over our home. The home was at a crossroads. I know now that the pilot was most likely reconnoitering to map the roads of the area. It is widely believed that Hitler did indeed plan to invade Ireland. On this particular afternoon, I had been detailed to mind my young sister, Anne, then less than two years old. She was in her "go-car," and I kept her happy by pushing her around. When I saw the plane coming, instead of going into the house, I remained outside to assuage my curiosity. Heretofore, when planes arrived I was in the company of an adult. When this plane began to circle, I concluded there was trouble ahead. I had read about the bombings in Europe. Was this plane getting ready to unload its bombs on our home? I wasn't going to wait to find out.

I ran as fast as I could, pushing my sister in her go-car, to a shed that was some three hundred yards or so behind our home. There I took cover, my young mind believing that if the house was bombed, my sister and I would be safe within the shed. It never occurred to my mind that perhaps I should first make my parents aware of the danger that might be looming. Through the crevices of the shed door I peeped out to watch what was happening. I prayed to the Sacred Heart to spare all of us, the prayer I had learned was so powerful: "O Sacred Heart of Jesus, I place all my trust in thee."

Within minutes, the plane gained altitude and flew toward the south. I watched it go and then returned to our own kitchen. My mother was there, and to my surprise she showed no real concern about the plane or the very obvious swastika on its wings. I recall the smile on her face when I told her where I had been and why. It was a smile of approval mixed with humor at the thought of a youngster who was going to save his sister by taking her three hundred yards to a shed that probably would have fallen in had there been any sort of explosion within a mile!

Time was moving on, and the world was changing before my eyes, but I didn't know it. Of course I appreciated little of the world that was passing away. But it seems to me the war put an end to many happy practices—or were those practices frivolities? For one thing, parties at our home became a thing of the past.

In her younger days, my mother loved to dance. Like her own mother she also loved company and the chitchat of daily affairs. She loved to sing, and she loved to listen to someone else singing. So it was not unusual that on a Sunday evening now and again a crowd of happy people would gather in our home around seven o'clock. A gramophone that had been purchased at an auction of the local landlords provided the music. It had a trademark of a dog looking into a large horn, and underneath was written, "His Master's Voice." The records were unbending and easily broken. The needle had to be changed after every two records so that it was essential always to have a box of needles at hand. And on the turntable was the marking "speed 78."

Then came the war. Changes were taking place before our very eyes, and the world would never be the same again. There would be no more Sunday evening parties.

The scarcities caused by the war made it difficult to have the normal commodities for hospitality readily on hand. Flour was available, but it was dark in color. There was little if any fruit. Raisins were not to be had. It would be five or six years more before I would see a banana. Varieties of breads simply could not be provided anymore. Even butter became scarce, and tea was rationed. Because the government insisted that each farmer provide so many bushels of grains, farmers had to go to bed earlier in order to get to the fields in the morning.

Something else was happening in Ireland too. The radio—or the "wireless," as it was known—was beginning to arrive on the scene. The family next door had a wireless that had been brought from America when one of the girls was returning home. Since there was no electricity in the countryside yet, the radio was run by a "dry battery" inside the set and a "wet battery," attached from the outside, that always stood by the radio. This latter battery did not last very long so that every radio owner had at least two wet batteries available. When one ran out, the other was attached and the depleted battery taken to be charged at a local store. Normally this procedure took about three days. The dry battery lasted a long time and signaled its loss of life by the decreasing volume from the radio itself.

Because of the wireless and growing interest in the war, people began to gather where a radio was available. The BBC news at nine o'clock in the evening and the Ireland news at ten minutes past ten became the order of the day. And at half past nine, just after the British news, listeners could tune in to *Germany Calling*—"the news in English with Lord Haw-Haw." Looking back, one must admit the German news was mostly unbelievable, and in dogfights German planes were, of course, always victorious. In 1945, Lord Haw-Haw would be charged with treason by the British government and suffer death by hanging.

The war had ended before the radio became commonplace in the west of Ireland. My parents were late on the scene because my mother believed a radio would be a distraction for us children and would distract us from our homework! Eventually we did get a fine radio, and our home once again became a gathering place on Sundays to listen to football games.

Every evening, we continued our practice of praying the rosary together as a family. There was more to be prayed for now than at any other time—and more reason to remind ourselves that we belonged to God. In the "trimmings" to the rosary, my mother added prayers for peace that were recited every night and a universal prayer to the Sacred Heart for peace. In those unsure times there was indeed great consolation in a prayer to the Sacred Heart—"We are thine, and thine we wish to be." We were indeed God's children. We asked His protection. He had instilled the desire for Himself in our hearts. Saint Augustine expressed the same thought when he wrote in his *Confessions*, "You have made us for yourself, O God, and our hearts are not at rest until they rest in you."

Chapter Sixteen:
Saving Crops and Standing Firm!

My memories of the early forties are sporadic. I was growing older. Life was changing. There seem to have been some lovely summers, and now they were taken up with saving the grain crops. Every farmer was obliged by government regulation to till a percentage of his farm. Some of the tillage had to be wheat crops insofar as that was possible. Some beautiful harvest days were spent in the reaping fields.

Machinery was scarce at that time. Most farmers were still dependant on the "crooked scythe" to help save their crops. Reaping two acres of oats or wheat could take as many as three or four days. The scythe-man cut down the standing crop. Workers followed him to gather it in sheaves, and then came someone who tied the sheaf, thus keeping the straw together. It was hard work, affecting the back muscles, but it certainly led to a good night's sleep.

Here and there in the neighborhood there was someone with a regular mowing machine. This cut the grain quickly and reduced the time by more than half. Unfortunately, because of the vastly increased amount of grain crops, it was not possible for the few mowing machine owners to cover all the needs of the area. The west of Ireland was poor, still recovering from the effects of the economic war. More often than not, if the crop were to be saved, a contract had to be made with the wielder of the scythe. Everybody leant a hand, the young and the old, and at the end of a hard day in the fields, there was a feeling of accomplishment.

And so from early morning into the bright autumn evenings we reaped and gathered as the sun sank slowly. Rumors would circulate of an air raid on a British town, or someone passing along the road would bring news that the German U-boats had sunk another British ship. On a couple of occasions, the bad news struck nearer home. German bombers had attacked the North Strand in Dublin City, causing loss of life and terrible damage to buildings. It turned out that the Germans thought they were over Liverpool. Belfast was bombed too, and the thought of an Irish city being thus attacked created antipathy toward the attackers. Border or no border, when the chips were down, fire brigades from the Republic rushed to the aid of their Belfast neighbors.

I retain recollections of those long-gone days and the field we reaped. Most likely it has stayed in my mind because it was in front of my grandmother's cottage which had been the scene of many a happy hour. My grandmother was, of course, living with us now. Her cottage had been abandoned. And unfortunately, there is no photograph of that lovely home. Cameras were a rarity in our lives then. The Kodak box camera was most prominent, and many of its owners had acquired it through saving coupons. The war was in its early years and would last a long time yet.

In September 1942, I began high school (secondary school), a totally new experience in my young life. And sometime in the fall of 1942, a well-known Hollywood actor—Leslie Howard—was killed when the plane in which he was traveling was attacked by the Nazis who thought that Winston Churchill was on board. Churchill had several look-alikes who were used as decoys. The one who got on the plane was the one reported to German intelligence who believed they had the prime minister of Britain in their sights. And so a planeload of innocent persons went to their deaths.

September 1942 was a watershed. My parents considered sending me to a boarding school but in the end elected to send me about forty miles from home to a secondary school (a day school as it was then known, because at the end of the day the students went home). In the Ireland of 1942 that distance was equivalent almost to being on another continent. It was arranged that I would stay as a boarder in a home in Castlebar that was owned by a very nice older lady named Mrs. Griffin. I was twelve years old.

Mrs. Griffin was caring, and she was kind. But when you are twelve years old and have never been away from home, and now you know you won't see your parents or your own fireside again for a few months, your outlook changes. In the early days of that September I learned that surely "there is no place like home." Gone was the sense of security, the sense of ownership, the familiarity with places, the memories that attach themselves to things, the ability to complain, yes, and the lack of want—and whatever else makes for the loveliness of the place we call home. And although Mrs. Griffin was thoughtful, the old home ritual was gone. For the first time in my life I learned about loneliness and perhaps how to deal with it.

The De La Salle Brothers ran the school. They were friendly and they were also good teachers. The jump from grade school to secondary was intensely exciting in those first weeks. Whereas in the grade school the same teacher taught us all day, now we had a variety of teachers. The first days of school were especially enjoyable.

Mister Nally was our Latin teacher. To this day, I have no idea what his Christian name was. Like many a teacher he had a nickname that outlasted himself. He was known as "The Bull." (Suffice it to say, looking back in my mature years, he was probably as gentle as they come. I cannot recall him ever striking anyone. But he knew how to use his large physique to instill attention edged with no little fear!) He was a burly man, not lacking in height, and he knew how to breathe fear without using any kind of violence.

In each class he kept a "bad list." This was a list of those he considered underachievers, and they had to surrender their homework first thing at the beginning of every class he taught. It would lie on his desk as he taught the class and went over the exercises he had given us. Now and again he would look over one of the exercises on his desk and shout, "Bourke, you got it wrong again. How many times is this you have made the same mistake? You remain on my list for two more weeks." Occasionally, he would call out the name of a "bad man" and bring him forward to answer questions, while the rest of the class sat in silence and learned much from the experience.

On the other hand, one could also gain points—which I must say were almost impossible to gain. If the homework was flawless just one time, Mr.

Nally excused the student from all homework for one week! This was a rare occurrence because Mr. Nally always found a period out of place (one was all that was needed!) or some other similar flaw to make sure the applicant did not gain the desired prize. Indeed, when the prize seemed to have been gained, Mr. Nally would ask two or three students to go over the homework "just to make sure." Oddly enough, and sad to say, the students (who were never the same group) were just as likely as Mr. Nally himself to find something incorrect. And frequently the student on the verge of joy found himself propelled back again to the hinterlands of despair. But one thing was sure: no student every wanted to be on "Bull Nally's" bad list!

Once only did I have a confrontation with "The Bull." He was also in charge of the lower grades' football games. Being a football enthusiast, I was always highly intent when I played the game, and I felt that all others should feel the same way. Don't mind that some were actually forced to line out because of school regulations.

On one occasion, during a game, I felt that our goalkeeper did not make enough effort in trying to stop the ball from entering the net. I shouted at him with an epithet that surely was not complimentary of his ability. It so happened that Mr. Nally, who was refereeing, was close by. He shouted to me, "Harte, do you want to go in goals? Why don't we see how good you are?" It wasn't an invitation. It was a command. Reluctantly and fretfully I took the goalkeeper's place. To my consternation, Mr. Nally stopped the game and announced, "Now we are going to see how good this know-all Harte is." He took the ball in his hand, stood about fourteen yards away, and looked as if he would blast me into kingdom come if I got in the way of the ball.

My mind raced. Should I turn and run? If that ball were to hit me with the sort of force he was capable of generating with his right foot, my earthly life might end. I was twelve. He looked every bit of forty-four and was probably four times my weight.

I made a decision. I would stand my ground, come what may. Life might be coming to an end, but I would not end it as a coward! I solidly faced the kicker, who was advancing ball in hand, and—knowing the end might be near—I also recited quickly my Act of Contrition. "The Bull" took a couple of steps made as if he were going to kick (my eyes were upon him) and then deliberately held back. He turned around and handed the ball to the original goalkeeper, said nothing, and signaled me back to my own position on the field. No words were spoken; none were needed.

On my way back to my position in the halfback line I drew some deep breaths. Never had I been on the brink of annihilation, but I was proud of myself that I had held my ground. From then on, whenever "the Bull" was refereeing, I was not to be heard from!

That first year of high school seemed to drag, but when one is young, time seems to be never in a hurry! The Christmas vacation came, and it surely felt like the return to the Promised Land. The song "I'll Be Home for Christmas" brings back the memory of those days. There was a discipline at home, but it didn't seem to matter anymore. Discipline is refined by love, and our home was a loving place. Nothing could compare to coming home.

The Church of Our Lady of the Rosary was just across the street from Saint Gerald's Secondary College where I was studying. The Brothers had encouraged us to make a visit to the Blessed Sacrament when school hours were over. Accordingly almost every student stopped in to make a momentary visit to the Lord. One evening, for some reason or other, I passed up the occasion and continued homeward. One of my classmates reprimanded me that I was reneging on my duty. I took him at his word, turned around, and accompanied him into the church. Of the two of us, I was the one who became the priest!

I suppose I knew I would be returning to the church that evening anyway. The Novena Booklet of Our Lady of the Rosary was among my favorite belongings when I went off to secondary school. I had followed the example of both my older sisters who were unashamedly devotees of the rosary novena. Every evening after my meal I would trace my way back to the church to recite the rosary and novena prayers before the Blessed Sacrament. The rosary would remain with me throughout all of the rest of my life. Praise God, the Lord and His wonderful Mother remained with me too.

Chapter Seventeen:
A Bend in the Road

My first year of secondary or high school was over. I can't say that I felt I had made any great achievement. In June, I left Castlebar and Mrs. Griffin, intending to return in September. The war rumbled on; it would soon be four years since it began. It had become a part of everyday life. The United States had become involved when Pearl Harbor was attacked by the Japanese. People were killing each other on three continents. No end appeared in sight.

Hitler's armies were in Africa as well as Europe east and west! To the onlooker everything was stalemate. Rommel, the "Desert Rat," was in Egypt. Newspaper headlines would announce his imminent capture. Next day they would carry news of his escape or his recapture of some Egyptian fortification. It looked as though Rommel was unbeatable. Newspapers were purchased at times simply to follow the activities of the extraordinary Nazi general.

I wasn't too long home from school for summer vacation when one day a letter arrived—a letter that would change the direction of my life and perhaps set it on an unalterable course. The letter was an invitation to join the Marist Brothers' preparatory school in Athlone with a view to becoming a Marist Brother in due course.

There are some things in life that are inexplicable. I had wanted to be a priest, but I had never discussed it with my parents. Both had such an unusually respectful attitude toward priests and their calling that I considered it would be a mistake for me to say anything yet. My father had frequently expressed the opinion that it was a difficult task for any young man to reach the standards required by the Irish Church for its clergy. They had to be of high intelligence, and their background had to be flawless.

My uncle Patrick had been a Republican soldier, taken by the British forces from a football game in Clonakilty, tortured by having his nails individually pulled off, and incarcerated in a British prison. During the torture, the objective of which was to get him to tell secrets about his comrades, he remained totally silent and never spoke again, even when he was freed from prison at the end of "the troubles." This state could have been regarded as a mental illness, though certainly not inherited. Indeed, the more one ascertains about Patrick's fate and the treatment he received following his arrest, the more one is amazed at his courage and determination. He was a true soldier for Ireland in every sense. But for some unknown reason my father feared that the Church authorities might somehow or other bring his illness to bear against any son of his who might wish for the priesthood.

Once when three Marist priests had given a "mission" in Killala, the town nearest our home, I spoke with him of the great impression they had made upon me, and indeed, at that time, I also intimated that I admired their lifestyle. It was a suggestion that got a deaf ear, with an explanation about what happened to my uncle Patrick. I knew what he meant: he did not want his son to be turned down for any reason. My father referred to Patrick's fate so often that it was ingrained on my mind as well as his. It did not dissuade me from my desire for religious life, but it might have played a part in my response to the letter I later received from the Marists. Becoming a Brother would be less taxing from the inquiry standpoint than becoming a priest.

How did the Marist Brothers find my name? I believe that the Brother who wrote the letter, a vocations promoter for the Brothers, had friends in high places, such as in the Irish Department of Education. They had provided him with the lists of those taking the preparatory colleges examination that spring. I had taken that exam and had done well enough to please my parents. Preparatory colleges were schools that guaranteed a teaching career for those who won scholarships to them. I did not get the scholarship that year, but my parents were optimistic that I would qualify when I sat for the exam the next year.

The invitation to join the Brothers' prep school excited me. I had just spent a year being taught by the De La Salle Brothers in Castlebar. I had a high esteem for the Brothers. I could easily see myself as a Brother, promoting the cause of Christ. I had no idea of the difference the sacrament of Holy Orders makes, and throughout the country teaching Brothers were looked upon with great respect.

My mother's reaction to my desire to respond to the letter was positive. She wanted whatever I wanted, especially if it was for the Lord. My father was at school that particular morning, and on his arrival home the matter was put to him. He hesitated a little, saying he would have to discuss it with my mother and that I should not mail any reply for the time being. However, a short time later, he too agreed that if this was really what I wanted, he would not stand in the way. I mailed my affirmative reply, and within a short time a Brother visited our home. Soon all arrangements were made for my arrival in their preparatory school. The road of life had taken a turn.

Chapter Eighteen:
A New Commitment

The day came in early September 1943 when I was to leave for the Marist School in Athlone. It was a day I had looked forward to, but a day that was not really so welcome when it arrived. I was to take a bus to Ballina (some ten miles from our home) and then take the early train to Athlone where the school was located. Preparations for my departure had been going on for well over a month.

As I walked out the door, after receiving the blessing with the Holy Water that my parents always gave to those of us embarking on a long journey, I turned my head just enough to see my grandmother at the window looking after me. The image of her face has remained with me all those years. It was a face filled with sadness and resignation—a face that told a tale.

I did not realize it then, but I have come to know it since: this day was the end of an era. My grandmother understood what was taking place. Yes, I would see her again, fairly often, and of course I would see my parents too. But my home childhood was over. I was embarking on a course that I had set for myself, a course on which no one had projected me. I believed I was following a call from the Lord. All at home were resigned and agreeable to my decision. It didn't mean that they wouldn't miss me. Nor indeed did it mean that they would admit they did! My parents never allowed any symptom of loneliness to pervade a parting moment by showing itself. And as for my grandmother, I am sure she remembered our chitchats in her home in the bygone years, the making of the butterscotch and the scones, as well as all the laughter. Now she was watching a young teenager leave home to follow a dream of adolescence.

In Athlone, the Brother who had done the recruiting met the train. Three or four other boys were on board, and we got acquainted as we walked the mile and a half from the station. The sun was shining. The future lay ahead. My mind was racing. It was only then that I began to realize the impact on my own life of the decision that brought me here. Might it be a wrong decision? Should I have continued my schooling in Castlebar, without responsibilities and with less commitment? What did the future hold for me?

It was my first time in a boarding school. The building was new. The Brother in charge boasted of the workmanship of the building, how modern it was, and how the ceilings had been lined with the newest and best type of materials called asbestos. The dormitories were long and narrow, probably ten well-made single beds on either side, a medium-sized locker beside each. So this was to be my habitat for the next year. I reminded myself it was September. I would be going to sleep in this place until mid-July.

That night I experienced my first communal "going to bed." We were quickly made aware of the rules, and a major rule was that after night prayer there was the "great silence." There would be no conversation until after breakfast next morning. There was something strange about preparing for bed with twenty others without being able to converse. About ten minutes were allowed for those preparations, and then the lights were turned out.

I could lie back on my pillow undisturbed now and reflect on the course my life was taking. I entrusted myself to the gentle love of God and began to pray the rosary. After all, it had always been my steady companion. Among the reflections on the mysteries came flying thoughts of saying good-bye at home that morning, wondering what was going on there now, thinking of what tomorrow might bring, and a loneliness that I knew I would have to conquer. I was asleep long before the rosary was completed.

Chapter Nineteen:
A New Life

I was awakened by the clanging of a bell. It sounded exactly like the bell that called the congregation to Mass in our parish church of Kilfian. It seemed to be the middle of the night. In fact it was half past five in the morning. No lights went on in the dormitory. Nobody stirred. I lay awake and wondered. Later on I would learn that the bell was the wake-up call for the novices. Their novitiate was just a couple of hundred yards away from where we slept. I would hear that bell for a good many years more, and in time I would have to obey it too.

Less than an hour afterward, at twenty past six, the lights went on, and a Brother came through using a clapper. It seemed very early, but I knew I had to get used to it. This ritual would continue until I reached the novitiate some years later. Twenty minutes were allotted to getting ready, then we made our way to the study hall for morning prayers, which lasted approximately ten minutes, and then to church for Mass. The church was a few minutes' walk across the courtyard, and in the dead of winter, going the short distance could be unpleasant, especially since we did not wear overcoats to protect us from the chill.

After Mass there was a ten-minute thanksgiving period in private, although all remained in their places. As the years went by, I found this a wonderful time. The Lord of the Eucharist was with me, and I was able to enter into dialogue with Him. The period passed so fast I hardly noticed it—most of the time too fast, in fact. Indeed, I think this daily ten-minute thanksgiving and the intimacy it developed between the Lord and me was to have a profound bearing on the rest of my life.

The noise of a clapper from the back of the church signaled it was time for breakfast. The refectory in which we dined was an elongated hall. The Brothers in charge sat at a table at the top of the room. Silence had to be observed, and in true monastic fashion there was a reader at every meal. Particular books were chosen—some religious, some secular, and the life of a saint or perhaps a religious novel. In the morning, we mostly heard about the life of then Venerable (and now Saint) Marcelin Champagnat, the French priest who had founded the Marist Brothers.

As we advanced into higher grades in the secondary school, we qualified for the honor of reading in the refectory. It was a dubious honor, especially in the morning! The Brother in charge believed he had a calling in life to help young people read better. He clung to every word, rang his bell frequently to correct and advise the reader, and generally made reading in the refectory at any time an embarrassing and unfulfilling occupation—a nightmare of sorts! Having corrected the reader two or three times, he would bellow, "You are spoiling my breakfast." But since we were aware that his breakfast was much better than ours was, our sympathies were always with the reader! And besides, tomorrow it would be our turn to spoil his breakfast.

With breakfast over, there was manual work to be done. I have never forgotten my first assignment. I was on the "toilet" group! It was our responsibility to clean the bowls of all the toilets, shine the toilet seats, wipe the floors, and generally restore the toilets to their pristine appearance after twenty-four hours' full usage. The task was not made easier by the fact that the flushing apparatus had been misengineered, and more often than not the floors of most of the toilets were covered in water by the time we came to clean them. Add to that the total disregard of a large number of the male inhabitants for careful sanitary usage. It was a task calling for humility and not for a delicate nose!

How did this first assignment affect me? Did it cause some rethinking of my situation? Well, of course! This was not what I had come to the Marists for. Nobody had told me the kind of life that lay in store. I had to work out the why and the wherefore for myself. It was a disgusting assignment, one that I could not have foreseen in my wildest dreams.

"God be with you, Mrs. Griffin, and Castlebar" were the thoughts that ran through my head. Yes, I could leave it all and go home. But it was too soon. And besides I knew that in a month or so I would be working on some other more acceptable task. I was learning that we cannot always foresee the future. But I was also learning stability and self-discipline. One must not down tools and run at the first signal of adversity. Time did indeed take care of the problem, and never again in my training period with the Brothers would I be faced with such a totally repugnant assignment.

Manual work time lasted about forty minutes until a bell summoned us to the study hall. The morning study hall period was short. For classes we joined the day students at the downtown secondary school, Saint Mary's. This meant walking the mile or so twice a day each way. We returned around noon for lunch and then went back to the school. In good weather and bad this walk was done every day, Monday through Friday. It was followed by dinner, recreation (usually football games when weather permitted), and study. Saint Mary's was a school of dedicated teachers. Brothers were in the majority on the staff, but there were also a couple of wonderful laymen who had been infected by the Brothers' intense dedication.

After the lunch-break we always gathered to recite the rosary in common. I had fond memories of the recitation of the rosary at home, and here again I found solace in this time of prayer. It did not take long for me to find out that the Brothers had an intense dedication to the Mother of God, not only through the rosary but also in the comments that would be made in the classroom and especially in the religion classes.

Each weekend the Brother in charge of aspirants, or the "Brother Master" as he was called, gave a spiritual talk to the gathered community of students. For the most part the talk would revolve around the community that was the Marist Brothers, their foundation, and their life. Time and time again he would refer to the Mother of God and the devotion and love for her that was called for in a Marist Brother. It was not without reason that Marcellin Champagnat had also titled his congregation "The Little Brothers of Mary."

Every three months or so we were visited by the Brother Provincial. He would also address the assembly, always insisting on the necessity for the spiritual life and the devotion of the Brothers to the Mother of God. The regularity and consistency of the advice given by the various speakers was bound to have its effect. In ways we were living the monastic life—praying, working, playing, and studying. And the objective was kept clearly before us: to be holy so that we could impart that holiness later to the students we would teach.

Looking back though, I have to admit a certain amount of brainwashing took place. The Brother Provincial, especially, would frequently refer to the sacredness of our vocation, what God was calling us to, and how important it was that we remain on course. Frequently he would quote a verse from scripture: "The man who puts his hand to the plough and looks back is not fit for the kingdom of heaven." This was a rather humongous threat in a way and a misdirection of the Lord's intent. The Lord was speaking about Christianity, nothing else. We were too young to understand the Lord's meaning, and possibly the Brother Provincial, who may have come under the same training, believed in his heart that what he was saying was correct.

Chapter Twenty:
Marist Novitiate and Beyond

The war in Europe rumbled on. News was scarce for us, because for some strange reason in those days there seemed to be a feeling among religious congregations that reading a newspaper could be injurious to one's vocation. The less connection with the outside world, the better! Whatever news of the war we got came from the day-students we joined for classes at Saint Mary's.

An announcement was made to all the students on a stormy morning of June 6, 1944, that Allied troops had crossed the English Channel and had successfully entered Normandy. We were told little though, just that it had happened. We were encouraged to pray for peace and an end to the fighting. Naturally, we had no idea of the sacrifices of those brave and wonderful soldiers as they faced imminent death on the shores of northern France. Thanks to their heroism, the war was won within a year.

Then gradually the dark bread disappeared. It was delightful to get back to the "real" bread of prewar times! For six years we had been eating the "black bread." Fruits that had disappeared began to reappear also. We had not seen an orange or a banana for years. Their return signaled that good times were back!

When I returned from vacation at home to the Brothers' preparatory school in 1945, I had mixed feelings. I had never been away from home for more than a year. Now I was facing a long period of uncertainty as regards homecoming. The very next September (of 1946) I would be entering the

Marist novitiate—a year of intense spirituality and study of the rules of the congregation.

When the day came, my parents attended the ceremony—the "clothing" as it was called—a ceremony during which the aspirant received the religious garb of the Society. For a full year I would be, as in the military term, "confined to barracks."

There were few privileges, and the Brother Master still believed in the virtues of manual labor. There was plenty of this since the novitiate was located on a farm. For several hours each day, we were called upon to rake and hoe, to dig potatoes, to save an oats crop. Two incidents I recall very well.

There was a huge ash tree on the grounds that for some reason or other the master of novices wanted removed. It was literally the kind of tree you envisage in the scriptural passage where the "birds of the air come and make their nests"—large enough indeed to shelter thousands of birds. The tree was to be dug out, a task that, on reflection now, seems a piece of foolishness.

But the Brother Master had a plan. If we were to dig carefully on one side of the tree, then dig some on the other side, the tree would fall in the direction of the deeper hole. This man had a strange sense of physics! We dug and dug and then dug some more, but the tree did not fall. We spent endless hours around that tree for more than a week. The tree refused to budge, despite the gaping cavernous hole that now housed its well-cut roots! We attached ropes to it and ten or more of us at a time pulled in an effort to get the tree to begin its fall. Nothing happened! No movement! This thing seemed monstrous enough to stand on its roots without any soil! It truly matched the mighty Cedar of Lebanon mentioned in the scripture.

Then one morning when we got up, the tree was lying on the ground. It had fallen during the night, and it had not fallen as it was supposed to fall! It fell in the opposite direction—toward the very place where the laborers had been daily assembled by the Novice Master. That tree could have killed all of us! The Lord spared our lives by bringing it down Himself when nobody was present.

The autumn of 1946 came wet. Farmers had difficulty saving their crops because of the constant rains. So severe was the weather that it caused the postponement of the all-Ireland football final. The farmer next door appealed to our Novice Master to send him some young men to help save his crops. The work was not easy. It was hard on the back! And the hours were long. The only reward was a spiritual one. The farmer gave us his verbal "thanks" but nothing of a material nature other than perhaps a few apples here and there if you were lucky enough to get one.

Father Greene was our beloved spiritual director. He administered the sacraments and provided daily Mass. He was also a sports fan, and in the absence of the daily newspapers, he made sure to convey to us the sports news of the day. Mondays were his busiest days for spiritual direction— naturally! Everyone was allowed "to see the priest," and no questions were ever asked as to why he did such a brisk business on Mondays. Father Greene gave good spiritual direction, narrated his experience of any game he might have attended the previous day, and had the newspaper on hand to allow us to read about our favorite team and how it got on!

In 1946, of course, the final was between Roscommon and Kerry. The Rossies seemed to have it won until Kerry kicked two unlikely goals in the final minute and tied the game! Much to the dismay of all of us Connacht men, Kerry was the victor in the replay.

In the following year, 1947, we were allowed to listen to the broadcast of the final between Kerry and Cavan, coming from the Polo Grounds in New York. The game made history in that it was the only time ever that the final of a Gaelic Football Championship was played outside the country and broadcast all the way from the United States, a feat of great magnitude at that time. As we listened, the sound of crashing waves could be heard coming from the cable that was laid under the Atlantic Ocean.

Cavan was the winner, and the exploits of their full forward Peter Donohue were compared to those of Babe Ruth in the newspapers the following day. At the time I had no knowledge of who Babe Ruth was! Nor did I have even the slightest notion then that I would ever be in his land.

Those were days too when "the schedule" governed the radio programs. If the game ran beyond its scheduled time on the air, it was simply cut off. But history was made here too when the radio station allowed the game to continue on the air even though it had gone long past the scheduled time.

When I recall my time in training for the Marist Brothers, I think with fondness of Father Greene and pray that his always smiling face is now reflecting the joys of the beatific vision. He was more than a chaplain. He was our friend and our sports outlet to the outside world.

We came to the end of novitiate days and took our first vows of poverty, chastity, and obedience, binding for one year. For anyone unfamiliar with the terms, they sound much more solemn than they are! Religious congregations may take "simple" or "solemn" vows. The "simple" vow allows a person to own property, but he may not enjoy its fruits. A religious in simple vows could for instance own a savings account in a bank but could not use any of it for himself! It is as if the person owned nothing at all. The "solemn" vow proscribes ownership entirely.

The vows of the Marist Brothers are simple vows. So on an August day of 1947 I formally renounced my right to enjoy use of any property I owned or might own. The vow of chastity carries with it an obligation to celibacy. The vow of obedience obliges the taker to obey the directives of lawful superiors and be always ready to take up a new assignment. These vows would be repeated for five years, and at the end of that period final vows were taken, that is, vows that were binding for life. In the intervening years, between 1947 and 1951, my education as a primary teacher was completed.

When it was all over, I found myself in Sligo, then and now a bustling town in the west of Ireland. The Marist Brothers had been in Sligo for a long time, and on my arrival I was the youngest member of the community. My classes there were mostly lower grades primary, boys who had come from families that were mostly middle class. They were easy to manage and enjoyable to teach. Father Tom Hanley was the administrator of the cathedral parish in which we worked, and I remember him as zealous and enthusiastic regarding education, especially the practice of religion.

It was during my time in Sligo that Father Tom came up with some "evangelical" work for the Brothers to do. He invited us to visit families in certain areas to encourage them to attend their Sunday Mass. So each week we spent a couple of evenings after school visiting homes and encouraging parents to give good example to their children by fulfilling their Sunday obligations. It was a work in which I was glad to be involved and something I especially remember from my days with the Brothers in Sligo. The families we visited were always receptive and always promised to do their best.

There were also the Eucharistic processions on the occasion of the Feast of Corpus Christi. The procession began in the cathedral grounds and traveled a good distance around the town before arriving back at the cathedral again where Benediction was celebrated. These processions were attended by thousands of people who joined in singing hymns and professing their faith in a very public way. The procession was a wonderful testimony to the faith of our fathers and an exemplary demonstration of Irish belief in Eucharist. And contrary to publications I have recently come across, no pressure was put on the people to attend. They were invited from the pulpit, and their faith did the rest.

In 1954, the rosary priest Father Patrick Peyton visited Sligo with his Rosary Crusade. It was an unusually warm afternoon, and more than twenty-five thousand people filled the show grounds for the event. Our school classes were taken to experience the occasion and hear the Holy Cross priest give his own testimony to the power of the rosary and the watchfulness of God's Holy Mother in His life.

Father Peyton was born in Attymass in County Mayo, forty miles or so west of the show grounds and about twenty miles from my own birthplace. He had emigrated to the United States before joining the Holy Cross congregation from which he later began his rosary crusades in both the United States and Europe. The gathering in Sligo was well organized, with members of the Irish army present to keep order and direct traffic. The occasion proved too much for one of the soldiers who passed out because of the heat of the afternoon.

Father Peyton's slogan was family oriented: "The family that prays together stays together." He was a good and holy man whose cause of beatification has been introduced. He did everything to spread his beliefs in the Gospel, even convincing some of his Hollywood friends to make a number of movies related to the mysteries of the rosary. As a fellow Mayoman, I would try to imitate his energetic zeal in later years by promoting the rosary at Mary's Shrine in Orlando.

School days came and went, and so did time! In those days, the town Gaelic football team, Craobh Rua (in English, "The Red Branch," from ancient Irish history) took part in the football championships of the county. Technically, Brothers were not allowed to play football. In practice, however, we did, and our superior, even though he was well aware of his men's sporting activities, chose to turn a blind eye. Those were the halcyon days of that football team, and sad to say, it departed the scene entirely a couple of years after I had left Sligo. But the student of the game looking into winners of the Sligo football championship in past eras will see the name Craobh Rua appearing more than once in the honors column. I might add that the same inquirer will find recorded a football team called "The Lily Whites" who took the Sligo town championship for a couple of years in a row. The team consisted of several Marist Brothers.

Those were times when vocations to religious life prospered in Ireland. Nobody at that time could have predicted the paucity of vocations within half a century or the lessening of the influence of the Catholic Church. Times would change drastically.

Chapter Twenty-One:
Rebirth of a Dream

⌘

In every life there comes a time to look back. I was twenty-three. I was committed to a religious life of teaching. It seemed to me I would be rising early for the rest of my life, preparing lessons, trying to impart knowledge and most importantly knowledge of religious faith. My life was set. Or was it?

It was the summer of 1953. It would bring sadness. On July 24 my beloved grandmother, Nan, one of the lights of my life, died at home. She had been suffering from gall bladder problems that apparently at the time were incurable. Her large funeral gave witness to the life she had lived and the friends she had made. She was buried in the family cemetery of Rathfran, on an inlet of Killala Bay where the Palmerstown River joins the sea. The cemetery was once the site of a thriving monastery until it was destroyed by the Cromwellians in the mid-seventeenth century. Then the immediate property surrounding the destroyed monastery was chosen as a cemetery by the local communities who wished to have their remains lie in a place hallowed by the prayers and activities of saintly and martyred monks of other times.

When Nan died, I came to be haunted with recollections of the ordination of my cousin, Father John, so many long years ago. I remembered my hopes of that time that I would follow him into the priesthood. Frequently in the past years, especially as I spent time before the Blessed Sacrament, I wrestled with the once great desire. But I always managed to put it away, consoling myself with the thought that God wanted something else from me, that somehow I was where I was because it was God's will.

Oddly enough, Nan's death made me think all the more. I reflected at her funeral that if I had entered an Irish seminary, I would now be nearing ordination. I had never shared my aspirations with Nan or anyone else in the family. But her death did something to me, for some reason that I cannot explain. Was it my childhood memories and my closeness to her in those early years? I cannot say, but I began to have doubts about where I should be and what I should be doing. A persistent gnawing about priesthood began to make its presence felt.

It wasn't that I didn't have doubts before, but I had always managed to overcome them. Now they kept returning. Whenever I went before the Blessed Sacrament, a great desire arose in me. I wanted to be a priest. I kept remembering my petition to Our Lady at Knock Shrine on that morning long ago. I argued with myself. I talked to the Lord about it time and time again. I resorted once again to my favorite rosary novenas. Every day, at lunchtime, while we waited to return to the classroom, I went into the oratory of our religious house and prayed the rosary novena before the Blessed Sacrament. In that oratory there was a beautiful statue of Our Lady. I prayed fervently before the statue every day, and I asked Our Lady to show me what to do. But no answer seemed to come.

I brought the matter up with my confessor. He didn't see any problem. If I wanted to be a priest, then why not take the steps to bring it about? I was becoming more and more inclined toward making the change, but somehow or other I lacked the courage. It seems I wanted everything to happen without any effort of my own.

Then something simple and yet extraordinary happened. My oldest sister, Maeve, was making her final vows the following January. Naturally I was going to be there, irrespective of how I got there. A couple who had become my friends over the past several years were also invited to my sister's celebration. They were indeed special people. Throughout a lifetime God sends His blessings in the friends He bestows. There is no explanation for friendship, and how this friendship blossomed I cannot explain. But blossom it did, and frequently we had all enjoyed a meal together. When the invitation to Maeve's ceremony arrived, it was agreed that the wife would attend the celebration while her husband looked after business interests, and she would provide the transportation that I needed to get there.

So on a dull and damp January morning we drove the fifty miles or so to the convent. The ceremonies were beautiful. My parents were there, and my father, especially, showed his pride at his daughter's choice of vocation. We didn't know it then, but it was to be the last family gathering. My father was closer to the great call than anyone could have guessed.

On the journey home the discussion ranged over many items—my sister's vocation, the history of her entry to the convent and why she had chosen that particular convent, located as it was so far away from her own home and not even within her own diocese. I said that my sister had been directed there by a Carmelite priest, who had been her spiritual director. Then, as a thunderbolt out of the blue, came a question that pierced my soul like a lightning strike: "Tell me, why are you not a priest too?"

This was the first time in all of my life that anyone had even remotely suggested anything connecting me to priesthood. Something exploded in my brain. I might be qualified to be a priest! "Why are you not a priest?" was ringing in my ears, filling my mind, taking possession of my whole being. This time there was no fight back—no excuses, no apologies. *I should be a priest!* I told myself. *Yes, it is a pity I am not where I should be! I can change the situation. And I* will *change it as soon as possible!*

By the time I got back to our community house the die was cast. There was no longer any doubt about what I was going to do. I was going to leave the Marist Brothers. I was going to begin my journey to the priesthood. I would try to be what I had always wanted to be, a priest of the Lord! It was the Marian Year of 1954, and I knew the Mother of God would direct my footsteps in the push toward a goal that was always alive within my heart. There were troubles ahead of me that would test my perseverance. Just as well God does not reveal everything at once!

Chapter Twenty-Two: A New Beginning

The fat was in the fire! The decision was made. Now to implement it! That was not going to be as easy as it might have seemed.

Self-preservation is inherent in every human society. The Marist Brothers were no different. I knew from the beginning that my resignation from the congregation would not be easily accepted. My years of training told me that much. It wasn't that I regarded myself as important within the Society but rather the urge to self-preservation which I knew was thoroughly entrenched especially in superiors. My years of training (brainwashing?) also compelled me to try to resolve my problems within the Society, and that allegiance would lead to major problems ahead.

But before I would do anything or make any announcement, I would first try to be sure where the road would take me after I had left the Brothers. I would have to find a diocese before I would sever the bonds. I made an appointment to see the local bishop. Bishop Hanly of the Diocese of Elphin in the northwest of Ireland (not to be confused with previously mentioned Father Tom Hanley) was thoroughly outgoing and a beautiful example of a good listener.

I well recall the Sunday afternoon he invited me to come see him at his home. He was totally in sympathy with my cause. He was effusive in his offer to help. He would help me to apply for the dispensation from my simple vows. The application of a bishop would have brought an automatic positive response. I made a major mistake there and then. I told the bishop I would prefer to apply with the blessing of the Society and from within.

It was a decision I would very much regret! The bishop then told me he would accept me as a priest of his diocese, but emphasized that even as a member of his diocese I would spend most of my life in England. (Those were times of a multiplicity of vocations in Ireland as previously noted, and many Irish dioceses sent their priests to minister in England until they were needed at home. At times the priests would spend the most part of their priestly lives in England). Bishop Hanly suggested that if I wished he could also help me get a diocese within the United States. This seemed an attractive possibility, and I accepted the offer. He knew a priest, he said, who recruited for the American mission, and he was coming home very shortly. He would arrange for me to see him. In time I did see this priest. He showed up at the school where I taught one day, and the Brother Principal came smilingly to my classroom to tell me there was a priest to see me. He would take my class while we visited. (He might have been unhappy had he known the reason for the visit!)

So I left my classroom to make my acquaintance with Father Maguire. He was affable and not at all confused about my plans to change my life. He could get me an American diocese without any problem. He suggested Yakima, newly formed in the Pacific Northwest. He drew wonderful pictures of the enticements and rewards for priestly work there. It was easy for me to agree with his suggestion.

When he departed, I was more certain than ever of my future course. Now I needed to talk to the Brother Provincial and ask for his cooperation with my plans. In my heart I had no assurance that this would pan out the way I had hoped it would. I did not have a good history with provincials. This one was of small stature, and I had previously found him peevish and perhaps unfair in his decision making in my regard. In my novitiate days I had gotten a name for my rough play in football. More than once I had been sent off the field. The referee had reported me to the Novice Master as having a bad temper on the field, and bad temper was not a sign of virtue! Teaching Brothers should overcome their tempers, and should not allow themselves to be overcome by their passion for football! I never saw it that way, and while I agreed that I should "behave" on the football field, I had little time for those who played the game as if they had just come out of a refrigerator. My father had an expression that "if a thing is worth doing at all, it is worth doing well," and for me, football was a game worth what the participant put into it. And winning was what it was all about! So I threw my body about and perhaps a few other bodies too. So what? Files were passed on—or at least their history was narrated elsewhere, that's what.

The provincial arrived at our religious house for his semiannual visit. It was now my opportunity to inform him of my plans. The interview was, to put it mildly, unfriendly. In political terminology, it might be termed a disaster. The provincial was aghast and would have no part of my leaving. I should not consider it. I should not ask him to cooperate in something so reprehensible. If I persisted, I could write him, and he would see what might be done, but he hoped it would never come to that. He asked if I fully understood what I was about. That particular meeting stays firmly in my memories. It was plain to see there would be no sympathy for my aspirations, and the Society was not about to cooperate in bringing them about, at least not without a struggle! When the meeting ended I knew the ice had been broken, but I would need a larger pickax. I should have returned immediately to Bishop Hanly. I did not, and I would live to regret it.

The provincial hoped I would drop the subject. But he was of course wrong! He was no sooner back in his provincial house then he got a letter from me stating my ambition and asking him to forward my case to Rome. It did not take him long to respond. I needed, he said, to ponder longer on what I was doing. I should write him again later in the summer. His letter did not faze me, but the hopes of starting in the seminary that fall were beginning to fade.

I did write him again in July of that year. I made it clear to him there would be no changing of my mind. I wrote a strong, but respectful letter. But no response was forthcoming. The days of early August arrived, and I was at home for a week or so. Then the postman brought a letter from the provincial. Basically the letter said I could do as I pleased. He was "giving up" on me. The letter was cold and unfriendly. There were no good wishes. But the letter stated I did not have to return to the Marist Brothers.

I was naturally elated. I called Father Maguire who was back in Ireland to tell him the good news. It was too late now to get into the regular seminary, he informed me, but he would make arrangements for me to enter the philosophy section of Mount Melleray, a college run by Cistercian monks in County Waterford. And so, in the first week of September 1954, I took a train from Dublin to Waterford and made my way by taxi from Cappoquin to Mount Melleray. I was at the beginning of a new life. I felt I was finally where the Lord wanted me to be. It was a dry, if somewhat chilly September day. But there was a lightness in my step. And a song in my heart! A great adventure lay ahead.

As it turned out, the script was not to be exactly as I had imagined!

Chapter Twenty-Three:
Bad News

⌒

I was back in school again! Mount Melleray was a boy's secondary boarding school run by the Cistercian monks. Attached was a seminary for the study of philosophy, and young men studying for the priesthood could begin their studies there. Sometimes too, the secondary students remained on to commence their studies for the priesthood in their alma mater. The boarding secondary school drew most of its students from the southernmost part of Ireland, perhaps 150 or more. The philosophy classes consisted of students from all over Ireland, men who were anxious to be ordained priests but for one reason or other had to await their entry to a major theological seminary.

The majority of the teachers were Cistercian priests, monks following strictly the rule of Saint Benedict. There was something special about being introduced to the monks. They lived a life that was totally different to that of the rest of the world. They were vowed to perpetual silence, speaking only a sign language among themselves and requiring permission for verbal communication. They retired at around seven in the evening and arose at three in the morning. Their day began with chanting of the Divine Office when the rest of the world was slumbering. They had periods of meditation and prayer long before daybreak. Their day was old when the rest of the world was just beginning to come to life. Indeed, the day was old when each Cistercian teacher faced his first morning class! It was clear the Cistercian monk had one, and only one interest, that of promoting and reaching Christ's kingdom.

But there was something uniquely different about these men. Those who were assigned to teach and had therefore permission to speak showed a contagious sense of humor. They were always happy. They knew each student by name, and it would appear they took a personal interest in each individual. Classes were always interspersed with laughter and learning. Better still, classes were something to look forward to. There was nothing boring about the teachers, and there was nothing boring about what they had to say about life either. Odd in a way for men who seemed enclosed behind monastery walls! But more than one had experienced life outside the monastery and had left a hurly-burly world behind for ever.

Our philosophy professor, Father Ailbe was one such. Whatever his background, something he didn't seem to share, he was able to regale his students with stories of the fight for Irish freedom and the civil war that followed. Some of the stories were horrendous, but he told them matter-of-factly, trying to imprint on his students the effects of the fall of man!

One such story has remained in my mind. An informer had been sentenced by the rebels for his relationships with the British that caused the loss of lives. He had been condemned to death by drowning. He was tied up and left in a hole on the shore for the incoming tide. It so happened that the tide that night did not come in far enough. So next morning the victim was taken further out for the next tide to encompass him. Father Ailbe was illustrating the depths to which human nature can descend and that as priests we must always be prepared for any eventuality without being shocked.

These men led exemplary prayer lives. On Sunday mornings there was a High Mass in the monastery chapel. (Vatican Two had not yet taken place). All the students attended this celebration, and for many it was a highlight of the day. Nothing compares with Gregorian chant when it is sung in its pristine purity. It was a wonderful Mass.

The philosophy students occupied the same quarters as the secondary boarding students. However, in many ways the philosophy students were less restricted and allowed much more freedom on the grounds. There was, however, one rule that was unbreakable: smoking was prohibited. Anyone caught smoking was immediately expelled from the seminary. This may seem a strange rule in modern times, but we need to remember that the philosophy students were expected to give an example to the rest, and obviously for a philosophy student to smoke was an encouragement for the lower grades of the school.

Even by the standards of the fifties Mount Melleray was a primitive place. There was, for example, no hot water, and each morning students attended to their toiletries as best they could in the cold mountain water that was provided. Neither were there facilities for showering, and hot baths were provided once a month. These were allotted during study time, and students were sent for individually as their turn came up for the bath, about four at a time. Primitive indeed! But somehow or other the Mount Melleray way of life bred contentment and tranquility.

Mount Melleray was a happy place. I had virtually returned to my teen years as regards my mode of life. I had lost a lot of my mature freedom. I was enclosed in every sense. I was back in a boarding school to all intents and purposes (only this time no manual labor was involved}. But in truth I had found true freedom. I was doing what I wanted to do and, more important, what God wanted me to do. And now I had the great hope for the future, that one day I would be ordained to the priesthood. And my hopes were buoyed by the other philosophy students around me who expressed the same dream for their future life. I was truly content.

Then as if out of the blue, my dream was shattered! It was October 6, 1954, a normal Mount Melleray day, with some drizzly rain as we walked the road up the hill to our classes. The morning went well, as did all mornings. The day had cleared as we returned for lunch. It would be a good evening for football when the last classes were finished.

Just after lunch the president of the college sent for me. When I entered his office the president was holding a document in his hand. He looked solemn. "I have some bad news" he said. He opened the document and read from it. It was the reply from the Sacred Congregation of Religious regarding the application for dispensation from vows that the Marist Brothers had submitted in my name. The opening paragraphs of the document had to do with my application—the standard opening.

The last line was to lodge in my memory. If it had been a shot from a gun, it could not have created any greater consternation. It read: "*Maneat frater in sua sancte vocatione.*" "*Maneat frater* ... let the Brother remain ... *in sua sancte vocatione* ... in his holy vocation." I barely heard the president say, "I am sorry this has happened. You cannot remain in the seminary." The floor reeled for a while until I pulled myself together. The president seemed truly sympathetic. "Go back," he advised, "plead your cause again, and when you are free, I will be glad to take you back here as a student."

Chapter Twenty-Four:
A Bishop Helps Out

ᗞ

Next day, with a heavy heart, I took the train back to Dublin. It was October 7, Feast of the Most Holy Rosary. I was glad the news had come the day before and not on the feast itself. I was glad that Mary had not allowed bad news on her own feast day. But the only thing to do was to return to the Marist Brothers.

The Brother Provincial of the Marist Brothers was new. He assigned me to the secondary school in Dublin. The Brothers, many of whom were my former confreres and all of whom I knew, were sympathetic. They couldn't understand what had happened or why. As one Brother put it, if I had applied for a dispensation from my vows in order to get married, it would have been granted on the spot.

Personally, I was confused. I had come full circle. I had been a brother, thought I was out of the Brothers to become a priest, had spent time in the seminary, and now I was back where I had started. What was happening to me? Was God laughing at me? Somewhere in the back of my mind I remembered lines from *Oedipus Rex*: "Men are the playthings of the Gods. They are like flies in the hands of cruel children." The temptation arose to give up on God.

That was a temptation I quickly repelled. My prayers had not been answered; indeed, it seemed that God was doing strange things with me. Then I remembered Jesus in the Garden: "Father, if you will, remove this chalice from me." The Father did not remove the chalice. He did better. He raised His beloved Son from the dead. God knows what is best for us. He writes straight with crooked lines.

114

So I refused to surrender to the notion that it was all over. I would still continue the fight. I would not give in. "Go back and submit your case again," the seminary president had said. That was exactly what I was going to do. I am glad I did! To this day, I sometimes dream that I gave up, that I am still with the Marist Brothers. And although this would not have been the most disastrous of fates, I wake up with the happy knowledge that I am and for a long time have been a priest, that I bear on my soul the perpetual mark of the priesthood of Christ.

A great advantage of being assigned to Dublin was that I was close to the place from where help would come. The Irish bishops held a meeting in Maynooth that October. Maynooth has been the center of the Irish ecclesiastical system, and the majority of priests working in their homeland have studied and been ordained from Maynooth, a major seminary steeped in Irish history for many a year. Situated only about twenty miles from the city, it was on the Dublin bus routes, making it easy to get out to the seminary at any time.

I went to see Bishop Hanly, the bishop of Elphin, already mentioned in this narrative. He was attending the meeting of the Irish bishops. When he heard what had happened, he was not only dismayed with my news, he was also angry. It was incomprehensible, he said. How could this be? Who had made the application, and how had it been worded? The bishop was totally incredulous. He made it clear he believed the application had been put forward to the Roman Congregation incorrectly and with hostility toward me. He would ask the professor of canon law at Maynooth to take up my case. He was sure there would be a satisfactory outcome.

He introduced me to the professor of canon law. I met with this man on a number of occasions, and by January of 1955 we were ready to resubmit. The professor had no doubt as to the forthcoming result. I would just need to be patient, he said. Most likely it would take six or seven months.

It took seven months. One morning in July of 1955 two documents came in the mail. One was addressed to me, the other to the superior of the religious house. Both documents were the same. I had been dispensed from my simple vows. I was released from the Society of the Marist Brothers.

This time there could be no doubt! A hurdle that lay in the way had been crossed. In September 1955, I returned to Mount Melleray to begin all over again. Only this time it was for keeps.

Chapter Twenty-Five:
My Father Dies

༄

hat first year at Mount Melleray passed quickly. It was marked by the death of my father, who fell ill on the Feast of the Immaculate Conception 1955, and departed this world in the early hours of February 27, 1956. I was allowed home for his passing and funeral, and I recall it as a time of great grief for all of us. He had been an anchor in the family, and his quiet wisdom and patience had their influence on every one of us. In all my years I never saw him angry, but somehow he had the respect and what I might call the godly fear of every member of his family.

Mother made the laws for the household. Occasionally she would call for help from my dad.. To bring a discipline problem to his attention meant immediate reform on the part of the miscreant. If Dad had to intervene, then we knew we must indeed be misbehaving badly, and somehow or other nobody in the family wanted to upset him. This despite the fact that we never saw him express anger, raise his voice, or physically punish any of us.

Throughout his waking I recalled his great affection for all of us and how as children we would look forward to his arrival home from town after a day's shopping for school requisites. We knew there would be chocolates and boiled sweets, and he never disappointed us. And we looked forward to feasting on the chocolate bar that was called "Half-Time Jimmy" with the representation of a footballer kicking a ball on the wrapping. To this day, whenever I visit my home parish Church of the Sacred Heart in Kilfian, I have memories of him making the Stations of the Cross—and above all, of one particular weekday morning (it must have been summertime with school out) when we sat together under a memorial plaque for a deceased priest toward the front of the church, and he put me through my paces in the responses before I went into the sacristy to serve Mass. (The new ritual had not yet come into being). *"Introibo ad altare Dei ... I will go to the altar of God.."*

His life, too, underscored his understanding of using opportunities to pray. His journey to school every morning took him at least half an hour, and the way home probably took longer since it was mostly uphill. One of the attendees at his wake told me it was common knowledge that my father would cycle to the school gate with his rosary beads in hand and had done so for twenty-five years.

On a blustery, wet day in March my father was laid to rest in the family cemetery of Rathfran. In that same cemetery many years ago, he had buried his youngest son. The wheel had come full circle. Time does not stand still. Nothing in this life ever remains the same. His time in this world had been completed. And I am sure as he stood before the judgment seat, he heard the words he had lived to hear—"Well done, good and faithful servant."

His funeral over, I returned to seminary studies with the monks of Mount Melleray. The Cistercian priests were spiritual leaders, wonderful spiritual directors, men of great faith. Each day we saw them trudging off to work, spade or shovel in hand, walking in a straight line, one after the other (no doubt to hinder the temptation to speak). Occasionally we had the privilege of hearing them sing the Salve Regina in the evening, that wonderful good-night to the Mother of God, which has become the last prayer of every monk following the rule of Saint Benedict. And I was influenced by their devotedness to the things of God in their everyday life. They have influenced my life much more than I could have imagined at the time. What was important to them was not the comforts of life but the sheer passion of their intimacy with the Lord.

In my two years at Mount Melleray, I formed friendships that have lasted to this day. The unusual fact is that even though I spent four more years at the major seminary, it is, for the most part, the friendships formed in the Knockmealdown Mountains where Mount Melleray is built that persisted. And indeed, when I get with those friends and talk about the Mount Melleray experience, we all have the same fond memories. We conclude that even though Mount Melleray Seminary lacked many of the ordinary comforts, those missing were compensated for in the atmosphere it breathed. That was an atmosphere of prayer and constant recognition of the presence of God. Add to that a wild enthusiasm for the coming of God's kingdom.

Chapter Twenty-Six:
Life in the Major Seminary

All Hallows Seminary is situated in that northern part of Dublin City known as Drumcondra. It was founded by Father John Hand in the 1800s for the express purpose of ordaining priests for the English-speaking mission fields. Hundreds of young men had gone forth from All Hallows carrying in their hearts the inscription over the main door of the seminary: "*Euntes docete omnes gentes*"—"Go teach all nations." Each June the daily newspapers carried photographs of the year's ordination class with sometimes a listing of names and the dioceses for which the newly ordained were bound.

I arrived there in mid-September 1957. (Mount Melleray did not cater to theology students, all of whom moved to another major seminary when their philosophy studies were concluded.) In my heart I longed for the day when my own class would appear on the daily paper, for then would my dreams be realized. Some of the men who had been at Mount Melleray enrolled in the college with me, so I began my theological studies with friends. One of them was John McMullan, a native of County Down, who was destined for the Archdiocese of Seattle. Father John would spend forty years there tending to his people. Life takes unusual turns sometimes! In later years he would join me in Orlando in the ministry of the Shrine, bringing the Lord to visitors from all over the world. But even though thousands of miles separated us for all those years, we stayed in contact, frequently discussing the Shrine ministry and, following Father John's retirement in Seattle, joining together to advance the cause of Christ in a unique ministry serving tourists.

My first impression of All Hallows was that it was much more institutional than Mount Melleray. It had a rigidity about it that was nonexistent in Mount Melleray. For one thing, there was little or no conversation with the teaching priests outside the classroom. About ten other students from other philosophical colleges enrolled at the same time. We were to be known as "supplementaries." This was a name identifying students who did not begin their studies at All Hallows and had joined at the beginning of the theology courses. While at the seminary we would always be known by this dubious title, thus distinguishing us from the other students who had begun their philosophical studies for priesthood here.

"Supplementaries" were placed at the back of every class. For me, this was a happy event! Given my own choice I would have chosen to sit just about where I was placed, with a clear view of everything that was going on in front of me. During class some of the theology teachers stopped short of asking questions of the "supplementaries," an unexplained conundrum, but one that caused no real hurt. We didn't have to bother about revealing our knowledge or lack thereof.

There was a sameness about every day in All Hallows. Variations from the curriculum were minimal. Newspapers were neither provided nor allowed until my final year, when some changes were made. Looking back on the militaristic training, one can readily agree with the changes of the Second Vatican Council. After all, here was a group of young men preparing to bring Christ to the world, who were not allowed to have any information on what was happening in the world which they would enter in a few years.

The rules were strict. Once within the seminary walls, there was no release until the following vacation time. This meant that if a student had, for example, a toothache, the burden of proof lay on him to establish the need to go "out town" to a dentist. He reported to the dean as he departed and again when he arrived back.

Quickly we learned which rules might be broken with impunity and which could not. Most could not. Seemingly unimportant regulations, such as the prohibition of newspapers and magazines, could lead to a delay in receiving the order of subdeacon or deacon if the violator was caught.

It was a way of signaling that the individual was under surveillance, and further breaches of discipline might lead to dismissal from the seminary. The announcement of the various orders was made toward the middle of each year, when the list was posted publicly. That list was sought out and read with some trepidation.

Returning from vacation could be quite depressing, especially in the darker days after Christmas. Suitcases were temporarily deposited in the long corridor outside the refectory, and the rows of suitcases were a reminder that the individual owner was a "prisoner" from the outside world until the days of midsummer came around again.

There was an oddity about the major seminary too. Here young men, and some not quite so young, were being trained in Christian virtue and their minds and hearts directed to the Christian way of life. Yet on entering this seminary, every student lost his Christian name in everyday usage as far as the seminary authorities were concerned. Teachers addressed the students by their surnames, calling them Mister Harte, Mister Murphy, Mister McMullan, or Mister Stretton. There were no exceptions.

One spring morning, just after the mail had been distributed, the dean, who was about forty-five passed by. "Mister McLaughlin," he said, "would you pick up that piece of paper?" Now it happened that the same Mister McLaughlin, known as Frank to his classmates, was a little older than the dean. Like myself, he too had been a Marist Brother in Australia. This kind of humiliating discipline was so common that it had lost its meaning. Students knew that the seminary was a means to an end. The end was the priesthood of Christ, and all were accepting of the discipline and sometimes the humiliation they would have to endure in order to get there.

Just a short few weeks after entering the seminary, I was requested by one of my fellow students to referee a football game. It seemed a minor enough task, and I acceded to the request. After all, I was twenty-seven years old. I had both played and refereed in my previous life, and quite a few of the students were familiar with my football history, especially those from County Sligo where I had been involved with the Sligo town team. Students gathered around the sidelines to watch the encounter. It was a tame enough affair, still early in the academic year—something I was to learn could not be said about every football game in All Hallows. County footballers who had studied there had remarked it was less punishing to play intercounty football in the All-Ireland Championship than to play in the league at All Hallows.

Toward the last quarter of the game I was refereeing, I noticed the dean standing among the students. When the game was over, a student told me the dean wished to see me in his office. I duly reported there. It was apparent the dean was not happy. "Mister Harte," he said, "while you are in this seminary, you will never referee a football game again." I was given no explanation why, and I knew better than to ask. Was the dean testing my acceptance of authority? I was not going to give him any reason for complaint.

"Yes, Father," I humbly replied.

"You are dismissed, Mister Harte," he said. I never refereed a game in All Hallows again. Nor did I ever find out what I had done wrong that particular evening!

Studies at the seminary were intense. Examinations in those days were mainly in Latin, and difficult questions had to be answered in the Latin language. As is always the case, theology professors differed. I recall some with special affection. One was Father William Meehan, who taught dogmatic theology. Father Meehan was affectionately known to his students as "The Billy Maw." In case you are not informed, "dogma" is related to Church teachings coming from the scriptures. It would be important for a future priest to have knowledge of the teachings of the church. I don't remember Father Meehan for his teaching skills but rather for his kindness and his deep attachment to his Catholic faith. He would at times give some personal advice to his students too, such as "whatever you do, save your own soul." "Priests" he would say "are conversant with sin, because they hear so much in the confessional. Be sure to keep yourselves holy and not take sin for granted in your own life."

Father Kevin Condon taught scripture classes. It did not take long to realize here was someone with an intense love for his subject that he wanted to communicate to his students. In the early days, I thought he might be somewhat "far out" in his theories, only to find later on that many of them were incorporated in the Second Vatican Council, which took place a short time after my ordination. His classes were always enjoyable and always gave food for thought. Naturally he too had a nickname. He was known as "Kilty," but don't ask me why!

Then there was Dr. James Rodgers, known as "The Buck" after the movie character of his name. Dr. Rodgers taught moral theology (relating to morality and ethics of the Christian). His classes were looked forward to because he could come up with examples that made us think about what might or might not be sinful. He could bring those examples right down to earth, like Our Lord Himself, by telling parables.

A golfer, for example, owned a putter. It was an old putter, but he could put the ball in the hole with it from any angle. He loved that putter and would not part with it for love or money. He had even turned down large offers. Then one day, while he was at the nineteenth hole, someone stole his putter. What kind of sin did the thief commit? Mortal or venial? Dr. Rodgers knew how to get his listeners involved!

Father Tom Lane was also impressive. He came on the scene in our dogmatic studies a couple of years before we were ordained. He was a "challenger," always examining the whys and the wherefores and getting his students to do likewise. We could always look forward to interesting deliberations in the classes he managed.

An abundance of time for personal prayer was afforded the students of All Hallows. After dinner a student could retire to the library or the chapel or head to the football field or ball alleys. I don't know if the ball alleys are still there. The rapidly changing religious atmosphere of Ireland has led to the closure of most of its seminaries, including All Hallows.

I have reason to remember the ball alley. It was a site of deep friendship and strenuous competition between Noel Stretton and me. Noel, another Mayoman from Claremorris, loved to play handball, and once a week or so we matched our skills. We might have been friends, but on the ball court friendship was nowhere present. There were no pleasantries. There was a game to be won, and all other relationship was set aside. After his ordination, Father Noel departed for Duluth, Minnesota, where he worked until his recent retirement. I am proud to say Irish priests have brought the news of the kingdom to many a land far from home. I wonder if we will ever see again the numbers of Irish missionaries who left all things to follow Christ. Is that golden era over?

Occasionally I revisit All Hallows when I am in Ireland. It is nice to go back and have memories rush at me like water over Niagara Falls. It is difficult to enter All Hallows without passing what once was the matron's office and the corridor close by that led to the college chapel. As the title suggests, the matron took care of those who might be ill or some way in need of medical attention. Normally she attended after breakfast, and she had the power to recommend seeing a doctor or a dentist or possibly spending a little time in bed.

The Asian flu broke out a few weeks after I entered the college, and I was among the majority of the students who were confined to bed for several days. It was the only time I had to experience medical care while in the seminary, and suffice it to say that Matron and her staff of voluntary helpers took great care of all who were ill at the time. I remember her because of her kindness and her caring.

It was the custom to arise at around 6:30 a.m. with morning prayer in the chapel followed by Mass. The dean always appeared a couple of minutes before prayers, and absentees never knew whether he missed them or not. However, the majority took the precaution of obeying the rule that required absentees to report to the dean with their reason for being absent. Each day after dinner the dean stood at the entrance to the chapel corridor and accepted the explanations of the few who might have been involved. Let it be said the dean was never difficult or challenging, and other than the time taken by the few who lined up each day (with some trepidation), there were no further recriminations against the violators. The 6:30 morning bell was taken by students in turn, though I have no recollection of ever being "on the bell" myself. On one occasion, when it was John McMullan's responsibility, he came up with a brilliant idea. He found a bicycle somewhere at the entry way, took it to his room on the second floor, and in the morning rode his bicycle down the various corridors as he rang his bell. To his great surprise he encountered the dean who happened to be already on his way downstairs to the college chapel. That the dean did not approve need hardly be narrated. The rest of the conversation with the future Father John has never been revealed!

Chapter Twenty-Seven:
A Priest Forever

❧

Then it was June 18, 1961, my own ordination day! That morning of childhood attending the Mass of a newly ordained was a distant memory. But had it led me to this day? Seminary life was over, the years had flown, and a young man was about to achieve his dream: the priesthood of Jesus, ambassador of Christ, proclaimer of the kingdom.

Each day at the seminary began and ended with prayer. There was ample time for prayer in the mornings before breakfast. By regulation students gathered in the church shortly after the rising bell. Time was set aside for personal prayer and reflection, which was always followed by Holy Mass. On certain evenings of the week the college spiritual director gave his talk to the assembly. Throughout the day there were many opportunities for personal and private prayer. The academic year ended with a retreat for all, concluding with the ordination of that particular year's senior class.

Here was a wonderful opportunity to do better with my own personal prayer. The various devotions I had accumulated in my life came with me to All Hallows. I made sure that I prayed my rosary novena every day. The Litany of the Sacred Heart was also a part of my daily prayer routine, as it still is. And I also took some extra time each day to pray before the Lord in the Blessed Sacrament.

The early days in All Hallows seemed slow. But soon we were second divines and then third divines, and the day came when we were fourth divines. The noun *divine* comes from the study of divinity—the science that pertains to God. Theology students were ordained at the end of their fourth year, in the month of June. The longing in my heart for the beginning of the year of fourth divinity was finally fulfilled. I began to realize I was but a short step away from priesthood. There was a euphoria pertaining to that final year of seminary.

Those were the days before the Second Vatican Council. Pope Pius XII died in my second year in All Hallows. He would be followed by the fabled Pope John XXIII. The winds of change were beginning to blow, although they had not yet reached the halls of All Hallows. At some stage along the way a convention of liturgists met at Assisi. The news media reported their dialogue about bringing the celebration of Mass into the vernacular.

In our liturgy class at that time, our professor expressed a horror that someone might have even suggested bringing the Mass into the vernacular. "Gentlemen," he remarked, "you will never see the Mass in English in your lifetime." He emphasized *never*. How wrong he was! Just four years later some of the Mass would be in English. Less than a decade later the entire Mass would have changed to the vernacular. The priest would also be facing the people! After the new pope called the Second Vatican Council, some of the old trappings of the daily liturgy would change for ever.

On another occasion an ordination student asked a liturgy professor if it might be possible to change the wording for the distribution of Holy Communion. Before the Council, the administering priest said in Latin, as he placed the host on the tongue of the recipient, "*Corpus Domini nostri Jesu Christi custodiat animum tuum in vitam aeternam. Amen.*" (May the body of Our Lord Jesus Christ preserve your soul to eternal life. Amen.) For his trouble, the questioner got a glare with the response, "If you want to be a priest, you do what the Church does." The answer was safe, of course! Within the decade the formula had been changed to "the body of Christ" in order to distribute more quickly to increasing congregations.

Tempus fugit! Almost before we could realize it, the month of June had arrived. The date of ordination was set for June 18, 1961, with the archbishop of Cashel, Thomas Morris, performing the ceremonies. I remember the day before the ordination as clearly as I remember the day itself. It was hard to believe I had reached the goal. Tomorrow would change my life forever, when I would make a commitment to the Risen

Lord that would truly unite me to His priesthood and mark me as one of His own, right into eternity. Tomorrow the imposition of hands by the archbishop would somehow separate us as priests from the secular world and yet bring us ever closer to it through our commission to bring all souls to Christ. Truly, we would be in the world but not of it, and the successes we might achieve would depend on God's grace and our own awareness of our special calling to priesthood. From tomorrow our lives would be spent for the Lord and in the service of His people.

These thoughts were a far cry from my first resolution to be a priest and my petition at Knock on that Assumption morning so many years ago. I was now fully aware of my calling. I didn't know at nine years of age that I would be leaving home, family, and country for the sake of the kingdom. But as I reflected on it throughout the final day of our preordination retreat, I was grateful that my early dreams would at last be fulfilled. I could hear the Lord's words to His followers: "I have chosen you." And the words repeated so frequently in scripture were ringing through my head—"It is the Lord." Tomorrow was to be the day!

The morning of June 18, came sunny and bright. Long before the ceremony began, friends and relatives of those to be ordained had taken their places in the college chapel. We did not have the opportunity to visit with them before the ceremony, but as the candidates for ordination processed to their places at the altar, I among them, I recall seeing my mother and my sisters among the congregation. My mother was dressed elegantly for the occasion. I am sure she had little idea of how the example of her dedication to Jesus in the Blessed Sacrament had influenced the path I was following.

My sister Ita was beside her. Monica was there with her fiancée and future husband, Jim Fitzgerald; Anne was with Michael Jackson, whom she would later marry. Carmel was there too, and my brother, Enda, and his wife, Mary, were among the congregation. Only one sister was missing, Maeve. The regulations of her congregation did not allow her to attend ordinations, but she would be allowed to attend my first Mass. Of course I also observed the presence of my great friends Aidan and Mary Murray. I knew that when I would speak to all of them again, I would be a priest.

The ceremony of ordination to the priesthood calls for the candidate to lie facedown on the floor at one particular juncture. During this time, the choir chants the litany of the saints, invoking all the saints in heaven to pray for the soon-to-be-ordained, that he will be faithful to his calling and fruitful in his ministry. During this time, my heart swelled with gratitude as, face to the floor, I knew that my prayers had been answered. The desires of my heart had at last been fulfilled, and I had reached the day when the aspirations of childhood had become the realities of my adult years. I belonged to the Lord. He belonged to me!

All Hallows Seminary Church, church of the authors
ordination and ordination photo inset.

After the ceremonies, there was the journey home. How I wished my father might still be alive! On our arrival, a group of neighbors had lit a bonfire to welcome home the new priest, one of two from the parish who had been ordained the same day, and the first ordinations from that parish for many years. The welcome when I stepped out of the car was overwhelming. There was also an aura of awe as those who had gathered all knelt on the pavement to receive my first blessing. I went to each individually, placing my hands over their heads and extending the blessing. The faith of the parishioners shone as on the following morning when I offered my first Mass. Another newly ordained, Father Ambrose Pryce, was also offering his first Mass on that same day. He had been ordained in the seminary at Waterford. The altar rails (still pre–Vatican Two) were packed with hundreds of people who had come for both masses and were not going home until they received the first blessing of their newly ordained priests. The faith imparted by Saint Patrick was indeed very much alive on that never-to-be-forgotten morning.

In the sacristy before Mass, I was searching for a maniple. This attachment was worn on the right arm of the priest while offering Mass. The tradition had apparently developed from the very ancient Roman dress custom of wearing a sort of handkerchief on one arm. Just as the missing maniple was found in the sacristy, the parish priest remarked, "Ah, sure the Mass would have been valid without it anyway. I don't bother with it most of the time"—words that seemed extraordinarily strange to a newly ordained, but a sort of prophecy that came true four years later before the conclusion of the Second Vatican Council. The Council removed the maniple as a requisite to be worn at Mass.

Chapter Twenty-Eight: Arrival in the New World

On August 28, 1961, I departed my homeland to begin my new assignment in a faraway land. Even though I knew it would happen, and I thought I was well prepared, the parting wasn't easy.

It was a morning I had dreamed about, the beginning of my ministry. But as in all dreams, there were shadows that somehow earlier had escaped attention. Perhaps it might have been that I didn't want to dwell on the painful aspects of parting during those times of preparation. Having offered Mass one last time with members of my family in Marino Church in Dublin, we gathered for breakfast. My mother was never a person to display her emotions, but one did not have to be a psychologist to realize her pain at my imminent departure. Mother never showed her tears when any member of the family was leaving, but to the very end of her life she failed to conceal her sniffles when family members took their leave. It was her way of being strong!

We had given ourselves sufficient time to get to the Dublin airport and be together for a while before boarding the plane. As I remember it, most of my family was present. I would be away for at least three years. Apart from their desire to bid me farewell, they also wanted me to know they would miss me. Indeed, I was the only member of the family now to be outside Ireland.

I had prepared for years for this day. I had fantasized about it. After all, was it not what I had been born for? Suddenly I found I was no hero. Yes, I had been out of Ireland previously but only to England or Scotland

and for just a few weeks at a time. There was something final about going thousands of miles away to a strange land and not coming back for several years. But I concealed my inner feelings. If my mother was thinking that way too—and I knew she was!—she said nothing. We were all very brave! Finally came the time to board the plane and the final embraces, the final farewells. My family would go to the observation deck to watch the plane take off. Observation decks were a common feature of airports of the day. Terrorism was a long way off in those golden years.

On the plane, we strapped ourselves in our seats. It was an almost new jetliner, purchased a short time previously by Aer Lingus. The jet age had just begun a year or two before. I was watching through the window for the observation deck hoping to see my family. Then came an announcement that air travelers don't ever want to hear: there was a mechanical problem, and the plane would be delayed two more hours. We should deplane and go within the waiting rooms of the terminal. The flight would be called again.

There was an amount of dark humor when I reunited with my family. "That was fast." "You weren't too long gone at all." "We hardly missed you." But in our hearts we knew the same parting emotions would have to be experienced again. Indeed, the second farewell was more difficult. There was a stop at Shannon where my uncle John Harte and his son Gerald had come to see me. Before the Dublin delay, the plane had been scheduled for an hour-long stop at Shannon. Now it would be fifteen minutes. My relatives were disappointed but glad to see me one more time. They told me they would have made the seventy-mile journey anyway even if they had known.

We arrived in New York several hours late. I was met by cousins, sisters of the same Father John O'Neill whose first Mass I had attended as a child. New York was a whole new experience. My relatives spared no pains in showing me the city. They introduced me to Irish next-door neighbors who knew our family before they emigrated. They had left for New York and married, never to return. By the time I departed for "the far west," I had been given a good introduction to the land where I would spend the rest of my life. And it didn't seem a bad place at all. Indeed, it appeared to be a land of friendly people. I had fallen in love with New York, a love that still persists.

How times have changed though. The only way to make contact between New York and Ireland at that time was by telegram through Western Union. I knew my mother would be awaiting that telegram, and it was duly sent with a scant message that reported, "Arrived safely. Enjoying my time in New York. Love." Today the traveler can simply take out a cell telephone and speak or text message as desired! The cell telephone was a long way off in those years!

At Idlewild Airport, more farewells! (After the assassination of President Kennedy the name was changed to Kennedy Airport.) Was this the stuff that life was made of? Arrangements had been made with an Irish travel agent to get me to Yakima. It turned out he was not a very efficient agent, but perhaps he did his best in circumstances that did not yield the easy communication afforded us today. I boarded a "milk flight" at New York around 7:30 a.m. *Milk flight* was the term given at that time to air journeys that made frequent stops; they should never be taken by the long-distance traveler.

The first stop was Minneapolis. It was going to be a slow day. We seemed to be getting farther and farther away from Ireland! It was becoming a strange sensation. Feelings and emotions I had never experienced brewed up within me. I have been to Minneapolis many times since, and my arrival there always brings back those desolate memories as well as an echo of emotions on the day I first touched down there so many years ago. Time, though, can change our outlook! Now I have friends in Minneapolis! I don't recall the number of airports at which we landed, but they were many, and Spokane was the last before Yakima. By that time there had been a couple of crew changes.

For a good part of the journey the plane flew low enough for me to be able to discern the fields of tillage being irrigated by huge watering devices, such as I had never seen before. There seemed to be fields upon fields, all being watered artificially. We may have been over Iowa. I took out a writing pad and whiled away the time by writing to my mother, telling her what I was witnessing underneath. It was the first letter she received from me in the States, and I believe she kept it locked among her keepsakes for many a year.

Finally, after many landings we arrived at my destination—Yakima! It was exactly 8:00 in the evening. We had been flying from New York in a prop jet for fifteen hours. Yakima bore no resemblance to Ireland. Its brown and scorched earth didn't remotely resemble the lush green of home. In fact, it seemed like a desert by comparison.

In the following days, loneliness was my steady companion. I was in a land without friends, I knew not a single person, and everything was strange in one way or another. The food was different. I suffered an immediate culture shock, so much so that I wished I could return home. But I was also penniless. I had come here to do the Lord's work. I entrusted myself into His hands. There would be no going back. By the same token, I often think of the modern youth who have flown half the world before they are in their mid-twenties. I admire their courage and I am glad they were born into such an advanced world. I had never sat in an airplane until that first journey to the New World.

For years to come, there would be no instant communication with the folks at home, correspondence would be entirely by letter, and worst of all, no Gaelic football games to attend and no Sunday afternoon results. I remember well in 1971 or thereabouts a game in which Mayo played Roscommon in the championship. I got the bad result three weeks later! Mayo had lost!

Still, I knew I had to adjust quickly to a new culture and a total change of atmosphere, and the youngsters at my new assignment would take care of that for me.

Chapter Twenty-Nine:
Early Assignment in the Priesthood

In those years the Diocese of Yakima was still in its infancy. It had been carved out of the Archdiocese of Seattle in the early 1950s. It consisted of that part of Washington that lay east of the Cascade Mountains as far as the great Columbia River.

The Yakima Valley is a fertile valley, helped in great part by the waters of the Columbia. Its towns at that time were not large, and the population mostly consisted of farmers who were involved in fruit crops, hops, and vines.

The new bishop was very education-conscious, and his awareness of educational ability in any of his priests was sure to lead to a teaching career for that priest. The Jesuit Fathers had been in charge of education in the Yakima Valley for half a century or more. In bygone days it was also Jesuit Fathers who brought the faith to many outlying communities, traveling by horseback long before the automobile came on the scene. The bishop was eager to oversee the educational process, and so it came about that the Jesuits agreed to turn over their school to diocesan priests who would now be assigned not only to the old previously Jesuit-run Marquette High School but also to the newly erected Central Catholic High School across town.

On my arrival at the Yakima airport I quickly learned my fate. The bishop was there to greet me effusively, take me for a meal, and inform me that I was just the man he needed at Marquette. "After all," he said, "you have been trained as a teacher; you have the experience we need here. It is quite providential that you have come to our diocese."

It was ironic, to say the least. I longed for pastoral work, to be with people, administering the sacraments and working with adults. But my previous life had caught up with me. There was nothing I could do about it. I had promised obedience to the bishop on my ordination day. I was not going to break that promise. The bishop told me I would join the Marquette High School staff and live at the Jesuit house at their Saint Joseph parish. The Jesuit priests were still in charge of the parish while the diocesan teacher priests—five of us—occupied the upper stories of their rectory.

My first living quarters were indeed sparse and monkish. The monks at Mount Melleray had more space for their sleeping quarters than did I now. The room was pokey, with barely enough room for a single bed, a chair, and a very small wardrobe. Washrooms were across the corridor. In the heat of Yakima summer it was almost unbearable for sleep, and a fan was essential. Here I would reside for five years—an introduction to the priesthood and a reminder that those who serve the Lord depend on His providential care in their lives.

"Providential," the bishop had said regarding my arrival. It turned out that way too. The Jesuit pastor of the parish was born in Spokane, Washington. His birthplace seemed to be the only non-Irish factor in his life. Irish customs and a great love for Ireland had been passed down to him through his family across the generations. He welcomed me with open arms and a shrewd awareness that I must feel lonely being away from home and country for the first time.

We discussed my disappointment about not being assigned to a parish, and he promised that he would involve me in parochial activities whenever I had time from school. My time with the Jesuits, almost as part of their community, has left many good memories, and the oldest member of the Jesuit community, was truly an inspirational mentor and advisor. Looking back, working with young people in a newfound culture was the very best thing that could have happened to me. Young people are bright and breezy, optimistic in their outlook, and expect their leaders to be of the same disposition. It didn't take long to get over my disappointment or my loneliness.

My classes in mathematics and English were filled with welcoming students, who made no secret of their delight in being taught by someone from fabled Ireland! They wanted to know everything about me first and then about Ireland. How interested was I in sport? I passed that one with flying colors. What kind of place was Ireland? Were there automobiles? Did Ireland have an army, a navy? Was there a president? And of course the perennial question of the time: "Tell us about Northern Ireland and why it won't agree with the south." Despite the questioning, we actually did quite an amount of teaching, even in the early days, and it became evident to me that my students were very accepting of their new teacher.

Early on I developed what I believed a clever little "trick." I would take questions on any subject for about seven minutes. Then it was agreed that we would all get down to work and cover the subjects in hand—algebra, geometry, trigonometry. When the subject of Ireland had been exhausted, I began to introduce to them something about the saint of the day. They would listen and ask questions that frequently were far-seeing and mature. I recall some very interesting discussions even to this day—one on the martyrdom of Maria Goretti, a subject that is always of deep interest to young people; another on Gemma Galgani, who was so disinterested in her appearance that she showed up at a wedding on one occasion very ill clad and most inappropriate for the occasion!

My life as a priest had begun. It was not as I had expected. But in no time I had accepted the fork in the road. Mathematics or not, I had decided that I was in charge of souls. Through our daily discussions on religious matters, I found a way of reminding the young people that God is always at work in their lives, just as He was at work in the lives of the saints we celebrated. I made sure they understood He was in their mathematics too, the Creator of order and certitude through whom we devise our formulas.

I am grateful to the boys of Marquette High School. They taught me to initiate myself into a new culture, how to love and laugh. Hopefully, I taught them to calculate and think and to have a better awareness of the presence of God in their lives.

And I never missed a high school football game or basketball game. These young men took their games seriously and were close to my heart.

Tom O'Brien was the football coach, as energetic and inspirational a coach as I have ever been in contact with. I recall a football game when Tom, having delivered his oration before the game, bellowed, "Go out now and show those fellows how football is played!" Unfortunately, someone had neglected to open the wooden gate on the way from the clubroom to the field. As the team swept out they took the gate from its hinges. Did they win? Of course! More than that, they were football champions of Washington State a number of times.

Hal Dodeward was basketball coach. He complemented Tom O'Brien in his enthusiasm and inspirational direction, winning a very famous state championship in 1965. The final was not all that exciting. Marquette had the lead at all times. But the semifinal was never to be forgotten. Down at halftime by sixteen points, our young men came charging out to hustle and take the lead with less than half a minute on the clock. They then defended their basket, and a delirious Yakima crowd charged onto the floor at the final buzzer. They say a way to a young man's heart is through his stomach. But there is a way there through sport as well.

Marquette High was eventually amalgamated with Central Catholic and closed as a high school. At that time, I was transferred to teach at Central Catholic and assigned to live in a parish about twenty miles out of Yakima. Here again I was blessed to have as a pastor a man who taught me much about hospitality and caring for one's fellow priests.

Chapter Thirty:
The Winds of Change

The walls of All Hallows Seminary in Dublin were decorated with group photographs of each year's ordination classes. During our time there, we would occasionally take stock of a particular year's class, mostly to see what diocese they were ministering in. (The name of the diocese was given after each priest's name.) In those days, there was one priest who had left the priesthood—and, as far as we knew, only one—from all those photographs. That would be incredible today.

All of that was about to change. When Pope John XXIII convened the Second Vatican Council, he could hardly have foreseen the changes it would bring about not only among the faithful but also among Christ's priests. I remember those early years of the Council for its changes—some straightforward, as in changing Mass to the vernacular and turning the altar around; some psychological, as in the newfound "freedom" that seemed to emanate from the Council.

After the Council parts of the Mass were recited in English, but not the canon. This was the last to be changed. Altars were turned around early on in the Council. This latter change appears to have caused the greatest conflict. Even to this day, there are those who argue for turning the altar back again, without being able to give the remotest reason why. Some will argue back to the Council of Trent, as if the latest General Council of the Church was devoid of the promptings of the Holy Spirit and therefore had no authority at all.

Perhaps the changes came too suddenly and without proper educative preparations. In our diocese the clergy were convened on a few occasions for seminars about the changes. Some of the older clergy, especially, resisted the new order. It was a resistance that appeared to raise its head in every diocese. That resistance has been passed on to the faithful, who have kept the argument alive to this very day. Looking back, there was very little effort to indoctrinate the people on the "whys and wherefores." To many it seemed to be change for change's sake. One has to believe, however, that some dissenting clergy have been at the root of the divisions, and while the majority of objectors have long since died, their faithful followers have succeeded in passing on their disagreements among the members of their own families and those who might be inclined to listen.

On the psychological front, change came more slowly. Among the clergy it made itself known by the departure of priests. As it became clearer that the times were changing, priests who were leaving the ministry moved quietly elsewhere. But as the sixties sped toward another decade, the numbers departing the scene rapidly increased, and the general public was no longer scandalized. It was a time when priests needed to recognize and reflect on their calling. It was no longer a world in which the word of the priest was taken for granted, and the winds of change had also blown in the practice to "challenge" not only the priest but the pope himself.

Fortunately for me, I was stationed with a kindly pastor who had a great sense of commitment to the local community of priests scattered throughout the Yakima Valley. Following the amalgamation of the high schools, my living quarters were moved to Toppenish, at that time a medium-sized city about thirty miles south of Yakima. Father John Maraschiulo was the pastor there. I remember him as one of the great priests of my life. He was exemplary in his hospitality and his care for brother priests, and his rectory was always open to visiting clergy. Born in Italy, he had first been with the Salesian Fathers before joining the Diocese of Yakima. Since my work was some thirty miles away, I would frequently arrive home long after dinnertime. It wasn't just once, but almost every time, that Father John would arrive on the scene to enquire if I had dinner. If I had not, he would tell me sit down "while I prepare something for you."

Somehow he managed to prepare a Sunday evening meal for any and every priest who would come to visit. And come to visit they did! There were many occasions when as many as fourteen or fifteen priests would show up, sometimes traveling long journeys to be with each other and to enjoy the hospitality. For many of those priests the Sunday gathering was the heart and soul of the week, affording the opportunity to meet as brothers, discuss their problems, advise each other, and generally relax in a tranquil atmosphere. I have no doubt that many a priest left this gathering fortified to face the ministry and problems of the week. I often think it is a great pity that in modern times, because of the priest shortage and the emphasis on parish committees and meetings, this kind of opportunity of priestly companionship has all but vanished.

Truly, I enjoyed those Sunday evenings that to this day remain up front in my memories. They added to my own spiritual well-being. They were times of camaraderie, good humor, and opportunities to share whatever burdens might be bearing down on the soul. Naturally, among so many priests there was also ample opportunity for them to hear each other's confessions and continue to develop their own intimacy with the Lord. Now and again the card games would run late. On a couple of occasions the "youngest priest" was delegated to take the morning Mass at 7:30, a service I was very glad to perform since I always qualified and everyone knew it was going to be me!

Let it be remembered that priests too are human. Every pastor is aware of the impositions from the chancery office that sometimes come out of the blue and tend to destroy mental peace for a day or a week and sometimes longer. I recall the following story for the humor of the situation. One Sunday evening, before the majority of "guests" had arrived, a pastor was in the middle of a deep complaint about a letter he had received from the chancery office that week. Looking around, he spotted the chancellor who had written the letter, coming up the corridor toward him. He jumped up, met the chancellor in the corridor, and began to remonstrate with no little sarcasm for the correspondence he had just received! The chancellor's guilt, of course, lay in the fact that he was the one who had signed the bishop's directive in the letter. In the "plaintiff's" enthusiasm for his own cause, he was vociferous in his condemnations, expressing his feelings with unusual passion.

It so happened on this occasion that the bishop had decided to join the gathering (invitations were never sent out; the occasion was open to all). It also happened that the chancellor had been the bishop's driver, and to the dismay of the plaintiff, the bishop was walking a very short distance behind and witnessed and heard everything that had gone on. However, the bishop showed only humor for the situation and simply remarked, "Jim, are we messing things up that badly?" to which of course there was no reply! Our hero returned red-faced to his chair. The bishop saw the humor in the situation too and never referred to it again. Bishop Con Power was known far and wide as a bishop who loved his priests and found it easy to join them in any kind of gathering.

I had been eight years now in the classroom as a priest. I had enjoyed my teaching duties, but I still yearned for parochial work. Indeed, I envied the confreres of my age, once teachers with me, now very contented in parish assignments. Often I had asked for a change, only to have my request denied. Eight years previously I had come to Yakima with great expectations of becoming a parochial priest, working with the people. It was not to be. Certainly I had enjoyed the teaching years, but I was beginning to wonder if I would ever be allowed to take my place in parish work.

The winds of change seemed to be blowing up a storm. Some priests who had worked in Yakima had already left the priesthood, including one who had taught with me. Men I had known quite well on a daily basis were no longer with us. There were rumors of imminent other departures. Vatican Two, for one reason or another, was bringing a kind of change that had not been foreseen. I found myself in a vacuum. I spent a lot of time in prayer, and that was my salvation.

I prayed once again about my childhood dream, this time from a different angle, since I was now a priest. That dream was about working with adults every day, living the Gospel with them, bringing God into their lives. I suppose I had been trying to do this in school too, but it didn't seem to be the same. I found the best time to pray was, as had been established in the seminary, early in the morning. The Lord and I talked together, I tried to listen to Him and sometimes found myself arguing with Him. Why was I being denied the aspirations of my priesthood? Was I to spend the rest of my life in the classroom just because I had the reputation of being a "good math teacher"? "Why are you allowing my confreres to be in the vineyard and depriving me?" There were prayers and beseeching, and like Hannah in the Old Testament who had prayed and wept for a son, the Lord smiled on my petition.

One morning, the newspaper carried a report that the Church would soon open two new dioceses in Florida—one in Orlando and one in St. Petersburg. Once upon a time, only the brave would reside in Florida because of the heat and humidity. Those were the days before the spread of air-conditioning to homes and businesses. Northern businesses were beginning to transfer to Florida for better living conditions and less expensive operation costs. The Catholic population was growing considerably. The Church in Florida was very much on the move. Florida seemed to be an attractive proposition for a priest to go about the work of the Lord. There might be a rich harvest there.

The idea of transferring to Florida ran through my mind. Many years ago in the seminary there was a kind of unwritten rule that a priest should not change from his diocese. But times were changing. Bishops had become more open to the idea of priests transferring. I decided I would first try to speak to the bishop of Orlando and take it from there. In August 1969, I visited Orlando and received an appointment with Bishop Borders. He was most gracious, even to the point of inviting me to stay in his own home while I was in Orlando. In short, he advised me that if I received permission to transfer from the bishop of Yakima, he would gladly receive me into the Diocese of Orlando.

Bishop Cornelius Power was a very kindly man who was supportive of his priests and a wonderful listener, by every standard a bishop who was still one of his priests. I asked for an appointment, and the date was set for October 7, Feast of the Holy Rosary. I was pleased about the date, which I had not requested specifically, and I saw it as a sign from the Mother of God that, come what may, she was still watching over me.

The bishop was sympathetic, but he did not accede to my request. "As Winston Churchill once said, I am not about to preside over the dissolution of an empire," he remarked. He wanted me to think further about my request and to write to him again in the New Year. I wrote toward the end of January and was given an appointment for February 11, Feast of Our Lady of Lourdes. Again, I took note of the unsought date, a feast of the Mother of God. Bishop Power was disappointed with my decision but told me he would not stand in my way. I remember his parting words very well: "If you are not happy in Florida, or it does not work out for you, remember we will welcome you back with open arms."

It had been nine years since I first arrived in the great Northwest. The years had evaporated quickly. There had been joy and sorrow, hope and disappointment. I had matured as a priest in those years. An inner voice kept urging me to a new beginning, to making a new start. God, I believed, wanted me elsewhere. I notified Bishop Borders that I had received permission to move. Even though I didn't know it at the time, the Lord had been preparing me for a great adventure. I was forty years old when I arrived in Orlando.

Chapter Thirty-One: Beginning Again

Change can be traumatic. In midlife I found myself in new territory. I thought back nine years earlier and wondered if time had stood still. Here I was once more, a stranger among so many priests and people. Naturally, I was tempted to doubt about the change I had brought about in my life. But I was also determined to stay put, to do everything I could to be a success in the new life I was beginning. New lives are begun with a smack and a shriek. There was a smack ahead for me. Perhaps I should have shrieked earlier and louder!

I was still in search of a dream, trying to climb a sunbeam to happiness, in my own way still searching for the Lord's will in my life. Orlando had a nice climate. The sun shone. It was good to arise each day to blue skies. But were the fates against me? The bishop assigned me, unceremoniously, to part-time parish work and as a part-time teacher to the city Catholic high school. Would I ever get away from education? I was not too pleased, but this time at least I was officially an associate in a parish. The pastor was quite willing to assign responsibilities to me. Each morning I drove to the school where I held classes teaching religion. The young people were friendly here too as in my former diocese and indeed open to new knowledge. And like all young people they were argumentative and at times ready to try to shock and be different!

But were my troubles following me? It was 1970. The religious world was turning. In the wake of Vatican Two, new and extraordinarily wild ideas were beginning to float. One of my students in Yakima had chided me that I was a teacher of "ancient religion." I had surprised the student by taking the reference as a compliment.

I was not given to newfangled ideas, especially where the teaching of the Gospel was concerned. It was inevitable that I would be thrown into the cauldron of argumentation these theories would cause. They seemed to hinge around the practice of Eucharist and the sacraments and sacramentals of the Church. But when the situation was put under the microscope, the vast majority of young people, mostly from truly traditional homes, wanted to keep up the beliefs that had been handed on.

That did not mean there would not be challenges for me! The senior class was dealing with the sacrament of marriage. The subject of birth control came under scrutiny. There were long and arduous discussions and examinations of the subject. Instead of a Christmas exam, to the class's delight, I gave them a paper on "birth control and the Catholic ethic." One young lady chose to challenge the Church teaching. She wrote an absolutely well-informed paper differing with the Church and quoting from many sources. It was obvious the student had gone to great lengths to find her information and assemble her arguments.

On the January morning I was returning the papers and awarding the grades I saw her eyes become somewhat tearful as the girls around her received their marks and compliments for their work. She was obviously frightened that her disagreement with the priest and Church teaching would be her downfall. When I got to her paper, I addressed the class. "Maura," I said, "disagrees with us. She takes an opposite view to Church teaching. But she has done a lot of study. She has read a lot. She has not proved her point. But she has written a wonderful paper. I am awarding her an A." Maura broke out in a big smile. I had made a friend thenceforth and forever! She was a beautiful girl in every way. I have not met her for many a year, but I am sure she has made her way well in the world. Faith is a gift of God. We can try to impart it, but we can never enforce it.

Soon the academic year ended. There was a Mass at the adjacent church to celebrate the occasion. The bishop was there. He had a surprise for me. "I am sending you to another parish," he said. "We need a mature man there. The pastor has an alcohol problem, and I think you will be able to handle it. I'd like you to be there in September." Just like that, my time at Bishop Moore High ended.

On my return to the rectory, I told the pastor of my encounter with the bishop and the forthcoming change. Being a wise man, he did not say much, but in some ways his silence spoke louder than words. "Yes," he agreed, "I believe you will be able to handle the situation."

Time would tell that he wasn't entirely correct.

Chapter Thirty-Two:
New Life with a Slap

My bishop had given me an assignment and a challenge. I had no idea what was in store. The assignment at first glance was attractive enough. The people in the parish were friendly, and there were many young families to be ministered to. I was to teach some classes of religion in the high school as well. But I was grateful that at least I would have the opportunity to continue with parish work. I moved into the rectory with hope and a certain amount of trepidation.

It did not take too long to realize that I should be anxious. The pastor was indeed an alcoholic, imbibing not just now and again but almost constantly. He was difficult to relate to and in a very gruff manner issued instructions regarding my work in the parish. For me, this was an entirely new experience. I had not had to deal with alcoholism in my life before. His early instructions became unnecessary when I began to realize that I would be doing all the parochial work. That did not bother me in the least, but when decisions had to be made, I frequently found myself like a cat on a hot tin roof. Discussion was almost impossible, so I learned quickly to minister, to guide, and to stay as far away as possible from new programs and whatever might have to be approved by the pastor.

It was, to put it mildly, an incomprehensible situation. The bishop was aware of it, but somehow he did not want to try to solve it—if he even felt a solution was possible. Then again, I doubt if he fully understood the plight of the associate appointed to this task. It was more a condemnation than an appointment.

What should a priest do in these surroundings? The answer is probably nothing. But when you are forty-one years old and still zealous to fulfill priestly duties, you will throw yourself wholeheartedly into the fray. That is what I did. I took on the responsibilities of the pastor in my zeal for serving the Lord. The pastor handled all of the administration side, and I was in charge of everything else.

All in all, it was, as a teenager might put it, "a weird situation." But I had my work to do, and thankfully there was plenty of that. There were many young families in the parish, and I was able to attend to their spiritual needs. I became involved with the youth, and we were able to form a wonderful youth choir. There were older people too, and I made it my business to make sure to visit them in their homes and whenever they had to go to hospital. From the hospital visits especially I learned that the sick are most appreciative of the visits a priest makes in their illness, and this is something they do not readily forget. Indeed, I made many friends through those hospital visits. We had a wonderful ladies' association and a very active men's club.

The assignment to this parish will always be foremost among my priesthood memories. Four decades later, a couple of episodes come to mind as if they had happened only yesterday. I can almost smell the coffee. Even to this day, sometimes in my dreams I hear a loud knock on my door and a gruff voice outside. The housekeeper always set the automatic coffeemaker to "on" as she ended her day's work. It was a matter to which I paid scant attention until one evening some friends came to visit. I had been involved in a car accident on the interstate a short time previously and had broken my collarbone. Some friends had traveled from Orlando to see how I was recuperating. The pastor had gone out for the evening, and rather than leave the house with my arm in a sling, I simply turned on the coffeepot for my friends. After their departure it did not occur to me to reset the coffee pot. I paid for that oversight.

At around midnight my slumbers were rudely interrupted. There was a knock on my bedroom door, and in my sleepy condition I saw the pastor come in. "You drank my coffee," he bellowed. "Get up, get up. Make more, who do you think you are?" He kept repeating that I had drunk his coffee. At this stage, however, it was very evident that the coffee was not the problem. Indeed, I could have thrown him out of my bedroom. After all, I was in my early forties, and he was years older and at this moment having problems with his balance! I took the peaceful route, however. I got out of bed, went to the kitchen, and as he supervised my work in his drunken stupor, I put the coffee pot in action. It would be the last time I would ever touch his coffeepot. Not that it mattered very much to him anyway. Through the paper-thin walls of the rectory in which we lived, the first sound I heard every morning was the tinkling of ice in a drinking glass. I guessed that perhaps he was drinking iced coffee!

The other memory is even less pleasant. I was going away overnight on one occasion, something the pastor did not care for. However, my departure was justified as I was attending the annual meeting of the diocesan council of Catholic women. On my way out to get into my car, we met in the garage. He had a pitchfork in his hand, and he stood there with glaring, wild eyes looking into space. I tried to make conversation by asking what he was doing—in reality a genuine question, as the point of his actions with the pitchfork was not in any way clear, and I had never seen the pitchfork before. His gruff reply sent shivers through my spine and had me upset all the forty miles or so to the meeting. "I am looking for snakes," he said, "and some of them are two legged." The tone of his voice made it clear to me he might have been issuing a plain threat.

I had had enough. I was beginning to fear for my own safety. When I got to the meeting, I reported the matter to the bishop. He would take action, he said. But time went by, and he took little action. Then one evening he showed up at the rectory to talk to the pastor. They were together for an hour or so, and when the bishop came out, he called me aside and told me he was appointing me co-pastor. I now had the same authority, he said, as the pastor. I wasn't sure how that would protect me from assault. Looking back, I should have refused the pretentious promotion.

A public announcement was never made. I never received a letter of appointment from the bishop. I was in a deeper limbo now than ever. Nothing changed at the rectory or in the parish. No one knew a change had been made. How could I tell them? I should have shrieked! The fact is, I didn't know how!

A short time later the bishop was changed to another diocese. There was nothing but trouble ahead for me.

Chapter Thirty-Three:
The Summer of My Discontent
⚬♪⚬

My life was in a mess—or so it seemed at the time. I was supposedly co-pastor now, with all the associated duties and responsibilities. The bishop never made a public announcement. Neither did the pastor. From the day the pitchfork was wielded, the situation had not changed except to grow worse. Indeed, I was now public enemy number one. The rectory had a housekeeper who was well aware of the situation. She befriended me, trying especially to please my palate with all kinds of tasty cooking.

I spoke to the bishop about the situation. He was noncommittal. I requested a change from the ordeal I was experiencing. "If you go," said the bishop, "he must go too." Then one morning the news broke that the bishop had been changed to another diocese. It was shortly after Easter. In no time the diocese was vacant. Then word came that my pastor had filed for a diocesan hearing regarding his situation. He had been wronged, he claimed. He had been made to share the pastorate of the parish with another. He wanted restoration of his rights through due process.

It all seemed so odd at the time but there was certainly method to his madness. A new bishop might enforce the edict of the previous one. The situation in the parish might be publicized. Then what? In my more mature years I am also aware that this hearing should probably not have been held in a diocese "*sede vacante*" (when the diocese is without a bishop). Indeed, it would appear very much against the spirit of canon law, if not against its regulations.

Spring and summer of 1974 were stressful times. I knew this hearing lay ahead, even though I had no clue as to how the hearing committee would be constituted. I would be called to give evidence. I also knew I was going to tell the truth. Since everyone, both clergy and laity, knew this pastor had a history of alcoholism, it seemed to me nothing new would come to light.

The hearing was set for early August. Sometime in July the former bishop returned to Orlando for a function. I spoke with him about the scheduled hearing. I remember his remark very well. "I am sure the outcome will depend," he said, "on your own report and on the reports of the other priests who have previously worked with this man. The man who was there before you should be a good witness."

I didn't feel reassured. Some days later I asked one of the aforementioned priests what his intentions were. He was going on vacation. He wouldn't be around in early August. And the chief witness the bishop had relied on, the one who should be a good witness? "Gosh, I am going to be away on vacation. I have my tickets purchased." Witnesses were disappearing like the last rays of the evening sun.

Things were not going so well, I thought. Was it the former bishop who was on trial? Was it the pastor who was trying to convince the world he was not an alcoholic? Or was I on trial myself because I happened to have been appointed to that parish, had tried to carry out my priestly duties, and had somehow or other got in the way?

There was a lot of tension in the rectory. I rarely saw the pastor, and that was nothing new. But he had a secretary who found ways to let me know which side she was on. Parishioners would call to speak to me to arrange a wedding or a baptism or for any other reason, and the secretary might inform them I was not in at the moment, and they would have to wait. I believe this was an effort to portray me as someone not dedicated to my work as a priest. The friendly housekeeper had left. She was aware of the discord. She didn't want to be around anymore.

I found solace in reflecting that over the past three years the various officers of the parish associations had frequently complained about the situation in the parish. Surely they would have some illuminating light to shed. I would comfort myself as I tried to sleep at nights that there was an abundance of evidence to make the entire affair look ludicrous and perhaps bring it to a happy ending.

It was the summer of my discontent. It was also the season when I learned a great deal about human nature.. If I had known then what I know now …!

But God has His ways, and the learning process also matures us. The summer of 1974 will always remain in my memory, for the anxiety and stress it caused and for the darkest days in my service for the Lord. But I also remember it as a time when I grew in intimacy with the Lord Himself. Never was the psalmist more correct than when he wrote, "For to His angels He has given command about you that they guard you in all your ways. Upon their hands they shall bear you up lest you dash your foot against a stone" (Psalm 91:11–12). I had recited the psalm many times, and now I needed the watchfulness of Divine Providence more than ever. No aspirant for the priesthood, in his wildest imaginings, would have been able to conjure up the situation in which I now found myself. There seemed to be an unfairness about it that beggared possibility itself.

And so, after I celebrated morning Mass, I would sit in the empty church just to be alone with the Lord of the Eucharist. I have no recollection of how I prayed or what I said to the Lord, although I do remember fighting tears on more than one occasion. I felt as if it were my own "agony in the garden." I wanted to be thousands of miles away like some of the other witnesses who were obviously fleeing the scene. But I was trapped. And God did not remove the chalice any more than He removed it from His divine Son. I remembered the words of Pilate in the Passion Story: "Take him and crucify him." But God's angels were around, and certainly they would bring me the strength to endure. On their hands they would bear me up!

Chapter Thirty-Four:
The Wait

ॐ

There can be times in one's life when things seem to be out of control. I wondered what I had done to cause what was happening. Was it entirely my fault? Other priests had worked in this parish and had not experienced the same problems. True, some of them had gotten out rather than be a part of what was happening. I should have gotten out too, but I had been trying to stay on, to bring Christ to the people, to carry out the commitments I had made to my God, to my bishop, and to myself. Then when I tried to get out, it was too late.

Now, here I was, in the middle of this horrendous situation with not a friend in the rectory. On the outside, my clergy friends urged me not to worry. But sometimes there was a tone in their advice that made my stomach feel a little queasy. In the middle of a conversation someone might ask when I intended to take a vacation, or was all this worth delaying a vacation for? (I really wanted to run, but frankly, even to this day I am not sure what I should have done! I was never one to run from adversity).

Mornings were the most wonderful time of day. I celebrated the morning parish Mass, and when it was over, I spent a long time before the Blessed Sacrament. Here, in the presence of the Lord, I found peace. There were times when tears welled in my eyes, when my spirit was near the breaking point, when I felt very much alone. But all those feelings were calmed by my awareness of the Lord's presence and His power in my life. So a lot of time was spent in thanksgiving for His goodness and in simple recitation of my problems. I could hear His answers in my heart.

I was reminded of His prayer in the garden, that prayer that had seemed not to be answered. And somehow I always heard Him say, "I arose at Easter. You are going to be all right. It's all going to work out. I am with you. Don't be afraid."

Throughout the day, I found myself going back time and time again to sit in His presence or to recite the rosary. Could I ever get away from the rosary? Here I was, in one of the most troubled times of my life, and when I knelt to pray the rosary, I was back again by my old fireside in Ireland, and my family was gathered around me as in days of old. What a wonderful gift parents give to their children when they teach them to pray! In the awful loneliness of that time I needed those memories!

I knew Our Lady would not let me down. Come what may, I was going to stand firm. No, I would not run away or make excuses. I would face whatever music might be about to start. On the way to visit the sick in the hospital or nursing home, I would pray the rosary. I had one intention—that the Mother of the Lord would take me through this crisis.

The parishioners were aware that something was taking place, that there was going to be some kind of legal maneuvering, and that the pastor was challenging some decision of the former bishop. They had always known there was an alcohol problem. A parish leader, who had frequently complained about his alcoholism in the past, wondered what might be brewing. I said nothing but wondered how all this information and opinion would be considered by the appointed "jury," who were already aware of most of it.

The steamy days of summer finally rolled into August. The agony of waiting was almost at an end. The atmosphere in the rectory was suffocating and tense. I was notified by the Due Process Board that I would be called upon to testify on Tuesday. When the day came, I drove to the location and awaited the call.

It was to be the kind of "due process" I would never forget.

Chapter Thirty-Five:
A Strange Court

☙

That Tuesday was a dreaded day. It was a day I had not wished for. Throughout the day, as we awaited the evening due process hearing, I knew it was going to be an awful experience.

I had heard the case being called one of "due process." The question was for whom? Somebody was going to be hurt in the process! As I drove to the location, I felt that something was over in my life. I had gone through some difficult years with this particular pastor. They had come to an end. One way or another, this man and I were going to part company. I couldn't help wishing the bishop might have listened to my previous requests for a transfer.

When I entered the hearing place, I was in for a big surprise. The pastor was sitting there with a lawyer. The lawyer had prepared his case. The rest of the Due Process Board was made up of seven priests. They listened to the proceedings, interrupting with questions now and again in the manner of the Supreme Court of the United States. There was a lawyer for the diocese too, but at this juncture it was not very clear how much preparation the diocese had made in presenting its case.

The pastor's lawyer asked direct questions and I answered them in a straightforward and truthful manner. I told of my experiences at the parish without rancor. I had a feeling some of the questions from the priest "judges" were intended to embarrass or have the answer avoided. The truth is the truth! Indeed, my recollection of this truly horrible situation is clouded, something that in itself is a blessing. Though it was an August evening, all I remember is a situation of darkness that has remained with me down through the years. The lawyer for the diocese remained silent. I was on my own. I must have been "in the dock" for at least half an hour, perhaps longer. Then I was asked to leave the room, and another person was called.

Next day, someone who had been involved in the hearing told me of the bias of at least one of the diocesan priests. The case being made for the pastor was that he suffered from diabetes, which caused him to be irrational at times. The disease apparently had the same symptoms as alcoholism. The argument being made was that reports of this man's drinking throughout most of the day, every day, should not be a factor in the case. He did not suffer from alcoholism!

One of the priests, supposedly unbiased and fair-minded, a man who surely knew the history of the particular pastor, asked an apparently "hostile" witness why he limped. When told it was a birth defect, the priest uttered a statement to the fact that his limping might have been taken for inability to walk properly because he was drunk. The writing on the wall was becoming clearer.

To this day, I well remember the atmosphere in the rectory next morning. Only Shakespeare might be able to describe it in one of his tragedies. There was a gloom that was heavy and depressing. The case would go on for another day or two, and I wondered how I might remain in this same residence where there was such apparent disunity and a pall hanging over the place. The pastor remained in his room, and fortunately we did not meet.

Thankfully, the vicar general of the diocese called and suggested I should now leave the parish. He invited me to take a vacation. I would get a phone call when the case was completed. Naturally, I didn't need a second invitation to leave. I called a travel agent, packed my belongings, and headed for Chicago—and from there after a week to my mother in Ireland.

My mother guessed there was something wrong. It didn't take her long to find out! I told her of the happenings in my life. I was awaiting the results. I was not sure of my future assignment. It was unlikely I would be going back to my previous parish. Before I left, the vicar general had told me that, irrespective of the result, I would be moving to another assignment. I yearned for the peace and freedom of a normal parish. I told my mother I was sure everything would be all right. She was skeptical. "I hope they are not making you a scapegoat for their own mistakes," she offered.

As it turned out, she was correct in her summation.

Chapter Thirty-Six:
Case Over

⟋⟍

I had spent several weeks with my mother before the result came. The nervous tension was beginning to leave my body, but nevertheless I could not forget the events of the recent past. How would it all end? What meaning would the "verdict" have for me and how did I get stuck with it in the first place? Somehow or other I was deeply implicated in the entire mess, and yet it seemed the case was either against the bishop or in favor of the pastor to restore him to complete autonomy in the parish. Was this really an instance of "due process"? The evidence suggested the possibility of a kangaroo court established while the diocese was without a bishop.

As the days went by, I became more resigned to what might happen. To this day, I don't know how long the hearings lasted or how the verdict was reached. I can recall a dream shortly before the news came, a dream indeed that was more like a nightmare. In the dream I was on the telephone with the vicar general of the diocese. Very bluntly he uttered the words "We have lost the case." The dream was so realistic that it awakened me immediately, and I sat up in bed making sure that it was a dream.

A dream it was, and it prepared me for what was to follow. I spent the next few days making peace with my situation in life. I kept reassuring myself that, come what may, my priesthood was my most valuable possession and an alcoholic was not going to separate me from it. Priests are not normally called upon to testify against their brother priests, and I had found myself in an impossible situation that was not of my making.

The former bishop's words kept crowding back into my memory: "The outcome will depend on your evidence and on the evidence of the other priests who worked in the parish." But no other priests showed up for the hearing. Nor was there any way of forcing their testimony to what this bishop had evidenced all along. He told me of the problem the day he gave me my assignment. Every priest in the diocese knew this pastor had a very serious problem of alcoholism. I found myself in a vast empty hole, on my own, lacking any obvious priestly support. I had to come to terms with a situation I had no part in bringing about.

We were having the evening meal at my mother's home some days after my dream. The phone rang. My sister answered. "It's for you," she said to me. I took the phone in my hand. It was the vicar general.

He was quick with the news. "I am calling to tell you we lost the case," he said. It was a rerun of my dream. I should have been numbed, but I wasn't. I was told that, when I returned to Orlando, I would be given another assignment. The conversation was very short.

Interiorly I felt at peace that the crisis was over or nearly so. Was justice done all around? A priest friend afterward opined that the clergy "judges" had no interest in punishing me. I simply happened to be in the way. They were taking care of "one of their own," he said, and the judges were intent on making the former bishop look bad for some reason best known to themselves. I recall responding, "But what about me? Why would they not think of me?"

"Because you are a lot younger" he replied, "and you'll get over it."

"And the people?" I queried.

"They'll get over it too," he said.

In many ways he was right. I did get over it—perhaps not as quickly as he thought I might have—partly with the remarkable influence of a friend I had not yet met. The parish has long forgotten the incident too, and like the ancient mariner, I can say of myself, "A sadder and a wiser man, I rose the morrow morn."

From this experience I learned that some people are not always as trustworthy as they might like you to believe. I lost some friends, people I thought were very close to me. They apparently accepted false stories that were circulated following my departure from the parish, or didn't want to be involved in taking sides in the outcome. A chairperson of a parish committee who had complained to me vehemently on a weekly basis for three years about the pastor's alcoholism testified in his favor.

To this day, I am still unable to comprehend how this affair was allowed to take place, either by diocesan officials or anyone else. I did not suffer payback from anyone involved, though one companion of the pastor, himself a drinking buddy, wrote a venomous letter about me to Barry University where I was studying for a master's degree shortly thereafter.

On my return to Orlando, I was given a new assignment as promised. It was to be short-lived. "The darkest clouds are just before the dawn." The proverb was about to be verified. The sun was rising. The best days of my life were just around the corner. Good Friday was indeed going to be followed by Easter Sunday! The Lord had indeed "given His angels charge over me," and I would later realize the promise of Psalm 91 that I recite every day: "In their hands they will bear you up." Angels' wings were fluttering around me, but it took me a while to hear the angelic sounds.

Reflecting on the situation, many years later, I know I did the right thing. I don't know how I might have fled the scene, and being true to oneself and one's calling was for me the only solution. Those who gave false witness, as some surely did, must resolve the situation for themselves, and for all of us my prayer is that we have the courage of our convictions irrespective of the outcome. The episode is still a painful memory that I try not to dwell on very much. Perhaps it made me stronger, but nevertheless it was an episode I would not wish in any priest's life.

Chapter Thirty-Seven:
Beginning a Tourist Ministry

There was a vacancy for an associate pastor in a parish not far from Orlando. I was assigned to fill it. At that time, I had not the slightest notion of what the future held in store. Despite the upsetting events of the recent past, I was still glad I had come to Orlando and determined to continue serving in my priesthood with all the zeal I could muster.

As things developed, my new post was a halfway house. It was a time for healing, a time for prayer and reflection, and a time to try and forget the past. The pastor here was a kindly man, who as I recall barely ever mentioned my previous disaster. Within the parish there was a hospital, and I found myself back again visiting the sick and repeating the various activities that had motivated me in previous years. The community was friendly, and here too, as in my previous assignment, I found myself sipping coffee with parishioners in a local coffee shop following parish meetings. The world hadn't stopped after all, but my scars were taking time to heal. When a newly ordained priest arrived and inquired about my past, I found great difficulty in narrating my story. It would remain thus for several months yet.

In the December of that year, Orlando was graced with a new bishop. He was Thomas Grady, a Chicago man of Irish extraction. Shortly into the New Year he began to make new assignments after he had first visited the parishes and spoken to the clergy. In early February, the call came for me to go to the bishop's office. He spoke kindly of my various ministries, and as we conversed he asked me about my previous assignment and what had happened. I told him I would prefer not to talk about it (mostly because I didn't want to have to fight tears), and with the graciousness that the diocese came to experience from him later on, he simply changed the subject. It was apparent to him I was still hurting within.

The great resort complex of Walt Disney World had been opened more than three years previously. What was once a wilderness was now teeming with vacationers. The Disney planners had made no provisions for church attendance within their established confines. Every weekend thousands of faithful Catholics were looking for Mass and Eucharist. The bishop invited me to begin a ministry that would care especially for the needs of vacationing Catholics. I was given a free hand in determining how this ministry might be carried out. A priest had preceded me but had not found the work to his liking. I could take up where he left off. If I encountered any problems, I was to report back to the bishop.

The base for this activity was to be provided by the formation of a new parish in southwest Orlando. The territory had already been proclaimed a "mission." The bishop would name a parish there as soon as I would report to him that it was viable.

This bishop was surely different from any other I had dealings with. "I want you to think about it for a while," he said. "Then let me know your decision." Never before had a bishop offered me the opportunity to say no. In my heart I had already accepted, but in accordance with the bishop's directive I left the chancery office without giving any commitment.

That evening, before going back to my own parish, I had dinner at Saint James, then the downtown parish for the city of Orlando, now the diocesan cathedral. The pastor there was encouraging in his remarks. "It's an assignment," he said, "that hundreds of priests could only dream of. You are going to be busy."

Little did he know how prophetic his words were. I arrived at my new assignment in the first week of March. Daily Mass had been scheduled in the priest's home. On my first morning there about thirty people showed up for Mass. I was quite impressed with the attendance in such a small and newly formed mission. I was to find out next day that the attendance was mostly through curiosity to see what the new priest looked like and what sort of person he was.

Just the same, even though the numbers at daily Mass dropped, my predecessor had done good work. He had assembled volunteers to help in the hotel masses, and when I made my first appearance at the scheduled hotel for Mass the following Saturday, I was greeted by eight or nine people, all gathered to help at the Mass. They were locals who were enchanted by the idea of a new parish, a parish of their very own, and they were more than willing to be a part of whatever ministry the new parish might provide.

There must have been around a hundred tourists at the Mass. They were jovial and friendly. And many expressed their delight that I was there to bring them Eucharist. In every way they made me feel a priest. There was something special about the demeanor and faith of those people. I knew it was the beginning of something good. But as is always the case in God's vineyard, it was obvious there was work to be done. This ministry could continue in a hotel setting, or we could develop our own special place of worship. It didn't take long to make this determination.

The offerings were not all that impressive. A parishioner helped me count the collection at my rectory on Monday mornings. His name was Dave, and he was one of those many people I was destined to meet in my new ministry. He had a veneration for priests and their work, and he was prepared to be available to help whenever he could. Since he liked to cook, he also made a habit of preparing breakfast afterward, and we always dined the Irish way on bacon and eggs and all the accompaniments. In those early days of the tourist ministry, preparing breakfast took longer than counting the previous day's offerings.

Somehow or other that situation would have to be changed around, and I kept thinking about it in my mind and in my prayers.

Chapter Thirty-Eight:
A New Light

⁓

Progress was being made. Daily Mass was available for the people in the rectory. Some ten to fifteen souls attended most mornings. They came for Mass and stayed for coffee. Most were women, and their concern for the pastor was helpful in keeping the rectory in good trim. Even on the lawn outside some people would gather in the evening time to plant flowers and to keep the place looking neat and proper. We were embarked on a new adventure, and there was a feeling of excitement.. Everybody felt they belonged. Each looked forward to the next step. I was quickly gathering new friends.

The next step would be the announcement of the development of the parish church, whenever that might come. Meantime, though, we had sixty or perhaps seventy families using their envelopes on a regular basis. They attended the hotel masses, welcomed visitors, and were active in many ways. The money was counted on Monday mornings and deposited in the bank. The totals were by no means large, and the hotel masses continued to generate only small offerings.

Divine Providence, however, has its own way of working. Small as the offerings were, it was necessary by diocesan regulations to keep accounts. I was no accountant, and I looked around for someone to be the bookkeeper. The pastor in a neighboring parish sent his bookkeeper for short intervals to help out. But it was evident that I would sooner than later have to find my own.

Then word came one day that a family who had previously lived in the area was returning and would be at Mass the next Sunday. The informant told me this family was one that would surely help. She spoke in glowing terms about Marcia and Carl, the parents, and felt certain Marcia was just the person I needed as bookkeeper if she would accept the job. She felt she was gifted in financial matters—just what the parish needed. There were Sunday masses at the Sheraton Towers hotel. Masses here were really intended for tourists, but the location, right in the center of the new parish, was convenient for those who wanted to belong, and at the moment there was no church. Let it be said that there were those who attended other parishes who believed the bishop was wrong and that he had no business developing a new parish "just for the sake of the tourists."

Every new family was a bonus. I watched, and the fledgling community watched for every newcomer into the area. Each was visited with a view to finding out his or her religious affiliation. And so I looked forward to meeting the returning family on Sunday. From what I had been told, this was one family I wanted to meet, especially since they might relieve me of my accounting tasks and more.

It was a happy meeting. I got my bookkeeper, whose name was Marcia. Every member of the new parish would soon know her. She would not only do books; she would keep records and take care of parish secretarial and managerial needs. She would play a positive part in the development of the tourist ministry too, and when the time would come to build the new shrine church (not even dreamed of at that time), she would be deeply involved in that as well.

Her husband Carl would also play a part in the development of the young parish. He was in the architectural field and looked forward to helping with the development of the future church building. Together they surely presented a whirlwind of evangelistic enthusiasm that gave a whole new injection of zeal to those previously on board. A new light had just been lit within the parish and the tourist ministry.

On that Sunday morning, God sent a lot of blessings to all of us involved in spreading His Word. I report the story here because I believe it was providential, part of God's plan, as were all of those who joined later in forming the new parish and in time the new shrine church at Lake Buena Vista. Nothing happens by accident. In one way or another it is part of God's eternal design.

At first Marcia came to help for a few weeks. Those weeks stretched through the summer months and into the fall—and on for twenty-three years thereafter. During this time she would make a lasting impact on my own life and on the life too of the tourist ministry.

Marcia was no "yes" person. She never believed in pretense. She had sharp insights. It was clear she loved the Church. Coming from a Polish background, she had a tradition behind her faith. We did not agree on everything at first—or indeed at any time. But Marcia knew that she could and should speak her mind, and I, for my part, accepted that. Indeed, I was glad for it. One of Marcia's favorite expressions was "If I agreed with you, we would both be wrong!" I did not wish to be surrounded by "yes" people. If progress was to be made in God's vineyard, it would depend on the guidance and advice of many people including Marcia, who in many ways was now as close to the scene as I was myself. Any priest who thinks he is the oracle in his parish is foolish indeed.

I was only a short time removed from the "due process" debacle. I wanted to forget about it, but in truth the experience had so devastated me that I found it impossible to keep it out of my mind. Not only that, but I felt that somehow or other I was under scrutiny and that I could not afford to make a mistake. In talks with Marcia I would always offer that my previous experience had taught me something or other—usually negative—about the situation under discussion. In truth, despite myself, I had become negative about many things.

Then one morning my negative attitude brought a retort that I needed to hear from someone. "Why do you keep quoting that?" Marcia said with a measure of feeling and perhaps some impatience. "You are not there anymore. Are you to live the rest of your life under the shadow of what happened there? Who cares anymore? It's over and done with." They were words of chastisement, but they were also wise words that I needed to hear. From that time on I took a huge emotional step forward. That episode of my life would simply be a memory. It would not play any part in future activities or decisions.

A great adventure of my life was just getting under way!

Chapter Thirty-Nine:
Walking the Pavements

The community to which I had been sent was small and quite friendly. It didn't take long to know that my new ministry had been endowed with some wonderful people. Indeed, I had not encountered such friendliness in all my priestly life. Perhaps I didn't realize the love our faithful people have for their priests, but I would soon come to that realization.

The majority of the people helping me came from all over the country. They had settled in Orlando for one reason or other, some because of the climate, some because it suited their business, some because of the Disney enterprise, some because the city had a large munitions factory providing weapons for the United States government. Perhaps it was because of their exile from their places of birth that they were inclined toward community. Together they wanted nothing more than their own parish and their own place of worship.

When I arrived, they had to drive long distances to a parish church. Of course they were few in number, well less than a hundred. But of that number, at least 90 percent involved themselves in the activity I brought to them, directed especially at this time to serving the tourists. In their own minds the reward would be a church of their very own someday—and perhaps sooner than later. They had a remarkable sense of church and evangelization, and they quickly came to understand my explanations of the ministry in which they were involved—bringing Christ to visitors from all over the world.

We organized ourselves as to our duties and our times to serve. There were problems though. The newly formed tourist ministry had no church, and masses were being celebrated in hotels. How would we get out the word? Which hotel, where, and what time would Mass be offered?

Naturally hotels compete for business. Herein lay a problem. Why should hotel managers send their people to attend a function, even a religious one, in a competing hotel? Masses were mostly at times when either breakfast or dinner was convenient after the service was over. Most certainly there was a possibility, even a probability, that after Mass the attendees would stay for a meal and thus give much-needed business to another hotel. It was 1975, and the country was undergoing a recession. There was a resultant drop in tourism; hotels under construction had halted work, and many hotels went more than half empty.

But I decided nevertheless that my best method of advertising tourist masses was to walk the hotels. Little leaflets, easy to fold and place in a pocket, were distributed in each hotel. I did the distribution myself. The leaflets gave the times of masses and the hotel locations where they were being held. Some hotel staffs were very courteous, others not quite so willing to cooperate.

I vividly recall my visit to one hotel on International Drive. The lady at the desk was, to put it mildly, quite hostile. She made no pretense of friendliness, and her impatience was visible as I explained my mission. "We are not interested," she said crossly. "Why don't you just leave?" I recognized the folly of any further conversation and turned toward the door. On my way out I saw a rack with tourist information and went over to view its contents. As I reached for one of the obviously free brochures, the lady said in a loud voice "Leave the rack alone. Don't you dare touch those things. Get out." I knew then there was at least one person in the world who was not overawed by the sight of a Catholic priest. But I understood that times were difficult, business was poor, and many people were hurting.

There were, however, times when seeming defeat was turned into victory. In one of the leading hotels I had heard that not only were people not being given my information about the hotel masses, but the hotel was posting the Mass times of a church eight to ten miles away. Having made no headway at the concierge desk, I asked to see the manager.

Unexpectedly, I was told he would indeed see me. Later I would find that this was indeed a miracle. Hotel managers do not readily acquiesce to requests for a face-to-face meeting here and now.

When I got to his office I explained my mission. I informed him I had been appointed by the bishop to take care of visiting Catholics to the area. "We take care of them," was his reply. "We send them all over to Saint John's."

"How far away is Saint John's?" I asked.

"Oh, about seven to ten miles," he replied.

"Do you think," I said, "you are doing a favor to people who have to pay a taxi to go that distance when they could have walked a few hundred yards over to our Mass? That being the case, why wouldn't those people stay in a hotel closer to Saint John's the next time they come and save the money?"

"I never thought of that" was his frank admission. He walked over to the wall and tore off the Mass times for Saint John's that had been on display there.

Over the next several years there would be ups and downs in our ministry success. We would become friendly with a hotel employee who would help us spread the message of the hotel masses, and then one day the employee would be gone and we had to start all over again with a new person. Some hotels would be always friendly, some totally unconcerned. Hotels in the larger chains were for the most part more likely to be cooperative.

The work would go on. At the beginning there was no great certainty about the direction we were going. The main objective was to make it possible for our Catholic people to get to Mass. In those early days the major battle for recognition from the hotel concierges consumed our attention. It would one day be won. I continued to walk the pavements, visiting hotel after hotel, making friends with the staffs, distributing informational materials about our masses. The day would come when hotel staffs would stand in wonderment at the devotion of Catholics and their desire for Mass. And if ever proof was needed that the Eucharist is at the very heart of Catholic faith, our tourist ministry in Orlando would certainly serve as verification.

Divine Providence was on our side. God's plan was at work. Three months into the new ministry there were palpable signs of growth and progress. Our volunteers were developing fervor for their commitment to the work of the Lord. We had become nicely organized and the winds blowing our way were showing signs of developing into a whirlwind.

Chapter Forty:
A Handy Gestetner!

❦

Disney World had been open for four years. We were heading into summer vacation time. This was the time for large crowds, and our expectations were fulfilled. The Mass attendance had grown. This was in no small way due to the work that a parishioner and I had done together. The parishioner was one of the most memorable men I had ever met.

He was a retired rear-admiral from the Coast Guard. His name was Robert Goehring. It didn't hurt that he played golf. In fact he loved the game. By way of the golf course he introduced me to a few other men who would also become involved in the new parish and in the tourist ministry. He had a small real-estate business that occupied his time, but he was ready to play golf at an instant's notice.

When I told him of my intent to place Mass time brochures in all the hotels, he immediately offered his services. We would go together. The actual city of Orlando covered a much smaller area at that time. Motels had sprung up in the most unusual places away from the city. (Today they are lost in a sprawl of buildings). Typical of Florida, there were also trailer parks in which travelers parked their recreational vehicles for the night or the week or even longer. And unlike some of the hotels, we never encountered any animosity in any of the parks. I have happy memories of people sitting contentedly outside their vehicles enjoying the Florida sun and welcoming us warmly into their midst. They would sometimes even tell us those they knew to be Catholic. In time Robert Goehring and I covered miles and miles of territory. We left home in the morning and returned in the late evening, taking lunch somewhere on the way. It became a ritual especially at Christmas and Easter time. Our objective was to make sure everybody knew where Mass was available.

When we formed a parish men's club, Robert Goehring was very active there too. He served as president, and his affable ways influenced other men to become active as well.

That first summer of tourist ministry saw us serving increased crowds. Nevertheless there was no major increase in the Mass offerings. Then one evening, as I sat at home reading my breviary, a thought crossed my mind. I tried to put it away as an unnecessary distraction, but it was still with me when my prayer was finished. It was a simple thought! Envelopes for offerings were used in church. Why not use them at hotel masses too?

Catching people's interest seemed to be the problem. They were all good people, seeking Eucharist. They were better than good. They had a great love for the Lord. But the majority came directly from theme parks, and who could blame them if they were still reflecting on the distractions of the day or appeasing worn-out children they had taken on the various rides?

Before each Mass, I made an appeal. I also tried to form community by asking where people were from, recounting sports scores, and generally seeking avenues by which to connect with the visitors so that they felt welcomed and at home. However, it seemed to me that when Mass began, people quickly forgot what I had said, and their forgetfulness was there for all to see in the offerings they made.

Perhaps if we gave out envelopes, it might help them remember. One thing about envelopes, which I had often seen in the churches where I had served, was that visitors took an envelope from the pew before Mass, put their offering in it, and then dropped it into the collection basket at the appropriate time. I wondered if the same principle might come into play at a hotel Mass.

I spent that evening designing an envelope, or rather the information that would be on the envelope. There was a message about the need to help the ministry and to help build a new church as well. There was a place for a name and address and the suggested offering was ten dollars. I wondered of course whether the fledgling ministry might be able to afford the cost of printing the envelopes.

In the morning, I talked about my idea to Marcia when she arrived at work. She was supportive and thought it a good idea. Furthermore, we had in the office an old Gestetner machine. (Today, the majority of people would not have ever heard of a Gestetner—a contraption that in no way resembled a computer or modern copy machine.) I had no notion how it worked, but Marcia knew. She took the idea I had come up with and printed a regular envelope. It looked quite good! So good in fact that she took four hundred more and repeated the same effort. The operation took all morning. I was fortified with a new idea for the weekend masses.

It was instant success. Not one envelope came home unused! People did not put in ten dollars per envelope, but many did. Others gave a smaller sum. But the offerings multiplied. Now we knew we could afford to get special envelopes printed. They would pay for themselves!

The system has been updated and has become more sophisticated with the years. It was born on a quiet evening while I prayed my breviary and fought a distraction. One might also say it was helped to birth by Marcia's enthusiasm and her creativity with an old and abandoned machine. And the Holy Spirit showered His enlightenment on both of us. Years later, when an envelope company singled out our shrine envelope for special recognition and an award, I remembered that evening and an old abandoned Gestetner that was brought back to life with the kind of enthusiasm that would one day give birth to a shrine of Mary.

A short time after the introduction of the envelope I began my appeal with an apology for "having to ask." Immediately a lady interrupted. "Father" she said, "you don't need to apologize. We are glad you are bringing us mass." The small congregation burst out in instant applause. For me it was a moment of grace! People were on my side. They understood the need to help. It was the beginning of a boldness in fund raising for the Lord that was to become a passion and would continue throughout the rest of my ministry.

Chapter Forty-One:
A New Parish Church

Meanwhile, in the other half of our ministry—nothing can compare to the enthusiasm of a group of people as they begin to develop their very own church in a newly founded parish. As the possibility of building a church for the community became a reality, there was no problem at all in gathering people to meetings.

Most of the meetings were held in my home, and soon it was far too small for the ever increasing numbers. I have memories of men sitting on the floor, their backs to a piece of furniture or the wall, as we thrashed out the various ideas for a church and discussed a possible architect. A few were skeptical of the project, but their negative outlook was quickly smothered in the enthusiasm of the majority.

There was one important matter that had to be addressed, however. Before the church is built comes the bank account from which to pay the costs. I was a learner at that time. I had to learn fast if a church was to be built. Though we had a small community, their numbers were outweighed by their enthusiasm and generosity.

I had formed a finance committee of men and women who were experts in their field. They wanted to go ahead and choose an architect. We did some interviewing and hired the man we believed would be best for our project. After that the train was leaving the station and gathering speed. Perhaps the driver wasn't too sure of where he was going, but God was. The financial requisites for diocesan approval were quickly completed, and in October 1976, we gathered to break ground for the new church.

Many people made time to take part in the ceremony on that beautiful October Sunday afternoon, and the prayers that were offered for the growing community were certainly answered. Time would be a witness to that.

Keep in mind that the erection of the new church was never intended to replace the tourist ministry. I had already witnessed the extraordinary faith of the tourists, and I knew that this church, several miles from the Disney complex, would not suffice to cover the needs of faith-filled travelers. But it was connected with the tourist ministry. All our volunteers in that ministry were from this new community. I had suggested to Bishop Grady that since a seeming majority of our visitors were young families bringing their children to a young people's haven, we should name the new parish for the Holy Family itself and entrust our community and all the visitors to their care. Bishop Grady had readily agreed.

By October 1977 the church was completed. A faith community had finally a place in which to worship. But of course in Catholic tradition the church is more than a place of worship. It is home. My parents, and especially my mother, were never as much at home as when they were in the presence of the Lord within the church walls. This is where Christ permanently resides in the tabernacle, and He is there for all who take time to visit Him. I can recall the happiness of those who came to visit when the church first opened its doors to parishioners; more than one had tears in their eyes. "We have waited so long for a church out here, and I am so happy to see it at last," one enthusiast remarked fervently.

We started with three masses, one on Saturday and two on Sunday mornings. But of course we retained every Mass in the tourist ministry. Salesian priests from Tampa continued to support our efforts to cover the multiple sites for Mass. Our valiant group of volunteers—still about three-quarters of the parish population at the time—continued to make themselves available for hotel masses. But now they were in the process of developing their community as well.

While the church was being built, there was a heated debate going on throughout the land about the placement of the tabernacle. We placed it prominently in the center where I always believed it should be. The

Eucharist is the heartbeat of the church, and I saw no reason why someone coming to visit should have to search for the tabernacle, as has happened in many new churches. At Holy Family we placed the tabernacle in dead center, facing the faithful as they entered through the narthex door. Should not the ever-present Christ be the first recipient of the gaze of those who come to seek Him? Jesus, the Christ, is at the center of the church's life. Surely then He should also be the main focus to the visitor upon entering His church.

I often think of my mother's faith. Whenever she made a visit outside of Mass, she headed first for the main altar on which the tabernacle stood, where the Lord and Creator of the world looked out upon those He had redeemed. She would whisper to us children during Mass to "keep your eyes on the priest, look at the altar."

At this juncture too, let me deal with another topic of frequent argument. The Church of the Holy Family, though somewhat in the round, had the separate statues of Mary and Joseph also toward the front, not in the sanctuary but close to it. In modern times liturgists and church architects have somehow contrived in many instances to place those same statues at the back of the church or in some inconspicuous place. When the Lord says, "Behold your mother," the congregation has to look around to find her. The old tradition is best, with Mary standing in a prominent position in close proximity to her Divine Son and not entirely outside the perspective of those focusing on the tabernacle.

I mention these things because I am a great believer in symbolism. Where the statue is placed should also inform the viewer of what is primary to our Catholic faith. The Lord in His parables indicated He too believed in the symbolism of place. "Friend, go up higher."

There is something special about opening a new parish. It seems to me our Christian faith excites the new community to extra special efforts in order to bring the Real Presence of Christ into their midst. When the church has been completed and the tabernacle is occupied by the Creator of the world, there is a euphoria among believers that has to be experienced to be understood. I well remember when our new church at Holy Family was completed, there were tears in many eyes as they gazed on the tabernacle for the first time. One of the great treasures of our Catholic faith is belief and love of the Lord in the Eucharist.

Those days of excitement and venture in my very first parish passed quickly. But they were happy times. The diocesan finance offices and the finance committee of those days were wonderfully supportive. So too were the building committee of the diocese. Bishop Grady came to see the construction a number of times and expressed his pleasure with the work under way. Never once did he express a negative. And when the day came for dedication, he was there as main celebrant. Our new community was so happy to have its bishop share their joy. And the ceremony had a much larger crowd than had been expected. A parish history that is still being written lay ahead.

Chapter Forty-Two:
Fund-Raising

 ⤬

At the time of its building, the new church cost around $300,000. By today's standards, that money might pay for a new parking lot! And I say "might." The regulation within the diocese at that time was that one-half the construction costs had to be on hand before construction began. The other half had to be guaranteed through pledges from the community.

Assuredly I knew nothing about fund-raising then. (All that would change later on.) My helpers were really not able to give advice either. We decided to hire the services of a fund-raiser. The gentleman duly arrived at the rectory, called a meeting or two at which he explained what we ought to do, and formed some teams for particular parts of the parish. For this he received a previously agreed fee. It was a learning experience, and having gone through it, I knew it would be no longer necessary for me to seek the help of a professional.

"Don't be afraid" was the advice of Jesus to His followers. The only fear a priest has in such a situation is the fear of having to ask. Somehow the seminary never trained us for that. Once that fear is overcome, the priest is working among friends, people who are truly on his side, and success will follow. The fact is, of course, that the benefices we seek are for the Lord and the spread of His kingdom, and that can be the only true motivation for those in the Lord's work. It doesn't mean that there won't be criticism. Any priest who has raised funds will acknowledge that. The most likely to find fault are of course those who don't give.

The fund drive was very successful, so I suppose I should have been happy. I was pleased with our success but not entirely awed by the fund-raiser's techniques. He was unable to stir up the enthusiasm of the workers. My conclusions were that the professional fund-raiser in many situations earns easy money. Indeed, I had learned that the leader is the one who must be able to inspire the followers. And in this case the leader is the priest himself.

Building a new parish church, as I have said, carries its own excitement. Surely the pastor is equally excited. All the opportunities for raising funds are there. People give, not because they are compelled, but because they want to do something for God. It's as simple as that!

Certainly there will be people who for one reason or another are not anxious to give. At my first parish we had a variety. There were those who said the parish wasn't necessary. We had to convince them it was. The professional fund-raiser did not do it. There were those who said the proposed church was too large. We had to convince them it was not. (The fund-raiser did not do it. Actually, time would tell that the church was not large enough!) Then there were some who believed there was no need for a church! We left them alone.

There were those who promised an anonymous donation in the basket every week, in cash. We had to convince them this was not a good idea and it would not help us with planning the new church. Here, we succeeded some of the time. The fund-raiser could not take care of this. Naturally, some were also unable to give because of circumstances. We excused them and asked for their prayers.

In the final analysis though, it is the pastor and his committee who do most of the work. My next church—Mary's Shrine—would not have the services of a professionally paid fund-raiser, although we did seek professional advice now and again. If pastors would help each other and share ideas and learned experiences, much time, effort, and money could be saved. But that, I suppose, is not likely to happen.

In every church building scheme and in every fund-raising effort, Christ is the focus. Saint Paul once wrote, "The love of Christ impels us." Saint Paul completed his passage with the assertion that Christians "no longer live for themselves but for Him who for their sake died and was raised up." It is in that love that new church buildings arise. And it is in focusing on the Lord Himself that the needed finances can be accrued. Everything we do is for Him.

Perhaps I learned quickly. I observed what the professional fund-raiser was doing and then improved on it. There should be no negatives in a fund-raising appeal. If we belong to Christ and attach ourselves to Him, then He has to be the focus of all our efforts. He must be kept up front. The people must be convinced that it is to Christ they are giving. This point cannot be overstressed. Funds sacrificed to Christ should belong to Christ and should be directed only to the purpose for which they were given. Careful accounting must be made.

On more than one occasion, I have heard people harangued about their giving or inability to give. For example, I have heard the accusation made to listeners more than once that Catholics give far less than Protestants. Not exactly true. The Catholic donor contributes not only to the local church but to an average of eight other appeals that come through the mail or in some other way. Catholic Action is widespread and not confined to the boundaries of any given parish. People of overflowing hearts are to be found throughout the length and breadth of the land. At the end of the day it is the Lord Who matters. The faithful will take care of their Lord if given the proper reasons. In the long run there is only one reason for church giving: "It is the Lord" (John 21:7). And our American people are exemplary in their generosity to His cause.

In time we would do further building at Holy Family, but without the services of a fund-raiser. People would give generously when they understood the needs of the parish in carrying out the mandate of Jesus to spread the good news of the kingdom. And so it always will be.

Some years down the road I would really need to be able to raise funds for the Shrine project—not just small sums, but large amounts. All of us working on the project knew we were talking about millions of dollars. We should have been frightened about it all, but we were not. (God's grace at work?)

I learned about an association specifically devoted to Catholic fund-raising. There was a fee if one wished to be involved, but since our plans called for us to be in the big time, the decision was made to join and attend the annual conferences that were held in various parts of the country. The knowledge gleaned at those conferences was far beyond anything I could have expected. The speakers were practiced, informative, and enthusiastic. At these conferences I learned the dos and don'ts of fund-raising. People had come together from all over the country to share their experiences and their knowledge. What I learned contributed to the success of Mary's Shrine in Orlando and helped me in every facet of fund-raising.

There was also another side to the conferences. They demonstrated the enthusiasm of Catholic Action. Here I met a conglomerate of persons involved in various Catholic activities doing everything they could for the advancement of the kingdom of God. This was their main objective in life. There were Catholic priests, working feverishly, humbly, and quietly to advance their mission, as well as sisters and lay persons all with one commitment in life, namely caring for the needs of the Lord in one way or another. It was all very inspiring for me and told me I wasn't alone in my efforts.

There was another facet too. Many of those people lived under a veil of practical anonymity, yet their giftedness could have won for them major success in the secular field had they chosen to go that road. One was to become a lifelong friend. Father John Farren was then in charge of a Dominican Order fund-raising venture. This man advised me wisely and humbly, and from sharing his ideas I learned much. Indeed, he would have a far-reaching effect on my abilities to derive the necessary funds to build the Shrine. Father Farren would later be chosen to go to the Angelicum in Rome to supervise translations of the works of Saint Thomas from the original Latin and to make sure that they were handed down in their pristine originality. At the time of writing, he is back at work within the United States.

This multitalented man is an example of the sterling qualities of our American priesthood and the caliber of the men whose daily lives are dedicated to the Eucharistic Christ and the spread of His kingdom. They are pastors and confessors, teachers and counselors. On any given day they may have attended to ten different things, all with respect to helping people and promoting Christ's kingdom. You won't read anything about them in the daily newspaper. They seek no power other than the promotion of the power of Christ in the world around them.

Chapter Forty-Three:
Parish Activities

ᑲᕧ

With the arrival of the new parish church came also the registration of many new families. For one thing, there were those who chose to await the completion of the new building before joining the new community. But the population of the area was growing too. The growing tourist industry was bringing many participants to Orlando. The theme parks of Sea World and Universal Studios had been planned or had already arrived on the scene. The population of the southwest area was rapidly growing. It would continue to grow for many years yet.

Gradually, we would be called upon to add to our parish weekend masses. This constituted quite a challenge since we already had five masses for tourists in other venues. But the great call of the priest is to celebrate Eucharist with his people. It was my privilege to make the Eucharist available for the many and to make sure that those we served were provided with the opportunity to celebrate the Lord in an atmosphere of prayer.

Along the way, we found priest helpers who were willing to aid us out on a regular basis. In time, Bishop Grady would also appoint an associate priest to Holy Family parish. The Marist Fathers came on board for several years in the mid-eighties, and their help was immense. These lovers of the Mother of God certainly left their mark!

Looking back, it is cleat that the parish was blessed with two wonderful organizations, the Ladies Association and the Men of Holy Family. The enthusiasm of these groups and their faith-filled dedication were plain for all to see. Their meetings were always filled with humor and apostolic zeal. Starting with around one hundred families, these organizations ploughed a lasting furrow. Both helped in serving coffee and doughnuts at Sunday masses, menial tasks, if you like, that contribute to daily service of the Lord. They also recruited for the Christian doctrine programs and generally made themselves available wherever needed. I cannot remember ever hearing anything negative from their ranks. They visited new families arriving in the locality, introduced them to the parish if they were Catholic, and made sure they were welcomed when they arrived at Sunday Mass.

On the community front the ladies ran a very classy and elegant style show every year. This became a community annual, and the numbers of non-Catholics supporting and attending the event was in itself remarkable. This show was a huge success year after year and was always held at a different hotel. Through it, funds were raised for many purposes, not the least being the needy of the area. As always, of course, these women were to the forefront in all parish spiritual activities.

One occasion is well remembered to this day. I am reminded of it when I meet old friends. As a fashion show they organized was about to begin, there was a Florida thunderstorm that created a blackout all through the district. Having waited for some time for lights, the committee decided to go ahead with their program with the light as it was. It was still a long way from darkness outside. I was called upon to say the introductory prayer, and having asked the Lord's blessing on our endeavors and all present, I completed the prayer with a petition: "Lord, let there be light." I had no sooner uttered the words than the light came on! For some, to this day a miracle! The truth, of course, is simply that the words were coincidentally timed.

The Men of Holy Family were no less eager to serve than their counterparts. They too contributed to parish fund-raising as well as to many other aspects of the parish, as for example, pancake breakfasts. At times it was hard to know who was having more fun—the workers or those who came to be served. The great annual event for them was a flea market that was held every spring. I think it is true that just about every man in the parish took part in this effort in one way or another. First a tent had to be erected on the church grounds and the materials for sale gathered and priced. These were no small tasks. Someone always had a truck to pick up articles for the event, and the gathering went on for several weeks.

Then came the time to assemble the goods in the tent—no small matter either, considering each had to be priced beforehand. The tent was loaded up the previous day, and since there are no doors on a tent, men had to be on guard all the previous night to protect from looting and stealing. Sales began immediately after morning Mass on Saturday and continued until the end of the day. The men always had their treasurer on hand to keep accounts as the day went on, and with a justified pride they reported their taking at day's end. On one occasion, a salesman made the mistake of taking off his blazer early in the morning, only to find that it had been sold when he went to retrieve it! He never did find the buyer either!

The new parish did not have a school, so it was necessary for us to attend to the religious education of our young people. For this purpose we consulted with an Episcopalian parish nearby and founded our educational program on their model. Wednesday afternoons were set aside for religious education since the public schools closed early on that day. We found in our ranks a lady who was very capable of heading the program. In no time she had assembled a volunteer teaching staff that held classes from first grade through twelfth.

The problem with religious education outside of the Catholic school is the challenge of getting the parents to send their children and of interesting the young people in what is being done for them. Our program started relatively early in the afternoon. Participants were introduced to classes but also given time for various outdoor sports, such as football and soccer. The program proved very successful as most youngsters like to be involved in sport. Older students arrived around six o'clock in the evening and shared dinner with each other.

The meal was prepared each week by members of our Ladies Association and Men of Holy Family. It was a full meal that most often was generously contributed by a local restaurant, and when this was not an option, the "kitchen staff" prepared it themselves. The majority of parents wanted to serve in the program and were glad to see their offspring sharing in a meal with each other while also learning Christian values.

I believe this program worked well and played an important part in the development of our parish at the time. And I have met quite a few adults since who reminisce on their young years learning and growing to adulthood through the Holy Family Christian education program. Later on we would introduce the Saint Lucy Sisters to run the program, and their faith and leadership strengthened the proclamation of the kingdom among our young people.

All in all the work of a pastor is intensely satisfying. I have had special blessings as a result of my work with the people to whom I was sent. Looking back, I have no doubt the work of a priest in any assignment begins and ends with love. The Lord washed the feet of His disciples and charged His followers to imitate Him. As priests we have been called to serve. That service is nothing more than the bringing of Christ to our people. The little Saint Thérèse wrote that "Love is at the heart of the Church." Our people have a right to see the priest as always being their friend. When we love each other and love our people, the kingdom of God is truly being established.

The sacrament of Holy Orders introduces us to a more special intimacy in the priesthood of Christ, and as Pope John Paul II stated in an Angelus exhortation in 1981, like the Mother of God "we daily learn to serve—to serve God in our brothers and sisters, to express in our service the royalty of our Christian vocation in every state or profession, in every time and in every place," so that the kingdom of the Lord may come. His address was fittingly titled "To serve is to reign."

Once, when we had been seated at the evening meal in our own home for just a few minutes, our housekeeper came in to tell us that there was an emergency call from the local hospital. They needed a priest immediately. Before she had completed her message my companion priest sharing the meal put down his knife and fork and was already leaving the dining room before I could even comment. That priest was among the caliber of great priests, servants of the Lord and His people, who have embellished my life. They are the jewels of the Church.

Weekends became busy times indeed! The time came when we had five masses for tourists at separate venues and six at the parish church. That made for a lot of "balls in the air," as Bishop Grady once described it, but through the grace of God not one Mass was ever missed. A priest was always available, and every priest was not only reliable but was also enthralled with his work. Father Leo Brown OFM was the first to help out at Holy Family, and despite having an artificial leg, he managed to offer two masses every Sunday. In time, he would make his prosthesis a tool for humorous fund-raising! Because of the smallness of our rectory, Father Leo lived in a rented apartment. Other clergy would follow him, one of whom almost caused a major fire when he tried to boil water in a plastic jug on an electric stove! And on weekends volunteers were developing an enviable tradition of service, making whatever sacrifices necessary to be a part of the ministry and join their priests in bringing Christ to visiting faithful.

With the growth of the parish and the tourist ministry, it became necessary to make some adjustments. A Redemptorist priest, Father John Barry, was appointed as administrator to Holy Family, allowing me to pay more attention to the development of the Shrine. Father Barry was most certainly not the fire-and-brimstone Redemptorist mentioned in an earlier chapter. His kind and soft disposition and his prayerful attitude are still remembered by many of his old parishioners.

The break from parish work was easier then as I still lived at Holy Family, still retained the title *pastor* there, and "came home to dinner" every evening. It was much later, in 1992, that Bishop Dorsey advised that I resign from the parish and devote all my energies to the Shrine.

Leaving Holy Family behind was a painful decision as I had formed many bonds at the parish I had founded, and though I now had a new and scattered community throughout the United States, I knew I was leaving behind memories of happy days and a truly loving parish community. Sundays would be different with new faces sitting in every pew. The weekly conversations with parishioners were gone. Gone also was the security of a unified community whose objectives were streamlined on the community itself. Henceforth, I would have to set my sights on serving the visitors and welcoming them home to their own church in Orlando. There was a lot of work ahead and a major challenge to be met. But there were many awaiting me to bring them the Lord, and in His own good time He would see to it that my work and that of those who joined with me would be carried up on angels' wings.

Chapter Forty-Four:
Serving the Lord and Country

The Brazilian bishop Dom Helder Camara has advised to *"watch how you live. Your lives may be the only Gospel your sisters and brothers will ever read."* Saint Francis of Assisi had given the same advice to his followers when he told them that the best sermon they could give was by how they conducted their lives ("Preach the Gospel at all times; use words when necessary"). Looking back on my time at Holy Family parish, I have indeed memories of men and women who influenced my own and many other lives—not by anything they said but by the depth of their dedication.

During my first years in the parish, a lawsuit took place between the government and AT&T. It appears Orlando was chosen as a site to be an AT&T defense location. It was my understanding that their representatives gathered here to prepare their case, and many AT&T workers were among those who transferred to Orlando. It turned out a blessed event for the new parish. Those were wonderful people who threw themselves wholeheartedly into the effort not only to form community but also to get the new church erected. I remember them for their devoted dedication to their Lord.

At the time also, a number of military retirees had settled in southwest Orlando. They captured my heart! They had spent years in serving their country, but their dedication to their faith was no less effective and alive. Someone trained in military ways knows how to listen, how to carry out a directive, how to stay the course. These families contributed in a wonderful way to the development of our new parish. There is something about military service that leads to commitment and true dedication.

The new parish was to benefit greatly from the commitment of all of those people.

The church had been built when General John Peter Flynn arrived as a member. He had just been released from a long prison term in Vietnam, being the highest ranked military officer captured by the Vietnamese. His was a simple story. As a leader of his men he felt he should also show them an example, so he undertook bombing raids along with them. On one such raid he was shot down by a Vietnamese missile. Having ejected from his seat, he remembered no more until he awoke to find a group of men staring down at him. His leg was broken, and he had other injuries as well. In time, he found himself incarcerated at the Hanoi Hilton, and later on, he spent four long years sentenced to solitary confinement.

There was torture too that he spoke very little about. His fear of torture was great. He did, however, recount the last occasion on which he was taken for the possible dreaded torture as his captors believed that, being a higher officer in the air force, he had secrets to share. On his way to the "investigation," he prayed for a sign. With that sign, he would resist the torture if that was what God wanted. During all the time he had been incarcerated, he never saw a robin. While he was sitting in the "witness" chair, a robin hopped into the room, hopped around, and then disappeared. General Flynn took the event as the sign for which he had asked and told his captors he had no secrets he would reveal. Instead of the feared torture, the leader simply dismissed him and never sent for him again.

The general had a great love for the Mother of God. From his meager rations, he saved some breadcrumbs each day—enough to make a complete set of rosary beads. He divided up his day into time for prayer and time to reflect on the passion of the Lord and various other time consumers. He attributed his mental salvation over such a long period to the intervention of the Mother of God through her rosary. When, in the closing days of the war, he was finally lifted off a hotel roof in Hanoi by helicopter, he was able to look back on years of suffering with the knowledge that higher authorities than this earth had taken him safely through the trauma.

He lived in Windermere (Florida) with his wife Mary Margaret for several years and was beloved for his easygoing manner and his contagious sense of humor. During many of those years he gave talks on his survival to many groups, including church congregations, both Catholic and Protestant. But irrespective of where he was, he always emphasized his belief that it was Mary and her rosary that had brought him safely back to his own country.

The general's generosity equaled his faith. Quietly one day he told me he would provide a national flag for our church. I thanked him, of course, but not enough! Later I found that this flag cost a bundle, and the placement in the ground of the pole from which it flew, a whole lot more. Here was a true American hero whose religious values did not remain hidden but guided his life. He had a wonderful love and respect for the priesthood, as did all of the servicepersons it has been my privilege to meet. And so often in my reflective prayer I have to examine myself, whether I live up to the standards those good people expect of me. Above all others, the priest must constantly challenge himself on the spiritual standards of his own life.

Chapter Forty-Five:
A Dream is Born

As the tourist ministry grew and numbers began to multiply, it became evident that we did not have the perfect solution in serving our people in hotel ballrooms. There were indeed those who believed we should leave well enough alone. These people were not around for our weekend masses and were not aware of the problems we were beginning to confront.

Orlando was growing. Hotel rooms were beginning to multiply. More and more people were coming to enjoy the theme parks. Hotels were hosting conventions, some of which frequently not only filled the hotel but also occupied every space within the hotel. Frequently the word would come late in the week that "there was no room in the inn" for our Mass. The hotel would try to make arrangements with another hotel to host the occasion. When they succeeded, it meant we had to post messengers at the appointed hotel to redirect the faithful to the new location. This would result in masses starting late, in people losing their way, and even in frayed tempers! And when the hotel could find no room elsewhere, we would arrange to hold Mass in the hotel foyer or by the swimming pool or—if it was morning Mass—in the stuffy bar filled with the cigarette odor of the previous night.

But Catholics are a unique people! Nothing fazes them when it comes to fulfilling their obligation to seek the Lord where He may be found. And so we celebrated Mass poolside with young children flopping around in the water, totally oblivious of the sacred event taking place beside them. Or we set up the altar in one corner of a room that would hold perhaps a hundred people, and three hundred crowded in, with another few hundred outside "watching from a distance." Calvary was being really reenacted! Somehow or other, the Catholic instinct and realization of Christ's immolation on Calvary lives healthily in the hearts of our people.

We had opened our new parish church. Parish numbers were growing. The parish was maintaining itself, and a fair amount of offerings were being transferred into savings. My local parish advisors and I knew we could not stand still. The present situation could not go on forever.

The question kept coming up: should another church be built near Disney World? How large should it be? How would it be supported since it would not be a parish church? Could the offertory at tourist masses be increased to the extent that a church might be erected and maintained?

The major problem was that there were no plans for development of housing schemes within the tourist corridor. This was a stretch of Interstate 4 reaching from the city to the newly erected Disney World. It found its name from its regular occupants: temporary visitors to Orlando, people seeking the sun and the added delights of the Disney World attractions as well as the additional theme parks that were beginning to crop up. On the other hand, as our numbers grew, it was quite apparent that somehow or other we would have to do something for our faith-filled visitors.

The conviction continued to grow as hotel business grew. The problem of moving the Mass at the last moment from one hotel to another was becoming more frequent. Saturday afternoons grew tense as we awaited the dreaded phone call that either there was no room at all, or we had been moved to another hotel.

A parish church? No; there were no people for the parish. Then in a moment of inspiration the solution dawned on us all. We would build! The church would be a place of welcome for visitors from all over the world. It could also be a refuge for them, a place where they would be able to retire to pray and rest—a spiritual oasis removed from the cacophony of noise and hurly-burly of the surrounding area. It would be their "holy place while away from their parish," their "home away from home." If Cinderella could have her castle, why not provide a fitting home for the Lord of the world?

The idea of a shrine church was born. For sure, I remembered my mother's devotion. She loved to make a pilgrimage to Knock Shrine, perhaps as often as three times a year. For her, if she was in Knock, heaven couldn't be far away. There had been a vision at Knock, of course. People went there specifically on pilgrimage. Might we have a similar place of pilgrimage in Orlando too, even though beginning from a different perspective—a place also close to heaven? More people were already coming to Orlando in one year than had ever come to Knock over the same period.

Our Lady would not be far away from her divine Son at an Orlando destination either. I had already experienced the faith of many of those visitors in their quest for the Lord on weekends. Could we provide a place of pilgrimage for them? A place where faith could be refurbished and spirits refreshed? A meeting place between them and the Lord? To borrow a notion from Oliver Goldsmith, "Those who came to play would remain to pray." In my mind I began to see the crowds, the daily confessions, the frequent receptions of the Eucharist, the quiet of the place that would enable people to pray, the total completion of a planned vacation. I shared the dream with my lay advisors, and they began to dream too.

Shortly thereafter, the diocesan bursar, who was a priest, paid us a visit. I decided to share the vision with him. I told him I believed, as did all my advisors, that Orlando would continue to grow and grow as a tourist destination. The Church could do something wonderful for many people. He wanted to help in any way he could, and since he met Bishop Grady every day, he promised he would mention the matter to him.

I didn't expect to hear much more for a long time. Instead, the bursar was back to me in a few days. He had spoken to the bishop, who wanted to see me to discuss the ideas. I recall well that meeting! Bishop Grady was supportive but careful. He liked the proposals but knew they appeared beyond obtaining, at least without a lot of monetary assistance from the diocese. He would write me a letter, he said, outlining the plans I had suggested and giving his approval to the stages we proposed to follow. Those envisioned the completion of a meeting space with offices for Sunday and weekday masses. The major shrine church would follow later if all went well. I left that meeting with a feeling that something good was about to happen! Now I knew exactly what sort of effort lay ahead.

The name for the shrine still needed to be chosen. In my mind there was no doubt that it would be a shrine dedicated to Our Lady, under one of her titles. That problem was resolved too when a letter arrived from Baltimore supporting our work. It was from someone who worked at "Queen of the Universe"—the Baltimore cathedral. Now we had found the title for our new venture.

Orlando was filled with "worlds." They included at that time Disney World, Circus World, Sea World, and a number of lesser "worlds" including even "Cloth World"! Mary, God's Mother, would reign over all. She is after all Queen of All Worlds! For a long time, she has been known as "Queen of the Universe."

Mary's example of fidelity and of humble service in carrying out God's will would be the spark to ignite our ministry. She brought the Lord into the world. We would bring the Lord into the lives of those coming to seek Him in Eucharist. Her interest was in the furtherance of God's kingdom: "Do what He tells you." That was the goal of our ministry too. The Queen Mother would be our motivation and our guide to Christ.

(Later on, when the signature statue of Mary Queen came to be designed, it was decided that Mary would prefer the designation of the "humble maiden of Nazareth," always ready to serve, rather than anything inclined to portray imperial majesty. And so the Mother of God does not wear a crown in that presentation even though she is our Queen, and the statue portrays the titular name of the shrine itself.)

When I suggested the name to Bishop Grady, he was pleased—and surprised. Oddly enough, he had been considering the same name for the future shrine! For that reason he was amazed that I would come to suggest the title to him. Looking back, I know the Mother of God was at work. Her shrine was in its gestation period. She would care for its development and growth in the days and years ahead. And she would help us defeat the opposition that would soon array itself against the plan to provide a place of spiritual refuge for tourists and all who might wish to go there for worship or prayer. Oddly, that opposition would come from a few Catholic clergy (working anonymously) and a laity most likely influenced by them.

Chapter Forty-Six: Writing to Our Friends

Time was marching on. Things were falling into place. We had the approval of our bishop for the future building. And he had also approved of the name. Still, there was no site. But that remaining item was soon resolved.

Bishop Grady was extremely interested in the project and wanted it to move forward. He himself took the initiative to procure the land for the future shrine. He called me one day and asked if he might meet with me on a dirt road just outside Lake Buena Vista. There was some property for sale there, he said, and he thought we should look at it. (Lake Buena Vista includes the Disney World Village, now known also as "The Marketplace," located about ten miles from the Disney theme parks.)

The property consisted of several acres. The bishop believed we should purchase ten acres. His only concern was that the place might be too far away from Lake Buena Vista. It might have seemed far away. It was around two miles from the center of the village. Personally, I believed the spot was ideal. I already knew that a distance of a few miles would not dissuade our Catholic people. I had seen the sacrifices they were prepared to make. I suggested this property was ideal for our purpose. Shortly thereafter the purchase was made. (Today the completed shrine stands among a profusion of buildings even though not a single one was there when the shrine was being built.)

Now the question arose, was ten acres enough? My advisors believed it was not. They urged that I go back to the bishop and try to convince him we needed at least another seven acres. Bishop Grady, a keen financial wizard himself and always concerned about finances, was not entirely convinced by my arguments, but he agreed I should take the matter to the real-estate committee; should they approve, then it was a done deal.

I recall that meeting very well. Once again it seemed to be David versus Goliath. Doubts were expressed about what we were trying to accomplish and the need for more property. Who could blame them? Here was this inexperienced priest coming in with a plan that seemed so far-fetched as to be ridiculous! Orlando was only a short time separated from the Archbishop Hurley era, when the Diocese of St. Augustine covered all of Florida and every church was built to the same design. Questions were asked of me that had no answer at the time of that meeting. But we had done our homework, and every prediction of the future foretold increasing attendances, growing theme parks, and an Orlando that was already rapidly changing in population and tourist services. By no means was this a "Build it and they will come" dream, but one that was based on solid statistics.

My presentation was well informed and well prepared even though it may have appeared somewhat audacious to the listeners. In the early stages of the discussion I was meek and humble, stating my case and asking for their favorable consideration. But as the discussion continued, I realized I needed to be more persuasive. Indeed, the case appeared to be lost just before a final vote was taken. It was not a time for me to be quiet anymore. I was not about to roll over!

I reminded the gathering that I agreed that our plan was uniquely different from anything presented to them heretofore but would one day be blessed by thousands of visitors and the Diocese of Orlando itself. These were the people we were trying to serve. Then I referenced some of the local churches. They were situated frequently in out-of-the-way places, and the best indication they were Catholic was the bingo notice nearby! We planned an outstanding edifice along the interstate that would be visible to almost every visitor to Orlando and would be the pride of every Catholic. My last-ditch appeal worked. The committee voted almost unanimously in favor of my presentation.

Soon the "dream" was materializing: we were planning to build a shrine church in honor of the Mother of God, and we had the property on which to do so. The church would be named for Mary, Queen of the Universe. Now all that was needed was to convince those attending Mass to be generous to our cause! It was the beginning of the year 1980.

It didn't take long to ready a weekly bulletin to massgoers, advising them of our plans. Soon there were envelopes bearing the title of Mary, Queen of the Universe, with various suggestions for giving. At each weekly Mass, our guests were greeted as they entered the hall. Our volunteer greeters handed them a package that contained the newsletter and an envelope they were invited to use. And of course, before Mass, when I went to the altar, I took a few moments to explain the whys and wherefores of our work. The results were indeed gratifying.

Money was being set aside, and it was growing. But it seemed to me we needed to do something to bring about the further involvement of the people attending the masses. Then in a discussion one day of "how to increase the offertory," Marcia came up with the suggestion that we might want to introduce some kind of memorial, one that would seize the attention of those attending Mass. Ideas were discussed and compared, and in the end a roof tile would be the answer to what we looked for. It was decided there would be roof-tile memorials. Not only that, each person purchasing a roof tile would be given a certificate of involvement in the project. Since there are innumerable tiles on every roof, the suggested memorial would last a long time.

"We have a roof over our heads for today's Mass," our priests would say in their introduction of the roof tile, "but that roof is not our own. With your help we can have a home for our visitors, a place we can truly call our own, and a place of respite and prayer for all who visit." The suggested donation was fifty dollars. Today, hundreds of those certificates may be found throughout the length and breadth of the United States, and even beyond. Such was the complete and immediate success of the new venture.

We also decided that we would try to procure a roof tile of the kind we had in mind for the shrine and display it at every Mass for visitors. For many years thereafter, a roof tile became a requisite item for packing in the baggage of the priest offering the tourist masses. Our dedicated volunteers who packed the priest's requisites for the Mass made sure to include it in his baggage. The tile was put on display at every Mass. It might be said there's an anomaly here: roof tiles laid the foundations of the shrine church long before the roof was ever reached.

Now we needed more staff. Roof-tile certificates had to be prepared and mailed. The persons receiving them had to be listed. These would constitute the very heart of our shrine family. Not only that, but the certificate was accompanied by a promise to remember the donor in masses and prayer. It was important their names be recorded. A little office was opened at Holy Family, in the education building we had developed. It was small, about ten by twenty feet. On the door a notice was posted that read "Mary, Queen of the Universe Shrine." The first office for the future shrine had opened—even though it was ten miles from the intended site.

Savings toward building the new shrine church were growing, but not fast enough. We were doing everything we could to develop the funds. But more could be done. It occurred to me we should write letters to our members, telling them of our success and asking for further help. In my childhood, I recalled my mother responding to such letters and in particular paying special attention to the Irish Salesians. On one occasion, while in about fifth grade, I had gone around to homes myself with raffle tickets that would aid a Salesian school. Now the wheel had come full turn. It was my opportunity to promote the Gospel of Jesus by my own poor efforts in somewhat the same manner, that is by writing to our friends.

I had absolutely no knowledge of how this should be done, other than mailing a sincere letter to the addressee. So one day I took a list of names we had acquired and wrote a letter to each asking for help for the future project. The results of the first mailing were surprising. Many respondents sent not only offerings and their good wishes but also included their prayer intentions to be remembered in our masses.

We continued with the mailing program. It grew larger with each passing month. Originally, we sent out only about three mailings per year. One was in the form of a printed newsletter, telling of our progress, our dreams, and our vision for the future. Let it be said here that we learned as we went along! The earlier newsletters were cumbersomely put together, poorly laid out, and most likely difficult to read for the average recipient. But such was the caliber of our clientele that quite a number of those receiving it wrote back praising the publication and recording their delight with it. Some too wrote suggestions as to how we might make the newsletter look better. With the passage of time and the advice of good friends, a worthy newsletter was produced on a biannual basis. When I retired, this newsletter, titled *The Magnificat*, was bringing news of the shrine's progress and its spiritual mission to benefactors throughout the length and breadth of the United States and even beyond.

In time, another employee would be added to our staff to handle and record incoming mail. And of course, as always, in the case of our letter writing, Murphy's Law came into play. As time went on, some subscribers were falling by the wayside. In one mailing I decided to begin a special letter to those we seemed on the verge of losing and another letter to those who were still contributing regularly. The first letter began with something like "Since I haven't heard from you for quite a while, I was wondering …" The second letter, to the regular donors, began, "I wanted to thank you for your continued support …" Unfortunately, the two lists got confused in the mailing process. The letters went to the wrong recipients and left many people wondering how I hadn't heard from them for a long time since I had written them a thank-you letter just a short time previously. We had to give some explanations and apologies, but people were wonderful and readily accepted our sincere regrets. It was an error we would never make again!

And so from small streams great rivers are born. The lordly river Shannon rises on the borders of County Cavan and Leitrim in a place where three almost unnoticeable and seemingly insignificant brooks trickle together. Ours too was a humble beginning. It would not have withstood the appraising eye of a seasoned fund-raiser. But God was with us. His Mother wanted her shrine. She would allow us to learn as we progressed!

With the passing years, we did indeed learn more and more. I attended fund-raising conferences, as previously narrated, and both my knowledge and my incentives grew more and more. More on how to ask for monetary help. More on how to publish a newsletter that would carry the message of the shrine. There would be more prayer too. The results of our work would be in direct proportion to the time we spent in prayer ourselves. Like Moses, I had to make sure my hands continued to be uplifted in prayer. Time had to be found each morning for an early session with the Lord.

We were progressing nicely. We kept writing to our friends who were interested in the proposed shrine. In their responses, they related their problems. Most were either health or family oriented. I began to note quickly how much thought and prayer parents give to their children. Probably 70 percent of petitions coming in were related to the well-being of offspring and family members. Now and again, early on, I made a few phone calls to chat with benefactors who had noted particular problems and assure them of our prayers. My calls were so well received that the habit grew of sitting at my desk later in the evening and calling friends throughout the country. It was amazing how those calls were appreciated.

Eventually, I was making calls to probably more than half of our supporters. I told them of our progress, and they discussed their own precious needs and desires with me. Since our recorded lists were growing, we had supporters now in every time zone in the country. California is three hours behind as a time zone. I would stay up late to get to the Californians well after their evening meal.

All this activity might be reckoned to have made for a busy day. I suppose it did, but my health was good, I was relatively young, and I was a man on a mission! At the same time, while helping our benefactors spiritually both through the mail and over the phone, I was building up a clientele that were becoming attached to their Orlando project.

Only once did I run into an awkward situation regarding a phone call. The call was to a lady in the Midwest. She had been to one of our masses and had asked for remembrance of a special intention. Of course I wanted to thank her too for her generosity. When I called, her husband answered. I explained who I was, and there were moments of silence. The vibes told me I was not in friendly territory. I was informed she was not there, and the call ended abruptly on the other side. Some time later I received a letter from the lady telling me her husband was not Catholic, and it would be best for me not to call or to send any further mail either. She would continue to support the cause, she said, and for many years afterward she kept her word.

I have good memories of all those phone calls. The obvious delight of some recipients that I would call them long distance gave me a good feeling. Now and again when the call was answered, an excited voice would call to the other spouse to "pick up another phone. It's the priest from Orlando."

Those were busy days. But as already mentioned, time had to be found for prayer also. I continued the morning routine ingrained in seminary, but most evenings I stole into Holy Family Church after it had been locked for the evening, where I spent considerable time asking God's blessing on the work. The parish offices closed at five in the evening. Unless there was to be a liturgy, the church was then locked. This was to be my time with the Lord. In my heart, I knew He was with me.

And directly in front of me too would be the statue of Our Lady. I recall gazing at her on many an occasion and asking her to give me the strength to carry out this project for her. Little did I know then of the power of her answer. She is the lady, one saint wrote, whose power is equal to her will. That power would most certainly be used on behalf of the tourist ministry.

And the time was not far off when I would need the Lord's strength and Mary's power to take on would-be Goliaths who would range themselves against our project.

Chapter Forty-Seven:
An Agreement with the Diocese on Taxation

✑

There were some stumbling blocks along the way. We were able to carry out a tourist ministry because the vast majority of our volunteers belonged to Holy Family parish. Finances of the parish were therefore twofold: directly as a result of the goodness and generosity of our small group of parish members, and, in addition, through the wonderful generosity of those attending our tourist masses. So, with less than a thousand families and because of the generosity of the tourists, we had an offertory that was beginning to rival that of many larger parishes. The only way a diocese can be run is by support from its parishes. It was inevitable that when the diocesan financial officers would look at our financial reports, they would surely be impressed by what they saw—and eager to tax our income!

When the annual bishop's appeal came out, whereby parishes support their bishop and his various works, we were taxed in a way that seemed outrageous. No consideration was given to the income coming from tourists. The good people at the diocese saw only one figure. But there was no way in which the taxes levied could be raised from our small community. We duly notified the diocese. Their response was both kind and understanding. Bishop Grady, always the great listener, dispatched members of the diocesan finance committee to meet with our own committee at Holy Family parish.

The diocese was represented by the comptroller, a priest, and a couple of other officers of the diocesan finance committee. It was a cordial and forthright meeting in which we explained the challenge we were undertaking of building a church at Lake Buena Vista, a challenge of which they had been aware. We explained as best we could that offerings coming from tourists were specifically given to aid the development of the proposed shrine church. Those donors were involved in supporting their own home dioceses, and we felt it would be injurious to our cause to ask them also to be involved in fund-raising for the Diocese of Orlando. But since many would be returning again and again, they would be willing to undertake to support the building of a church to serve their spiritual needs.

It was agreed that from then on we would develop two accounts—one for the parish and the other for the new project. There was to be no taxation on the shrine account at all. Thus the taxation on the parish would be considerably reduced. This arrangement, of course, called for honesty and fairness on our part. We promised truth and honesty in our reporting, and that promise was kept to the very end of my administration of the tourist ministry and the shrine itself. As toilers in Christ's vineyard, we must all work together.

From then on, we could sleep peacefully in the knowledge that our efforts for the tourist ministry would not be hurt by a command to turn some of the income from tourist masses over to the diocese. Bishop Grady readily approved the arrangement. His successor, Bishop Dorsey, did likewise. Occasionally, people would ask if their donations were being taxed by the diocese, and I was able to tell them truthfully that every cent they gave went to the development of Mary's shrine. This arrangement was kept in place for many years.

Bishop Grady had confidence in our ability. He knew we would keep a promise and work with him as bishop. We were very careful not to commingle tourist funds toward the proposed shrine church with parish funds. When a priest knows he has the confidence of his bishop, he can climb any mountain. Undoubtedly, the arrangement that was made at that afternoon meeting at Holy Family many years earlier contributed handsomely toward the development of the shrine. I knew that every cent would go into the building. My enthusiasm for the cause contributed to successful fund-raising. And our benefactors were happy too that their donations were being used according to their wishes.

Our accounts grew, and as the 1980s progressed, we set our sights on starting the project. Bishop Grady had given his wholehearted approval. We believed that by early 1984 we would be in a position to get the project under way.

Neither my committee nor I were prepared for the opposition that was just around the corner as the sun dawned on the early spring days of 1984.

Chapter Forty-Eight: A Roadblock

Dear Reader, come down the road with me, perhaps nearly half a century! The little boy facing the "monster" in the school classroom has grown to a man and has been an ordained priest for almost a quarter of a century. He is in the process of trying to have a special church erected for tourists to Orlando. He sees the need, and his bishop has already approved the idea and given it his blessing. But this time, some people with considerable animosity towards the project see a tiger, not a mouse. The invisible tiger bothers them, though it can't be seen at all by those promoting the project.

Nothing worthwhile is accomplished easily, especially if the work is for the Lord. The devil doesn't mind who he works with as long as he achieves his goal. He may have enlisted a few unlikely helpers on his side, perhaps even diocesan employees as well as a few well-intentioned but misguided priests.

Easter 1984 … our shrine committee continued to meet. We had the bishop's approval after all, and erstwhile shrine supporters were getting impatient with the seeming lack of progress. But in the back rooms much time was being spent planning and anticipating. A roadside sign, for example, announced the "Future site of Mary, Queen of the Universe Shrine."

Besides, the hotel ministry was growing. Throngs of people, upward of eight hundred to a thousand were showing up for weekend masses. The writing was on the wall. The church needed its own space. Anybody even remotely involved in the ministry knew that.

And so we got to work with the architects. The first question that arose was where to place the buildings on our seventeen-acre site. This question was readily resolved. We all wanted high visibility for our future shrine church. The property on which it would stand was very close to the interstate. The closer the church was to the interstate, the more easily it would be seen, and the better statement it would make about its own presence and the presence of God in the lives of the people. By its prominent location it would issue an invitation to passersby to "come and see."

Availability of finances would play a major part in the decision making. There was no likelihood that all finances to build the entire shrine at once would be available. It was decided to develop a master plan and build in stages, so that the financial burden would be bearable. And of course, friendly though the hotel staffs were—and by this time some staffs and managers could not have been more supportive—the church needed a place to call its own, not only to provide masses for the visitors but also to provide a sacred space for believers wishing to recreate their spirits.

By the spring of 1984 all was ready to begin the first phase of the building. Bishop Grady agreed and recommended we meet with the diocesan building committee. A couple of meetings with the committee took place, and everything seemed to be progressing favorably. We decided the groundbreaking would take place in Mary's month, since May was on the horizon.

It was not to be.

None of us was fully aware of the undercurrent of hostility to the proposed shrine that lay still beneath the surface, all of it being furthered by just a small group. It was incomprehensible, but it was very much alive! Names of particular clergy kept recurring in connection with the opposition. All who worked in the tourist ministry were aware of the need for a church. A priest or two, working within the diocesan offices and with absolutely no connections with the ministry, were suspected as the root cause of the trouble. One did not have to belong to a detective organization to arrive at that conclusion. There were lots of clues.

Had we been building a parish church there would have been no recriminations. It seems to me that because it was a national rather than a local effort it somehow drew not only the attention but also the ire of some objectors, for reasons known only to themselves. I should add here that the majority of my brother priests only wished me the best and were solidly in my corner, even to the point of a number being benefactors of the proposed project. A priest friend of mine from another diocese attending a priest's conference in New York was told by an Orlando priest that the diocese had a "man who was about to build a nonsensical monument to himself at Disney World." Naturally, when my friend got home I got a phone call. And I immediately knew the identity of one priest who disagreed with my plans.

We had come to what we thought would be our final meeting with the diocesan building committee. All was ready. Every directive had been followed. We all looked forward to the beginning of construction. Approval for a groundbreaking date in May seemed certain. It was shortly before Saint Patrick's Day 1984.

We had a surprise in store for us.

First, let me explain that building committees have been the normal way of life in diocesan governance since Vatican Two. They are an excellent and, in my opinion, the only way to make sure that the proposed construction will be the very best possible. Every diocese throughout the length and breath of this great land is blessed with knowledgeable and often brilliant people who are prepared to share their talents for the good of their church. At that time, and to this day, the Diocese of Orlando has had wonderful building committees. There can always be the possibility that one or another member of a building committee is biased, and in turn this may shade the decisions of the committee. (Our own shrine committee was blessed with a couple of wonderful architects in addition to those we contracted for the project.)

As we presented our final plans, the committee was friendly as always and indeed gracious and receptive—all except for one person, a diocesan lay official. He constantly objected to a variety of "problems" he found in the architects' drawings. Many of those had been discussed at this level before, and changes had been made in accordance with the committee's suggestions. The question arose in my mind, was this member on a mission?

Was his positive participation in the meeting being dulled by the exigencies of preconceived theories?

It seemed clear he might have come to the meeting with an agenda—to prevent or at least postpone the start of construction. His arguments were countered by the other members time and again. But he was not to be put off. Somehow he kept finding fault. When one objection was ruled out, he found another. As the meeting dragged on for no reason, the negative atmosphere that he planted finally succeeded. And his success was to all intents and purposes based on a triviality.

Bingo! How wide was the driveway into the proposed construction site? Oops! A foot short of regulations. The dissenter was delighted. At last something concrete! But how important was it? A paper error! And since the plans would have to be submitted to the building department of Orange County, Florida, it would have to be corrected first. How long would it take to redraw the driveway? An hour? A day? The arguments we advanced, sensible as they seemed, were rejected. This man was about to accept no immediate solution.

"I am here to represent the diocese," he proclaimed. The other members of the committee obviously felt it would be improper to oppose a diocesan representative, although each participant of our own committee wondered if his stance was really a façade. The architects would have to go back to the drawing boards and have new lines drawn on paper widening the driveway and then come back once more to the diocesan committee.

Had we been torpedoed by a preconceived plan from an enemy within? We all believed we had. There was surely a tiger in the room that nobody could see except this gentleman, who had made himself the monster. Nobody of course could see the tiger. What was his bias? How do you respond to make-believe that is only in one person's head?

A meeting before Easter (April 22) was impossible. The next diocesan committee meeting would not be scheduled until after Easter. In fact the meeting would not take place until the following October. A date in May (Our Lady's month) for groundbreaking at the shrine had just gone out the window.

Chapter Forty-Nine: Follow-Up to a Crisis

❧

From the outset, we had taken the road less traveled. We might have opted for a small building in which to offer weekly masses and possibly a weekday Mass too. It would have been easier! But did we not have an obligation to the Lord? And an obligation to visiting Catholics? Should we not be doing everything in our power to affirm their faith while they were vacationing in Orlando? Was there not more to life than Cinderella and her castle?

Now we had hit a bad rut! Or was it a landmine?

I recall a feeling of aloneness. David was once again pitted against Goliath, and thus far Goliath was coming out on top. Would faithful Catholics to Orlando continue to have to endure the uncertainties and problems of having Mass in a hotel? Would they not have a church of their own in which to be with their Lord? Would the hotels get tired of "the Catholic Mass" intrusion? Would dedicated volunteers continue to stay with a ministry that seemed to be going nowhere? Above all, would a golden opportunity be lost whereby the Diocese of Orlando could proclaim the kingdom of God in an attractive and faith-inspiring environment?

After the meeting, a committee member invited me to dinner. He was as deflated as was I, but he suggested that perhaps a nice dinner might raise our spirits. It was a good restaurant, but it might have been a fast-food venue. We were both discouraged. There didn't seem to be too much light over the horizon.

I slept fitfully that night, awakening often to recall the major setback of the previous day. The dreams of yesterday, of yesteryear, seemed to have evaporated into a foggy mist, and indeed this mist kept recurring in my sleepy delirium throughout the night. Hours and hours had been spent on the project. But when we were ready to build, intangible forces seemed to have carried the day. And for how much longer would this nonsense continue?

When morning arrived, getting out of bed was easy. I had been awake for hours previously. My mind was a whirlwind of conflicting thoughts. I offered my scheduled Mass and began my day as usual, taking care of parish responsibilities. But try as I might, my mind kept returning to the previous day's disappointment. By midmorning, I was back in front of the Blessed Sacrament, sitting there, looking at the Lord. Few words escaped my lips. I tried to place my dejection in His heart, to try to end my deep depression. I can't recall how I prayed or whether I prayed at all, but somewhere along the line I whispered to the Lord, "Not my will but Yours be done. I am here if You still need me."

I have no idea how long I remained in the church. I recall someone coming to tell me a priest friend of mine was in my office waiting for me. I never found out what he wanted to discuss with me because, although I told the messenger I would be over almost immediately, I totally forgot about him, and my friend had long gone when I returned to the office building.

I had been sitting close to a statue of Our Lady holding the divine Infant. As I left the church, I approached the statue and looked into the face of my great friend, the Mother of God. I whispered a prayer that told her, "I need you now. Do you want this shrine? If you do, you will have to help me. I think I am coming to the end of the road. Please tell me what you want, what God wants from my life." I remember placing my hand on the foot of the Virgin and looking up into her face. And at that moment, my anxiety was gone! I left the church with more determination than ever. There might be grenades, landmines, and missiles further ahead on the road. But I knew this shrine was going to be built.

My prayer was heard that morning. Goliath would fall, and a much higher power would overcome him!

I didn't know it then, but it was the beginning of another new era in my life. I wasn't going to be afraid or allow the small-minded picayune adversaries to bother me again. The Mother of God had heard my prayer. More incidents hostile to the shrine would follow, but those attempted roadblocks would make no impression. The Mother of God was squarely on my side. I knew it!

As I write this story, the main shrine church is more than a decade and a half in service. And it is more than a quarter of a century since that dark and dismal meeting. I now realize that in every organization there will always be someone with a different view, a strong will, or a tendency to be political. Had I known then what I know now, I would have been disappointed with the result of the meeting, but certainly I would not have been so distressed about what had taken place. To this day, I have no notion why such hostile opposition should have developed. As we go through life, we learn, and frequently the learning is in itself a grace that brings us closer to God and develops our maturation in the intimacies we experience both in life and with the Lord of Love.

Along the road too I learned that incompetence can breathe hostility and jealousy. These latter may be found in places high or low, and there are those who have never been at the edge of the storm because they have never had the courage to accept a challenge or, in the case of a priest, try something unusual for the Lord. It is easier to hang back, sit on the fence, inquire into what others are doing, and make Monday-morning quarterback judgments. Or as they say in Ireland, "The hurler on the fence is the best hurler." Thirty-six years into the history of the tourist ministry, there are those who affirm "it was easy to bring about. Look at all those tourists!" To this day, I hear comments about the "cash cow" and how easy it all was! And I have to endure those comments even from some in high corridors of Church power. But I am glad the Lord chose me! The story of Columbus and the egg continues. "The invisible mouse" doesn't ever seem to go away. For my own part, I forgive my misinformed opponents. The storms in life can come from any source, even well-intentioned people, but I am consoled by the words of the psalmist who prayed about danger and crisis: "But God has heard; he has harkened to the sound of my prayer.

Blessed be God who refused me not my prayer or his kindness! (Psalm 66) Saint Paul expresses it well in his letter to the Ephesians when he gives glory "to Him whose power now at work in us can do immeasurably more than we ask or imagine" (Ephesians 3:20). So often Jesus had said "Do not be afraid." I was among those to whom He spoke! His response was far more positive than I could have ever imagined!

Chapter Fifty:
Controversy Plus the Arrival of a Dignitary

‿

here were some psychologically difficult times ahead. Our tourist
ministry volunteers and I had been working feverishly toward a
building that would house our weekend masses. Truth to tell, our volunteers
were just as committed to the project as was I. Occasionally a visiting priest
would help out at a Mass, and it was not unusual for a volunteer to register
a complaint that the priest had not given a worthy appeal for help. Here
indeed was a group with a passion for the work of the Lord!

To this day—long after the project has been substantially completed—I
am mystified about why the original dream drew so much adverse attention.
But the hostility toward our plans developed and grew among an apparently
small but influential group. Perhaps it was because the idea was something
new and different. Or perhaps it was because myopic minds were not able
to foresee the future. Perhaps too, there were some who misjudged my
ability to be involved in the creation of something as truly unique as had
been announced in our plans. After all, "No prophet is received in his own
country." The critics became noisy. But not one of them had any inkling of
the passion and determination of our team. And they knew nothing at all
about the ministry itself or the need to be of service to visiting Catholics.
To put it mildly, and for reasons best known to themselves, our project
had developed both "hurlers on the fence" and lots of Monday-morning
quarterbacks!

There were critics within the diocesan offices. There were some clergy
there who were unimpressed. Gradually the opposition widened. In the

early days of 1984, I received a letter from Bishop Grady. He was forwarding to me, without comment, a letter he had received. To say the very least, the letter was hostile, both to me and to the project we had in hand. The writer saw no need for a church for tourists. He proceeded to try to take apart—with poor argumentation, I might add—the entire purpose for the proposed shrine. He had never been to one of our hotel masses.

Soon the Catholic newspaper took up the issue against building a shrine. It was done with no little subtlety. As I recall it, the paper published a long letter from a lady who was a former employee of the diocese. I found this letter painful, as I thought I knew this lady well and wondered why she had not contacted me first for details of our ministry. Putting it plainly, she said there was no need for a shrine in Orlando. Later on this good lady lauded the new Baptist church that had been built in the city and held an estimated six thousand persons. I was at a loss to understand why a building for Baptists could be so beneficial and a project for Catholics unworthy!

Further letters were published in the same paper from persons very often living far away from Orlando. For some reason, there seemed an effort to create a general consensus that the gifts being given the Church by our tourist visitors were somehow being extracted by false pretenses and without justification.

Our bishop took no action at that time with the newspaper editor. In modern times, our Catholic newspaper editors are in many instances members of a union. Bishop Grady was in no way given to controversy, and while he was certainly unaware of the anguish I was enduring, most likely he believed the harsh criticism would not affect me. (In passing, let me pay tribute to the *Orlando Sentinel,* whose reporting on the shrine and its ministry was always positive and often filled with praise even to the point of mention in an editorial.) With the passage of time, the hostility died a natural death. Contrived arguments contain the seed of their own undoing. And so it was in this case too.

The Catholic newspaper did not, however, give up all that readily. More than a year after the campaign against the building of the shrine had begun, the animosity was still alive. It came to its climax as the roof of the first shrine building (to be used as a temporary church) was being put in place. On one weekend the paper had a surprise for us. When we opened its pages we came face to face with a familiar scene—our own new building, with the information underneath that it was "a recreation building being erected by Holy Family Parish."

Throughout the paper's hostile campaign I had remained silent. This, however, was too much. I had been making personal appeals to various individuals in Florida and throughout the country, and here was a report that we were simply building a recreation complex! I called our bishop and asked to see him. As always, he readily gave me his time. I carried the paper with me into his office and showed him the picture with its offensive caption. I explained one would have to be totally stupid not to get the message.

The bishop was equally incensed. He had been away, he said, and had not seen that particular issue. This nonsense would have to end, he promised. He was a man of his word. For whatever reason, whatever he said or did, it was the end of the paper's campaign against the project. I suppose it may be asked why I was so concerned about the opposition, since the project had been approved by Bishop Grady. In truth, I was afraid that the hostility being stirred up might lead the bishop to change his mind. Years later I now know this would most likely never have happened. Not only was Bishop Grady totally behind the work at hand, but he also saw the opportunity for the diocese to do something special for our visiting faithful. Besides, the hostile campaign was hurting our fund-raising.

Through all this, Divine Providence was at work. As we were undergoing this trauma, the Apostolic Delegate to the United States came to visit. He wanted to see Disney World for himself. This was during the presidency of Ronald Reagan, during which time the Apostolic Delegate would be elevated to Papal Nuncio. And the delegate—Archbishop Laghi—would oversee the establishment for the first time of diplomatic ties between the United States and the Vatican. His arrival in Orlando was the beginning of a lasting friendship, and shrine family members will remember with affection the man on whom later was bestowed the highest honor of the Church in 1991, Pio Cardinal Laghi.

Archbishop Laghi, a man obviously powerful in public diplomacy but steeped in personal humility and faith, lauded our plan, foretelling the spiritual effect this proposed shrine would have in Orlando. When I showed him a newspaper letter adversarial to our efforts, he simply smiled. He assured me the Holy Father would be pleased with my efforts, as he was very much in favor of shrines and their work. The archbishop was so enthusiastic about the project that his advice was easy to accept: "Keep going, and with God's grace you will realize your dream."

He would come many more times to Orlando, always inspiring us with his enthusiasm and his good-humored friendship. He came on the scene at the right time, a gift of Divine Providence to me and indeed to the Diocese of Orlando. He was one of the rare and memorable personages one meets in life. While I lived at Holy Family, he liked to stay at the rectory. On his first weekend visit, as I was going out to offer early Sunday Mass, he had already arisen and was sitting in the kitchen sipping coffee he had made for himself. This prince of the Church had no grandiose notions.

Chapter Fifty-One:
First Artist Is Commissioned

There was nothing to do but wait—and hope! There were forces out there against us, but we felt the Lord was on our side. There wasn't a lot more to be done as regards the architectural drawings already completed. Meantime, there were visiting Catholics to be served, and we went about our business as usual, taking care of them. I recall advising our committee that Jesus wept over Jerusalem, but He still proceeded with the divine plan. In His footsteps we were called upon to do the same. In the long run, time would take care of another year added to the history of the shrine's beginnings.

Easter was approaching, the season that reminds us of the Man-God's victory over evil and hostility. It was celebrated with the feeling that somehow our designs for the Lord had been buried too, but the wait would end as it did and does for all believers in Christ. We knew that there was little likelihood of groundbreaking in the foreseeable future. Another meeting with the diocesan building committee could not be arranged until the fall. On the positive side, we had more time to add to our financial savings.

We knew nothing was going to stop us! First, we looked at another possible date for groundbreaking. The Feast of the Immaculate Conception would provide a wonderful opportunity for us. The new shrine was to bear Mary's name. Why not place the first shovel in the ground on one of her greatest feast days? And not only that, but on a feast that celebrated Mary Immaculate as our national patroness! And so it was decided.

When the time came, we took our case to the diocesan committee again. The individual who had caused all the problems was no longer in the employment of the diocese. Without him, those hostile to our plans were without a leader. Permission for groundbreaking was readily granted. But a new fly had gotten into the ointment: the chairman of the diocesan committee felt we could lower costs on the project by giving it a shingle roof.

This of course flew in the face of our previous fund-raising efforts. Hundreds of people had subscribed for roof tiles. Every appeal for funds had featured the roof tile. I had to make a stand, and I simply told the truth. Shingles, I said, were not an option on the new building. We were not going to be accused of raising funds on a falsity. It was difficult to get some members to understand. Fortunately, Bishop Grady was in attendance at this meeting. (Had he learned about the previous meeting?) Not only was he a good listener, but he had been in charge of the major portion of the completion of the basilica of the national shrine in Washington DC. He listened quietly to the argumentation and after a while interjected with a simple statement: "I think we will go along with Father Harte's presentation." The discussion was over. We could look toward setting a date for groundbreaking.

There were months to go before December 8, 1984, the day that was to become the birthday of the shrine. But we had work to do. We had our dreams—and plans to fulfill them! Everything in the future shrine would hint at the majesty of God. There would be lots of artwork to provide such reminders of our relationship with the Creator. We would need artists to provide us with artwork, and we wanted only the very best. Outdoor statuary of the Mother of God and the Divine Child was foremost among the plans. We needed to find an artist for this first piece. Our liturgical architect, Bill Brown, long on board, was familiar with some well-known artists. We invited them to Orlando to make a presentation. There were eight in all.

I recall a fluttering in my heart as we entered the meeting with the competing artists. We had decided to meet with them at a local hotel where masses were being held on weekends. The owner had very generously provided the meeting space gratis. I reflected as we entered the hall that in a way history was being made. The outcome of this meeting might well have an effect on future generations of visitors to Orlando. Groundbreaking would take place sooner or later. From this meeting might come a work of art that would convey spiritual hope and desire for the many. A spirituality fostered by religious art might raise minds and hearts to God. And surely, spirituality was foremost among all our plans.

The statue was to be placed under the proposed bell tower. We knew there could be a multiplicity of concepts. We had hoped for a variety of presentations. We got what we were looking for!

Each of the early artists to address us presented himself meticulously well dressed, and each gave his own impression—and his hopes—as to what the future statuary would look like. It was an enthralling afternoon. There was a break halfway through, after four presentations. Then the rest gave their presentations. The decision was going to be difficult!

The final presenter made his appearance. He was different! The meticulous dress of the previous hopefuls was missing. Here was someone who had on a leather jacket, sported a beard, and looked like a member of Hell's Angels. The latter might have an artist in their midst, of course, but I had never heard of one! A committee member seated beside me leaned over and whispered "How did this guy get in?"

The question was soon answered. The man was Jerzy Kenar. Born in Poland, he had escaped the Communist regime to Sweden and later had made his way to the United States where he had set up shop in Chicago. His workplace there was named the Wooden Gallery.

His presentation held us spellbound. He dealt not with any proposal but instead gave a beautiful presentation of the relationship between a mother and her child. His talk was sprinkled with examples. This relationship should, he said, be illustrated in whatever sculpture might be created.

His casual appearance was forgotten or attributed to his artistic leanings. This man was inspirational. He was chosen unanimously. And he had the better part of two years to get his work done!—that is, if we could find a benefactor to underwrite the costs.

In many ways, things were looking up. The committee and I got together and arranged for an informational evening on the shrine at the

Holy Family social hall. There was a great deal of local interest, and the gathering was well attended, so much so that we were surprised with the turnout. The burning enthusiasm and excitement of those days is still fresh in my memory. We explained the project and told of the dream.

The plan called for the building of a magnificent shrine church that would bear the name of the Mother of God. The church would not be a parish church but a place of prayer, surrounded by beautiful and tranquil grounds and fountains. It would be centrally located near Lake Buena Vista so that tourists to Orlando might not only be able to attend Mass there but also be attracted to spend time with the Lord in an atmosphere of prayer. It would provide a very special chapel of adoration that would be open almost every day. The Eucharist would be the primary ministry of the shrine, but the sacrament closely connected with it for Catholics—Reconciliation— would also be administered on a daily basis. The surrounding gardens would also be places of quiet prayer and reflection, and we hoped to have the Stations of the Cross on the outside as well as within the church. We described this development as "a place like no other." The care of souls was our main and, in fact, our only objective.

We also explained the predictions that at the present rate of tourism Orlando would match Jerusalem, Athens, or Rome as a destination. We felt it would be beneficial for the Church and the spread of the Gospel if there were a fitting place of spiritual respite for vacationers during their visit here. There was enthusiasm among the attendees, but truth to tell a few naysayers too.

I suppose in a way our dream did indeed seem overly ambitious at the time, and I recall describing it some time later to a priest friend in Ireland. We were walking by the ocean at Howth Head outside Dublin. He listened and then asked, "How much money do you have for this project?" When I told him our present financial situation, he stopped walking, looked me in the eye, and said, "Joe Harte, you are out of your mind." We often joke about that statement of his, and he has been to the completed shrine many times and rejoices in its success. "God gives the increase."

On that informational evening in Orlando though, Divine Providence was at work. A good gentleman who "looked in to see what was going on" was so impressed with the Jerzy Kenar presentation that he committed there and then to underwrite the cost of the shrine's first piece of sculpture – the courtyard mother and child beneath the Bell Tower. The meeting was a success! "Come to me all you who labor and are burdened, and I will refresh you," Jesus had said. That evening's meeting was a time to realize the Lord was indeed to be found within our efforts. And His Mother wasn't far away either!

Chapter Fifty-Two:
Designing the Shrine Church

Perhaps here we should address the frequently asked question, "How did you decide on what kind of church you would build?"

The question is indeed an important one when one considers the varieties of churches that have been built in the years following the Second Vatican Council. The freedom to attempt the modern frequently overlooked the tradition of faith that was embedded in the more classical structures. Many of the newer churches were more in keeping with the principles of the Protestant revolt than with retention of an architecture that somehow reflected the Body of Christ. In the earlier years especially, after the Council, churches were erected that were notable for their bareness. The crucifix seemed to be the only Catholic element. All too often the tabernacle was hidden away. The baptismal font could be anywhere. Statues and works of art were either removed or made inconsequential. It seemed that the theories of the reformer (Father) John Calvin were once again alive and well.

I always found it difficult to understand the chief objective of the "new architecture." It was not unusual to hear of the renovation of a church where traditional stained glass was removed and replaced with faceted glass that mostly showed color, nothing else. There were incidents of marble statues being taken out of churches and at times broken in small pieces to form a garden walkway. (In one such incident, I am told, the parishioners refused to use the walkway paved with marble stones that came from their beloved Sacred Heart statue. Did the ordinary faithful have a greater understanding of faith in tradition than those who wrought such havoc?)

The fact is, visual aids are very much part and parcel of our Christian Catholic belief. The statue of Saint Peter in the Vatican is a fine example. The toe of the saint is almost worn away from visitors touching it. One is reminded of the story in the Gospel of the woman with the issue of blood: "If only I could touch the hem of His garment!" The faithful want to come as close to their Lord as they can. Touch is one of God's gifts to us. The work of art evokes that desire to be closer, to touch, and to make known not only one's presence but also one's love and the inner thoughts of one's heart. It is much the same as when a parent runs her hand over the photograph of her son or daughter who is fighting a dangerous war in a foreign land. Touching the image fills the parent with feelings of warmth and contributes to a spiritual connectedness. The tomb of Saint Peter in Rome was discovered partially because of an inscription on a nearby tomb that reads something such as the following. I can't recall the exact words but the inscription tells that the parents of the young person being entombed wanted their child to lie "close to Peter, the disciple of the Lord."

The shrine church today has a window recalling seven very important councils of the Church. The Second Council of Nicea is among them, for the very reason that it was this Council that declared the veneration of images to be not only permissible but recommended. As human beings, living our lives among objects created by man, the early Church understood the usefulness of using manmade objects to remind the viewer of the presence of God in his or her life.

Our shrine committee members were not conservative in their aspirations, but neither were they too much devoted to modern church design. This proposed shrine church would serve people from all nations, and it was important therefore that it be faithful to universal traditions. Before construction began, several members of the committee took time to attend one or more conferences on church building. I have vivid recollections of the posture taken by one of our members at one such conference. The discussion was regarding seating: the advantages of replacing pews with chairs, the savings garnered by omitting kneelers entirely.

It was advocated that the pew could be an obstruction by its immovability. Chairs could be moved around in different arrangements according to the need or the occasion. The church could serve a second purpose as a hall. Our committee member voiced his objections in no uncertain terms! Pews, he told the group, had been with the Church for a long time. They provided solidity and were a symbol of strength. They were what the faithful "expected" to find in a church.

There was a constancy and strength about the arrangement that was significant, he said. And as far as designing a church to also be a meeting hall for purposes other than worship, he told the group he found this to be upsetting, for the simple reason that he had early come to understand that the worship space was always just that and not to be viewed as a utility hall. This man had no previous liturgical or theological education. But perhaps he exemplified the desire of faith that so often fills the hearts of the faithful and tends to be overlooked in the construction of many places of worship.

Later on, after the first phase of our shrine had been built, we found out how correct he was! Because the first phase was a temporary place of worship, it would not have been wise to introduce pews. We installed steel chairs, which brought us a directive from the county authorities that the chairs must be connected so that in the case of fire they would not constitute dangerous obstacles to persons trying to exit the building. Admittedly, the chairs were steel and inexpensive. But it seems to me that there is no replacement for the time honored pew—immovable, strong, permanent, unchanging, just like the teachings of Jesus espoused by His Church!

The design of the main building came easily enough. It was to be a shrine church. None of the great shrines of the world are rotund, where people often sit face to face because of the geometry of the architecture. It would be a traditional edifice, spacy, high, reaching toward the heavens, and totally in keeping with the older edifices worldwide. The design itself was finalized when the designing architect came across a rendition of the first great Christian church of Rome, built in the time of Constantine the Great. He took it as his model, and today Mary's Shrine in Orlando in its exterior form relates very closely to that first of Christian churches.

The placing of the tabernacle was always going to be a subject of debate. "Prominent but not central" seemed to be the liturgical mind at the time.

This frequently resulted in subjective interpretation in the construction of churches. The Eucharist is at the very heart of Catholic faith and worship, as previously mentioned. For hundreds of years Catholics were accustomed to seeing the tabernacle in a central position over the altar. There was no need to search; it was always there. My mother, in her visits to Ballina Cathedral when doing her shopping, always knelt first at the middle of the altar rail, where she was exactly facing the tabernacle. She knew the Lord was there, and I quickly learned that too.

All too often we have seen new churches with the tabernacle obscured. I have seen one church where the tabernacle was enclosed in a space smaller than a confessional, with one kneeler and no room for a second person. Tabernacles have been placed in their own chapels to the side of the church, at the back of the church—almost as if to keep them out of the main assembly. The faithful coming into church found themselves genuflecting from habit—to nothing! The "sacred space," terminology that was so much in vogue after the Second Vatican Council, found its sacredness only in the celebration of the divine liturgy. But after the people had departed, what was left to the onlooker was merely an empty hall.

Was this what the faithful wanted? Was this a part of our faith tradition? Absolutely not! To many it appeared to be a downplaying of the importance and meaning of Eucharist. If the church was sacred, that sacredness came through the Lord whose commanding presence remained even after the liturgy had concluded. The place for the King was His throne—at the center of the assembly.

Time and time again, before the shrine church was completed, visiting faithful asked me, "Where are you going to put the tabernacle?" It was quite clear to me that those visiting Orlando and supporting this ministry to tourists were keen to see the tabernacle placed in the center, where they had grown accustomed to it in their younger days. (Some too were saddened by modernizing developments in their home parishes.)

And in the center the tabernacle would be! When the time came to place the tabernacle, Orlando had a new bishop. We weren't sure whether he would permit the center tabernacle. We didn't have to worry. He asked no questions and readily accepted our explanations regarding the placing of the tabernacle. Jerzy Kenar would in time create a tabernacle that not only gave grandeur to the place where the Eucharist is maintained but also rendered its own statement about the presence of the Lord. Kenar wanted to symbolize energy in his creation of the tabernacle, something he attained through the installation of the ornamental glass at the back as well as in the door of the tabernacle itself. And certainly the Eucharist is that great sacrament that bestows the energy on all of us to be Christ-bearers to the world at large.

Titled for the Mother of God and Queen of the Universe, we also decided that the signature statue of the shrine would display Mary in a prominent location. That location would be to the front of the church. When planning the daily adoration chapel, it was decided to place the statue of the Queen just outside the sanctuary and in such a position that those on their way into the adoration chapel would first pass the statue of Our Lady. It would be good to greet the mother while on the way to spend time with her divine Son. This statue of Mary stands today, a beautiful work of art, close to the sanctuary and a reminder of the sacredness of not only this area of the church but indeed of the entire place of assembly.

We were, of course, living in the twentieth century when the church was designed. Along with our architects, we believed it would be useful to incorporate some modern aspects to the design. Most of those aspects took place almost automatically, without too much attention being paid to design at all, as for example the placing of the glass division between the narthex and the nave, and the creation of the blue glass windows for the day chapel. This was a more contemporary addition that added a look of modernity to the building, a look that both pleases the eye and adds to the ambience of the general design. The placing of some of the artwork also contributed to this notion of modernization without taking anything away from the traditional layout of the church. Considerable attention was paid to the placing of the pews in the side aisles. It was decided to place them at an angle so as to face the altar rather than the old system of facing straight ahead into empty space. The church lighting might also be considered as modern: there are no hanging lamps, and the light comes from fixtures that are high overhead without being in any way prominent or distracting. Practicality took precedence in some areas, leading to an edifice that is both prayerful and tranquil.

Today, our Catholic people, on visiting the shrine church, are for the most part drawn into an atmosphere that is traditional, warm, and conducive to prayer. The presence of the Lord is foremost, and with a central tabernacle the faithful are immediately invited to awareness of Him who invited all of us to keep Him in our memory when He offered Himself on our behalf. The beautiful altar of white ash constructed by Jerzy Kenar looks out prominently toward the congregation, reminding those who visit on occasions other than Mass that this is indeed the place where the sacrifice of Jesus is renewed and His faithful followers accept His request to continue His presence according to His words: "Do this in memory of me."

Chapter Fifty-Three: A Shrine is Born

The summer of '84 wended its way to autumn. We waited patiently as the Florida oaks began to shed their leaves in the latter part of the year. The architects had designed the location for groundbreaking. Now and again, returning from a hotel Mass, I would drive by to take another look, just to make sure the spot was still there.

Indeed, the chosen location was a considerable distance from the dirt road that ended just before our property. Frequently, I took interested parties to see the site, always assuring them that one day a shrine to the Mother of God would adorn the place. Some were skeptical and in their charity expressed the hope that the dream would come true. Many others were true believers, and the vigor of their encouragement and willingness to help added to my determination that success would be ours. A lot of people were depending on me.

Time passed. In mid-November invitations went out to clergy and others who might have an interest in the project. The first earth for the building of Mary's Shrine in Orlando would be broken at 3:00 p.m., December 8, Feast of the Immaculate Conception of Our Lady.

December 8, 1984, is a day that has affixed itself in my memory. It was one of those beautiful sunny days that winter visitors dream about, temperature around 72, with a whisper of a breeze. Our volunteers had amassed at the site. This was the day they had waited for. The first phase of the longed-for shrine was about to begin. A loudspeaker system had been provided as well as a couple of shovels for the actual groundbreaking. Clergy are not used to digging, but the extra shovels afforded an opportunity to one and all to be a part of the celebration of beginning to build a shrine to Mary, the Mother of God.

Bishop Thomas Grady uttered a prayer asking the blessing of the Lord on the work about to commence. Then he took one of the shovels and ceremoniously dug into the earth. He then handed the shovel to me and I followed suit. Many of the other clergy then performed the symbolic task.

Since protocol called for our bishop to be the final speaker, I was asked to express my sentiments. I was loud in praise of the Lord who had brought us to this day. I told the gathering that we would build something inspirational, a building of which every Catholic could be proud, and a place where people could come close to their Creator. This would surely be a place like no other! I believed it was important for me to continue to keep the plan before our people, and I spoke in glowing terms as if the shrine were a positive certainty. In my mind it had to be! I recall the occasion because, when I really think about it, I wonder how I could have been so determined and so positive. Perhaps the Lord was driving me, as I think He was.

Bishop Grady had a more sober view. We were, he said, preparing a place where Catholics visiting Orlando might come to Mass and fulfill their religious obligations. He most likely approved the sentiments I had expressed, but he wanted to bring reality to the situation. We were only beginning; the fulfillment of the dream might be a long way off. It was the desire of our Catholic people for Sunday Eucharist that had brought us this far. Perhaps too, the bishop had his own reservations about future success, and who could blame him? (Let it be recorded, however, that when the building began, he was most supportive and always gentle in the advice he would give. And he made himself readily available whenever I wanted to approach him with a problem or an idea. This bishop had a wonderful gift of making his guest feel at home, and the quiet and gentle manner of his words had a tendency to remain in the mind.)

As the traffic hummed by on the adjacent Interstate 4, about five hundred yards from where we were gathered, I couldn't help reflecting on the symbolism of the occasion. Undoubtedly, some of those drivers out there were ardent Catholics who would sooner or later join a faith community within the walls of the future building. Others may well have been concentrating exclusively on their own ventures in this world apart from God. But their journey to Tampa or Tallahassee or wherever would come to an end. The better journey they were on was to eternal life. And here we were, erecting a structure to remind them of God and hoping one day to help steer their journey to eternal life through the ministry of this future shrine. There would be a permanent placard right by the interstate, and that placard would be the building itself.

On the eighth of December, 1984, Mary's Shrine was born. Masses would continue to be celebrated in local hotels for one and a half more years. Volunteers would still have to journey here and there with the priests. We would still have to make arrangements with hotels more or less on a weekly basis. As far as the ministry was concerned, nothing had changed at all. But it would change someday, we now knew. A brightening horizon lay before us!

As for priests associated with the ministry, they would have to continue to make sure that the "roof tile" was carried to each Mass venue and displayed to the people in an appeal for their support. That support was forthcoming. And the roof tile had already become a become a bone of contention for those on the diocesan building committee who wished to cut back on expenses by giving the shrine a less noble and less expensive roof. That crisis was past! Little did we know the shrine roof was destined to bring future pain for those of us involved in the tourist ministry. But that tribulation was a long way off.

One might add that the spot of the first groundbreaking is now marked with a plaque bearing a scriptural passage. The passage is from Saint Paul: "You are strangers and aliens no longer. No, you are fellow citizens of the saints and members of the household of God. You form a building which rises on the foundation of the apostles and prophets, with Christ Jesus himself as the capstone. Through Him the whole structure is fitted together, and takes shape as a holy temple of the Lord: in Him you are being built into this temple, to become a dwelling place for God in the spirit" (Ephesians 2:19–22). For those who take time to examine the wording, the message is that God dwells in His people. Each is a temple, contributing all the more to the sacredness of the building into which they carry their own holiness.

Chapter Fifty-Four:
First Buildings Completed

⤬

Sometimes we understand better when we look back. I should have caught the signs of fervor for the shrine among our supporters, but I did not. There were many who were as desirous for the shrine of Mary as were the volunteers or I myself.

The contractors needed time after the groundbreaking ceremony. January came and went and most of February too. Nothing seemed to be happening. But behind the scenes there was a lot of activity which could not yet be seen in construction of any kind. Formalities and legalities were being taken care of by the construction company. The necessary documents were being prepared. Of course, as is always the case in such circumstances, no one seemed to be in a hurry!

Only the shrine supporters wanted action. During these weeks of delay, I got several complaints. The complainants wanted to know why nothing had happened since the official ceremonies in December. At Mass, people would inquire about the progress. Others were close to complaint! "I pass by there frequently, and nothing is happening. Why?" "Father, it's high time the building got under way." And not infrequently a letter came as well, either asking about progress or uttering the same disappointment as the locals.

It seems that in the public opinion, the shrine was needed. Catholics were looking forward to it; more than that, they would frequent it. They looked forward to it as a haven. Had I understood all that at the time, I might have been less apprehensive about the future. What was also being illustrated was the wonderful Catholic love and devotion to Mary, the Mother of God, that is deep in the hearts of our American people. Mary Immaculate is patroness of the United States—and not without reason!

In late February, work did indeed start. Slowly but surely the building began to rise. Workers took over the marshy area behind the building site, and soon a lake was evident. Then came the work to build the bridge across the lake from what would be the parking lot. Good things were happening.

Bishop Grady made frequent visits to view the progress. It was evident he was pleased. On one occasion, he asked what the plans were for the courtyard. I explained to him that it would be covered with concrete, just enough to enable the faithful to walk in and out and nothing more. "Why don't you tile it?" he asked. This would give a finished appearance to the courtyard, where pillared lamps had been scheduled to stand. I responded that the building committee of the diocese had not given permission for that. "Go ahead, do it," he replied. This small permit and departure from his own building committee rules told me the bishop was squarely in our corner. The tiling would add to our costs, but apparently the bishop believed the money would be forthcoming.

As the roof was placed on the building, he came out again to look at the interior. He was quite pleased with what he saw. "What will you do with the floor?" he asked. It was a concrete floor at the time and destined to remain a concrete floor. I told him we had no plans other than to leave it as it was. He suggested carpeting. On this occasion I offered that carpeting would add to our expenses, that this was a temporary building, and that indeed we shouldn't give it a permanent look. He agreed with this sentiment, and the floor was never carpeted for the six years the building was used as a place for Mass.

Soon it was the summer of '85. The summer is memorable for two reasons. With the new building well under way, we made a decision that it would be good to offer Mass on the grounds, even before we occupied the structure. We sent out word to our supporters, many of whom turned up on a Saturday morning in July to participate in Mass in a small tent erected for the purpose. Father Charles Pfab (a Marist priest and associate at Holy Family Parish), Father John McMullan (my seminary classmate and friend who journeyed all the way from Seattle to be present for the historic occasion), and I were the concelebrants. It was a beautiful Saturday morning. The majority of our volunteers were present, along with some well-wishers from far away. Supporters from all over the United States sent wishes and associated themselves with the Mass.

We commended the work to God and dedicated the entire shrine grounds to the Lord at that Mass, asking God's blessings on those who would come to worship or even simply visit down through the years. A place becomes sacred only if God reigns there, and these acres on which the shrine would stand were consecrated to God. In many ways, it was a family occasion; people who had been involved with bringing Christ to the tourists now enjoyed the fruits of their labors in witnessing the new buildings being constructed not a hundred yards from where they now prayed. The sun shone that morning, and the light of Christ warmed the hearts of all present. In my heart I remembered the words of Jesus, "I am the light of the world. He who follows me will walk not in darkness or in the shadow of death but will have the light of life." We all wanted that light to continue to shine.

Indeed, that would not be the last tent Mass. Every Easter since we occupied our first building, Mass is celebrated in a huge tent adjacent to the new shrine church. Easter massgoers far exceed the hospitable space provided for normal attendance. The extra numbers to Mass are welcomed in the tent outside.

There was another reason too for remembering the summer of '85. Progress was being made, and as the project developed from the ground, we had time to reflect on our fund-raising efforts. The finances set aside at the moment were for building purposes only. There would be a mortgage facing us at completion of this first phase. The plan was to pay off the mortgage and then begin to plan for the final phase, the shrine church itself. We already had chosen a sculptor in the person of Jerzy Kenar. Now we needed another artistic firm on board that could provide us with stained glass.

No stained glass was scheduled for the initial buildings. However, we had to look to the future. If somehow we could provide a showcase within the temporary edifice for one stained-glass window, then the visiting faithful would be able to see for themselves what was planned for the future main shrine church. Surely some might want to be involved in this facet of the project too.

And so we got to work. There are many stained-glass companies in the United States. A letter was sent to those we considered capable of being involved. We invited them to respond if they were interested. The responses were enlightening. Quite a few returned our own letter with their response on the bottom or on the back of the page. They were immediately struck from the list of candidates. Professionalism calls for courtesy. These letters told us all we wanted to know about the firms. If they couldn't afford a secretary, then we couldn't risk contracting them.

In the final analysis, we interviewed eight applicants. These were whittled down to two, one in California and one in Philadelphia. Both came across as highly qualified. After one of our committee members had visited both establishments, Judson Studios of California was chosen. It was one of the oldest stained-glass companies in the United States and had won renown for work it had done elsewhere. They would install our windows.

Walter Judson owned the firm in Los Angeles. He was a very personable man with a wonderful knowledge of scripture. Stories from the Bible flowed easily from his lips. After his contract had been signed, I met him in San Antonio to discuss future arrangements and how we might go about designing the windows. (San Antonio is about halfway between Los Angeles and Orlando. I was able to stay with my good friends of former times, General John P. and Mary Margaret Flynn who had been wonderful friends while at Holy Family, the parish of which I was still pastor.)

The installation of stained-glass windows in churches developed before the Middle Ages to help bring the message of the Gospel to an illiterate people. I had been to Chartres Cathedral, outside of Paris, a number of times and had seen the wonders of stained-glass art in the magnificent pre-Renaissance church. Chartres Cathedral in every way presents "the Bible in glass." Down through the centuries, people had viewed those windows and learned about God's love for His people. Personally, as I gazed on the windows for myself, I thought of the effort and the dedication of the artists and the passion of the church so many centuries ago to bring the Gospel story to the world. Could we emulate them in Orlando? We couldn't, of course, provide that amount of glass in our forthcoming shrine. We knew our limits! But we did want to reflect the wonders of God's love at our Orlando edifice too.

The future shrine was far from being designed. The first building was not even completed, and no move could be made again until its mortgage was paid off! (Frequently, I recalled my priest friend's amiable reproach some time previously: "Joe Harte, you must be out of your mind!" On the other hand, I balanced that statement with the angel's message to God's future Mother: "Nothing is impossible with God.")

At that San Antonio meeting, we decided to tell the Bible story in our windows. Walter Judson was a convert to Catholicism and had insightful knowledge of the scriptures, both Old Testament and New. As at Chartres he would create windows with little medallions, thus providing the opportunity to tell a multitude of Bible stories. But we didn't know how many window spaces there would be! We would wait and then put all the windows together later on. Meantime there would be a first window that would illustrate "The Fall"—or, as it was called by Saint Thomas Aquinas, "The Felix Culpa" ("Happy Fault"). And since the future shrine church would be dedicated in the name of Mary, Queen of the Universe and Mother of God, she would be the centerpiece in the very first window. "The Fall" did indeed provide the opportunity for the Son of God to come among us. At the moment of the Fall, was the Word envisioning the beauty of His own Mother? We believed so.

The dream for a wonderful place of Catholic witness near the theme parks was unfolding. Cinderella had her castle just a few miles away. But Cinderella was nothing but a fictitious fairy tale—the story of an imaginary midnight and a dawn that really never blossomed. The shrine would be "the theme park of reality" and one day would, please God, help people on their own pilgrimage to God. Its adornments would tell tales of the infinite love of the Son of God for His people. No "small, small world" here. Rather, a world of love and life and God's beneficence! And in this world the song we would sing would be "Jesus Christ." There would be no holding back the dawn!

It had been our hope to have the new facility completed in time for Easter services of 1986. Easter came early that year, on March 30. As the time grew closer, we knew it couldn't be done, and so we set the inaugural Mass date for the third Sunday after Easter of that year, April 20. Even as Easter arrived, Jerzy Kenar was still working on his statue for the outdoor chapel. The statue would not be ready until mid-November.

But on April 20, the new temporary building experienced its first full house at the opening Mass with Bishop Grady as the main celebrant. Progress was being made. A couple of weeks later, we ended all hotel masses other than those within the Disney World resort complex. We were at last in our own facilities.

In September, I visited Jerzy in Chicago to see his project for the outdoor chapel nearing completion. With bronze there is time to correct problems before the clay model gets to the furnace. I learned that being an artist is a laborious occupation. The collar-and-tie part and the glory only come when the work is completed. (Occasionally Jerzy wore a collar and tie!)

But I also learned something special about Jerzy Kenar. Like all artists, he truly wanted to please. It was toward late afternoon, and we had planned to go to dinner together. I had expressed reservations about Our Lady's face and head. Jerzy was a little distraught. When it came time for dinner, he asked me to go on my own; he wanted to continue work on his project. There was no arguing about it, even though I encouraged him to join me. He asked me to return after dinner to see the changes he was about to make.

When I got back, he had completed the change, and better still, he agreed that I had been correct in my observations. The statuary arrived in Orlando on the Friday before the ceremony of blessing of our new building. There was just one day left to get it in place. Jerzy got to work early in the morning and as we watched he pulled and dragged the statues of the mother and child until he had them in the place designated. He attached them to the floor beneath and put on the finishing touches. When the finish had been reached at about three in the afternoon, Jerzy looked like a fatigued and beaten individual. But there was a look of satisfaction on his face. The artist's work was done. Tomorrow he could wear his collar and tie. Or perhaps his leather jacket, though he was now lacking the beard.

Sunday, November 23, 1986, dawned a beautiful day. For us involved in the shrine project, the forthcoming ceremonies would make it even more beautiful. Bishop Grady and all the bishops of Florida, together with a large number of diocesan clergy, gathered for a ceremony of blessing of the new temporary church. That particular date was chosen because it was closest to the Feast of the Presentation of Mary, which fell on the previous Friday. It was a tribute to the undertaking of our Diocese of Orlando that every Florida bishop was in attendance at the ceremony other than one who could not attend because of illness. Archbishop Pio Laghi, now Papal Nuncio, presided at the Mass. It was an opportunity to look back on the work that had been achieved with God's blessing and a time too to utter a prayer for our future plans. The ceremony was completed with the placement of a time capsule in the ground at the entryway to what is now the main shrine church. As the November sun sank a little lower in the sky, the atmosphere was warmed by the voices of the congregation led by the many clergy present, singing the Salve Regina—a fitting conclusion to a beautiful ceremony. The shrine was titled for the Queen, and here were her family singing her a song of praise and commending themselves and the future ministry to her loving care.

Chapter Fifty-Five:
Absentees from a Celebration

∽

We gradually got used to the new surroundings—and to all the new invoices that were now coming in, a sizable mortgage on the new buildings as well as the new expenditures on maintenance and staff. But crowds at masses continued to grow, especially now that there was less trouble for visitors finding the location of Mass. People revisiting from times past were also excited to see the progress, and supporters of the project were reinforced in the decision they had made to help. I knew that if we were to begin the next phase, we must first wipe out our mortgage, and the committee and I threw ourselves wholeheartedly into the challenge of doing just that.

Success came our way! Two years later, the new project had cleared its mortgage. We were in a position to look to the future! Indeed, we had continued to plan for the new shrine church, and as previously, "the long day's journey into night" had also repeated itself many times with late night meetings, discussions, and dreams among the shrine committee members.

Early in 1990, a new bishop was appointed, as the beloved Bishop Grady had reached retirement age. The new appointee was the Most Reverend Norbert Dorsey, who had been an auxiliary bishop in Miami. Bishop Dorsey came to Orlando with credentials that make priests happy. He had been well loved in Miami, and his characteristic gentleness of spirit and personal affability had endeared him to all with whom he came in contact.

It was natural for us working on the shrine project to have concerns as to how the new bishop might relate to our ministry. We did not have to worry. He had previously attended the blessing of the first building, and he was very much aware of the service being rendered to the tourists. Indeed, apparently the reports were so good that he had to come see for himself! When a volunteer reported to me after a Vigil Mass one Saturday evening that she thought she had seen Bishop Dorsey at Mass, I dismissed the report as imaginary. But it turned out the volunteer was correct: the bishop had come anonymously to the Mass and had seen for himself what procedures were in place. He was impressed with the fervor of the volunteers. Afterward he remarked that with such dedicated volunteers the future shrine would have to be successful. We quickly learned that the go-ahead for the main building had been given.

The landmark day came for us on August 22, 1990, Feast of the Queenship of Mary. The ceremony was scheduled to take place at 5:30 p.m. We had chosen the occasion in keeping with the name of the shrine and also to continue the practice of groundbreaking on a feast of the Mother of God.

It was a short ceremony indeed. It was to be followed by Mass, and the many who had arrived for the occasion sheltered themselves from a thunderstorm as bad as Florida can produce. The only people braving the storm were the two bishops, myself, and one or two other attendants. So amid the crackling of lightning, the roar of thunder, and a downpour from the heavens above, Bishop Dorsey, then-retired Bishop Grady, and I put our shovels into the earth. Then the bishops quickly blessed the spot, and we retreated to safety for the celebration of Mass.

I couldn't help contrasting the day to the first groundbreaking ceremony. That had been a magnificent eighth of December, sunny but not too warm, allowing priests and people to participate in a joyful event. Perhaps the Mother of God was reminding us that in the service of the Lord there can be stormy days as well, and no one is excluded or prohibited from carrying the cross behind our Lord. Our speedy retreat to the Eucharistic table to celebrate the greatest gift of her divine Son was symbolic of the life of the Christian amid the storms of life.

In life, one cannot foresee the future. Neither can one be always ready for the travails that may beset our weak frames. There would indeed be more storms ahead, storms that would cause a lot more pain than the sporadic flashes of lightning. But those days still lay ahead. What mattered this evening was that another start had been made on completing the dream. The last great shrine of the second millennium was under construction.

The Mass that evening, with a large congregation, was one of gladness and satisfaction that the Lord was propelling us on our way. His Mother was still watching over us. The size of the overflow congregation which filled the temporary church on a weekday evening gave testimony once again to the excitement of the faithful for the work now under way.

While some members of my family were able to attend this major beginning, there were a couple whose absence was conspicuous and sadly missed. Both my sister and my mother had been called from this life during the preceding years.

My mother had been quite proud of the work. Throughout her life she had been a humble woman whose main objective was the upbringing of her family to be independently able to care for themselves while they walked in the fear and love of God. In true motherly fashion she had approved of the project, which appealed to her because of her own devotion to the blessed Mother of God. But she would also occasionally remark that she hoped I was not taking on too much and wondered if the people would continue to subscribe to what surely would be rising costs.

My sister Ita had survived serious illness before. During her early twenties, she had received a blood transfusion following surgery. It turned out that the blood was infected, and Ita fell into a coma from which she was not expected to recover. I was in college at the time in the south of Ireland, and after she had been about three days in the coma, I called the hospital to inquire about her. The nurse who answered informed me of the situation, remarking, "You do realize, don't you, that we don't expect her to recover?"

The nurse had reckoned without knowing my mother! Every priest she knew, every monastery she supported was petitioned for masses on Ita's behalf. Lots of prayers were ascending to God. After a week or so, an extraordinary thing happened. It was early morning, and Ita awoke from her coma, sat up in bed, and asked for her breakfast—just like that. Medical personnel were astounded.

Twenty years later, I had occasion to seek out a doctor in Ballina for a minor ailment. I told him who I was, and he immediately responded with a question as to whether I was related to the girl who had made the extraordinary and inexplicable recovery at the hospital two decades before. That was in 1950, and Ita went on to live a happy life until Easter of 1982 when she received very bad news from her physician. Cancer had attacked her body. This time prayers on her behalf would go unanswered. God had a better idea.

Ita entered hospital some days after that Easter, never to return home. She died July 15 after her condition had worsened with each new day. Before her death, I spent about three weeks at home, and I was able to visit with her every day. In the early days, we did not discuss the seriousness of her illness, which was a mistake on my part.

At that time in Ireland it was not normal custom to tell patients they were terminally ill. There were exceptions, but mostly it was considered destructive to tell the patient the whole truth. When I arrived—at an abnormal time for me to be in Ireland—my sister immediately suspected something. I parried her questions, arguing within myself that I should not be the one from across the sea to bring the bad news. Later, when she had drawn her own conclusions, she would quietly admonish me, letting me know that I had done her no service and that I had kept a secret from her that she should have known all along.

I was wrong. She was right. The medical people had concealed from her that her situation was terminal. I should have told her the truth, even when it was bad news, and surrounded it with the other truth of the immeasurable love of God. We are all on a pilgrim journey to eternity. Certainly Ita had earned her stripes for the Lord's abode. She had been a daily Mass attendee, had supported her parish church on a weekly basis, and had been active in many charitable organizations. Because of the illnesses that beset her life, she had not married and had been the caregiver for our mother for many years.

Ita died in the very early hours of July 15, 1982. In every way she had fought the good fight. She held death at bay as long as she could. And when the time came for her to return to God, it provided a moment that impressed itself on my memory.

The hospital nurse had just attended to her needs and placed her head back on the pillow. Without warning, a truly angelic smile lit up her face, and she raised herself slightly, peering toward the foot of the bed. Then, with that memorable smile still on her face, she sank back and left this world in as peaceful a death as one could wish to have.

I am convinced that someone or some angelic presence had come to escort Ita to her eternal home. What she saw delighted her, and before her soul had departed her body, she had become unaware of any further involvement in this life.

Her death broke my mother's heart. Ita was fifty-seven at the time of her passing, my mother eighty-three. My mother never recovered from this loss. She began almost at once to lose her memory, and even though she managed to live on her own for several more years, she was never the same person again. Family members came to her aid and watched over her, providing for her situation until, in November 1989, she was moved to the same hospital in which Ita had died.

Her peaceful passing on the shortest day of the year, December 21, 1989, was for me the end of an era. The previous evening, when in a semi-coma, she was heard to narrate the names of all her children, one after the other. Was she making a final commendation on our behalf to the Lord with whom she appeared to have been so intimate? My return visits to Ireland would be different. I would never again experience her superb cooking, nor would I experience the warmth as well as the occasional reprimand (even in my mature years!) of a mother's love. At bedtime, we always prayed the rosary together as in my childhood years. That joyful custom too was over.

The family laid her to rest beside my father in the family graveyard of Rathfran, overlooking an inlet of the Atlantic Ocean. She had loved Christmas. There was something poignant about her coffin almost touching the crèche at her funeral Mass in Kilfian Parish Church. When I was a child, she had sent me on the bus to Ballina cathedral with my older sister to see the much larger crèche the cathedral had on view. I remembered the day she had taken me to this very church in which her remains now rested, on the back of her bicycle for my first communion. In my mind's eye I remembered her love for the Lord of the Eucharist, a love that through her example had invaded my own life. With my father she had lived a full life. Her children had all been successful and faithful to the Lord and her work was done. She was now with the Lord to whom she had eagerly cycled for weekday visits on those many schooldays of my early years.

As her grandsons carried her coffin from the church to the hearse for the graveyard burial, I remembered her dedication. She would have wished for nothing better at her funeral. She had seen her children's children and had been proud of their success. The promise of Jesus would be fulfilled for her too: "Whosoever eats my flesh and drinks my blood will live forever." There would be a glorious resurrection for her, and for all of us. We would meet again.

Perhaps I should tell you here, dear reader, that both my parents had a wonderful devotion to the Holy Souls. Remember the *toties quoties* indulgences? Before the Second Vatican Council, the church granted a plenary indulgence on the occasion of a visit to a church or cemetery, applicable on All Souls Day, November 2. There was an annual custom among parishioners to gain as many indulgences as possible. A "visit" was fulfilled by entering the church, offering the prescribed prayers, and then leaving. So individuals would go in and out of church several times during the day in the hope of gaining as many indulgences as they could for the Holy Souls. I can tell you now that my mother would be among the numbers entering and leaving. Not only that, but many a time she instructed me to remember my grandparents and relatives who had died. And so I would join with her on her visits. And my remembrance for the Holy Souls continues to this present day. On All Souls Day, my mother is the first person to come to mind.

Hope is one of the great virtues of the Church. We Catholics are unique. We never give up hope. The story is told about a grieving widow who, after the death of her husband, sought consolation from the Curé of Ars. Her husband had been killed in a fall from a horse. His life was not the most exemplary, and so she worried about his eternal salvation. The response of the curé has been recorded in poetry in the lines "'Twixt the saddle and the ground, he mercy sought and mercy found."

The Church doctrine on purgatory is about hope that springs eternal, about the infinite mercy of God, about the price that was paid for our salvation which the Father will most certainly not overlook. Purgatory, we learned once upon a time, is "a place or state." We do not know what it is, where it is, or how it is. We think of the "punishing flames" but only because those same flames are also associated with hell. Our Lord did talk about the fires of Gehenna, but students of scripture argue he might have been referring to a "garbage dump" outside the city of Jerusalem. One way or the other, the comparison is good for hell. Garbage dumps were frequently set on fire, their contents being considered useless. Saint Augustine said it well when he wrote in his Confessions, "You have made us for yourself, O Lord, and our hearts are not at rest until they rest in you." The true Christian panics at the thought of winding up on God's scrap heap.

Purgatory, however, is no scrap heap! It is a preparation for heaven, a looking forward to the good things to come. It reminds us of mortality and assures us that God's mercy will not be stingy toward those who love Him. Perhaps too the thought of purgatory reminds us of death and judgment. We know we will die. We look forward sometimes in fearful anticipation to our judgment. One of my priest friends who died in recent years had a great fear of judgment. He needed to be reminded time and again of the mercy of God. Returning from his funeral, the conversation centered around his fear. One of my friends expressed the opinion that "only the righteous fear judgment" and he strongly added that "the profane have no time for God or man."

Before his passing, my father had the same fearful anticipation seeking prayers for his soul from his family members weeks before his death. My mother, of course, who lived much longer, solved her problem in another way. She had her priest son agree to offer Mass for her once a week! It's odd, though, how parents' faith and concerns can be passed on to their family. Every year when I return to Ireland, I visit the family graves. How could I not, with all the teaching of my mother on the subject? My brother always accompanies me on my cemetery visits. I can tell you he looks after those graves with great filial devotion. In the United States, graves are not cared for privately. The down side of this is that the dead can be forgotten.

My experience has been, though, that the majority of our Catholic people remember their dead, especially in prayers and masses. In Ireland there is the custom of "the month's mind," as it is called—a Mass for the departed one month following death. This is regarded as the first anniversary—a sort of closure, if you will—when the family gathers with friends and relatives for a further church remembrance. These are beautiful customs that hopefully will live on. They provide opportunities not only to remember in prayer but also to share happy memories once again of the departed soul. And every Eucharistic celebration is a joining with the resurrected Christ even here below and a guarantee of future happiness for all of us. It was the great Saint Augustine who wrote "Those who die are no farther away than God, and God is everywhere."

Memorial Stone over parents' grave at Rathfran
cemetery, formerly a monastic site.

Chapter Fifty-Six:
Faith-Filled Matchless Volunteers

⚭

It seems to me also that a new impetus, a new sense of mission, was brought to the hearts of our shrine volunteers when we took over our own sacred space for worship. Now they knew exactly where the weekend masses would take place. No longer would there be any need to display placards on the streets redirecting massgoers from one hotel to another when changes took place at the last minute. They knew exactly where the crowds would gather for Mass. The gathering place was a certainty. Now there was a new sense of excitement. The first step had been completed. They longed for further progress.

Nor was their longing something wistful. They were aware there was a mortgage to be paid. They knew the plan, and they were determined to make things happen. One example of this enthusiasm was to be found at the outdoor mother and child sculpture every weekend. Visitors could light candles there. Our volunteers took the candles to the sculpture, and each Sunday three or four volunteers were to be found not only providing candles for those who wanted them but also enthusiastically informing the visitors of future plans and relating the history of the ministry to this point. Frequently, a volunteer would drive a visitor back to a hotel, and volunteers organized themselves in many conspicuous places, always in readiness for whatever service might be required throughout the evening or morning masses.

It was a beautiful example of faith in practice. As a priest I felt exceptionally blessed to have been able to work with such faith-propelled people, a privilege I will always cherish. This giving spirit has prevailed among the volunteers to this day. Shrine volunteers practice Christ's message to love each other, and their spirit of love extends itself into the ministry too. They embody the petition in the prayer of Saint Francis—"to give and not to count the cost" —which has become to a great extent the very essence of the ministry at Mary, Queen of the Universe Shrine.

The question is often asked, "Where did all those volunteers come from?" Those never-to-be-forgotten people joined the tourist ministry from many sources and occupations. As previously recorded, many came from the original seat of the tourist ministry, Holy Family Parish, which the bishop had assigned me to found in southwest Orlando. They were enthusiastic about the founding of the new parish, and often I heard them express their opinions that there is nothing like being involved in the formation of a new community and building a new church.

Having studied Vatican Two intensively, I was prepared to "empower" my people to be actively involved in every phase of the development of the new parish. Somehow that empowerment lit a fire! It seemed everyone in the new community wanted to be involved. And many too wanted to play a part in the tourist ministry. Just about every member of the original Holy Family Parish took part in serving the tourists. There is a great deal the lay person can accomplish in the name of Christ, and given the opportunity, those people threw themselves heart and soul into the ministry.

We needed ushers and lectors in the tourist ministry before the church was even contemplated. We needed responsible persons to meet the priests at the various hotels where Mass was scheduled, help carry in the equipment for the service, set up the altar for Mass, greet the visitors as they entered the area, and distribute the missalettes. During Mass, they kept a close eye on their surroundings, welcoming latecomers and generally providing a sense of security for the priest at the altar.

When Mass was over, the volunteers were so organized that in minutes they disassembled the altar, repacked the baggage, carried it to the priest's car, and left everything packed for his next Mass at a different hotel. If I had been delayed speaking to a visitor after Mass, as I frequently was, a volunteer would come to remind me of the time and escort me to my car so as to get me to the next Mass venue on time.

Naturally, a new set of volunteers would be on hand to greet the priest celebrant at his next venue. One of my fondest memories is related to arriving for a hotel Mass and always being greeted by happy and good-humored volunteers who were already awaiting my arrival. Almost instantaneously, they whisked the Mass paraphernalia from my car and carried it to the place for Mass, guiding me too to whatever hotel meeting place had been designated for the occasion. The tourist ministry was not the operation of one priest or a few select people. It grew from the combined energies of many people to further the kingdom of the Lord.

I suppose that, to the unacquainted, all this seems inconsequential. But consider that those volunteers never missed Mass without a good reason and made it their business to escort the priest wherever he went. At Easter, when the numbers attending Mass skyrocketed, they covered many masses, and with masses scattered in various hotels, some of the leaders would make it their business to travel from hotel to hotel to make sure there were sufficient hosts, wine, and so on, often remaining there themselves to be of assistance. Without them, there could have been no shrine ministry.

Many of those wonderful people have been with the ministry since its inception. They have put countless miles on their autos helping bring Christ to the tourists, and they have taken pride in the numbers they have served. In the years after the main shrine church opened, those people brought service to perfection. They loved their priests and associated themselves with the ministry of the priests. This is Catholic evangelization in its very best form.

I truly believe the zeal of the Mary, Queen of the Universe volunteers is unmatched. For example, when then-Cardinal Ratzinger issued instructions for the distribution of communion and a few other minor changes to the Mass, these volunteers, without any directive from me, went about finding out what exactly the cardinal had ordered. The inquiry went a step further when their coordinator composed a test to be administered to every volunteer, with questions regarding their particular duties. The test was taken very seriously, and nobody wanted to score low marks. I have never seen that kind of inspirational zeal anywhere else.

I should also remark that they made life wonderfully easy for their priests. They had so trained themselves in greeting and handling the crowds that the priest's main responsibility was to vest himself and ready himself spiritually for Mass. There was no need to worry about anything. The volunteers had thought of everything, whether it be Christmas or Easter or any other festivity. And that included the preparation of the altar, the numbers of hosts, and having everything in readiness for the Great Sacrifice. When the masses were transferred to our own facilities, the volunteers maintained all the traditions they had developed. When special feasts occurred, such as Christmas and Easter, the volunteers were assisted by some members of the shrine staff in ordering and arranging the flowers to decorate the facility.

The shrine has developed a Mothers' Day tradition of "Sunday of ten thousand roses." The tradition started as a fund-raiser for the shrine. People were invited to send an offering for a rose or roses to be placed at the altar in honor of their mother or grandmother or some other beloved lady of their family. The practice grew and grew until the numbers of roses reached approximately ten thousand. Imagine how long it takes to prepare ten thousand roses and place them around the altar! The chore is quite effectively taken care of by a special group of volunteers—some of whom live almost in Daytona Beach, fifty miles away—who assemble early on Saturday morning and have completed their task before the evening Vigil Mass.

Shrine volunteers are beyond comparison with any other group. I am reminded of an incident that took place one Easter Sunday. In case you have never been to the shrine, Easter Sunday is a day for the crowds. The street leading from Lake Buena Vista is normally backed up with the autos of families trying to get to Easter Mass. On that Sunday, we normally employed the service of at least half a dozen sheriff's deputies to control the traffic leading to the shrine grounds. Many drivers abandon their cars by the roadside and walk the last quarter-mile or so to the church.

Volunteers are on hand at the shrine long before the sun rises. They are there most of the day, well into midafternoon, and many return for the last Mass of Easter in the evening. It became the custom for the volunteers to take food with them to the shrine to help them through the long morning. The volunteers, of course, always thoughtful, brought food for their priests too!

On one particular Easter morning, an aged and venerable lady arrived in her car at the front door of the building in which the food was placed and partaken. A deputy happened to be nearby. He immediately directed the lady that she could not park where she planned. He came to her car and said something like "Lady, please move. You can't park here." Everyone in the ministry knew Peggy, the driver of the car. She would not be put off her mission by an officer of the law or by anyone else!

She rolled down her window and told the deputy, "I am bringing Father Harte his breakfast. He hasn't had anything to eat, and look at the time it is. Do you want him to pass out?" The deputy stood aside, and the priest got his breakfast! The story illustrates the devotion of the great group who are known as the volunteers at Mary's Shrine in Orlando.

The volunteers fill many positions. They help with the mailings, of which there are about one per month. They are to be found helping in the gift shop on a daily basis. If you have been to the gift shop, you have most likely experienced their warmth and zealous devotion to all things of God. They work on the grounds tending the flowers and trees. And of course they are at their assigned tasks in the shrine church and its sacristy on Sundays and Holy Days and for regular weekday masses, plus the other occasions that demand their presence. And long before there was a church and we had weekend masses in the hotels, a group of dedicated people came together every Friday to pack the equipment the priests would need and make sure that everything was ready. Let me tell you, this group never once erred. Never was there anything missing that might be required.

Shrine sacristans are uniquely devoted to their calling. I cannot ever remember being let down by a sacristan. They are knowledgeable yet humble in carrying out their duties. They know that what they do is for the Lord. They want nothing more than the spread of His kingdom in the service of their fellow Christians.

Today, volunteers come from the surrounding parishes. When Bishop Dorsey led the diocese, an agreement was formulated that volunteers who served at the shrine would support their own home parish financially. The bishop was rightly concerned that there should be no competition between the shrine and the local parishes. With these great people, the shrine gains while their home parish sometimes loses their services but is most likely compensated through their weekly support.

It is fitting here also to pay tribute to another group of shrine volunteers. They form the shrine committee, which has been instrumental in developing the project from start to finish. Some wear more than one hat, also volunteering in other areas. Among the committee is a gifted and experienced architect who is an ex–vice president of one of the building contractors of Walt Disney World. An architect employed by the Diocese of Orlando was designated by Bishop Grady to the committee as diocesan representative, and both those men made invaluable contributions to the success of the project. Another committee member was an executive of a manufacturing company—a mathematical wizard and the genius behind the financial management of everything pertained to the shrine. A past scholarship winner at MIT, he collaborated with a previous manager and owner of an automobile sales company, a community housing developer, and of course the lady previously mentioned, who was gifted with wonderful insights, a depthless love for art, and the ability to keep the fires of enthusiasm burning.

All have left their mark on the shrine church and on its ministry. Every one of them has also made a major financial commitment toward the development of the shrine. Their names are to be found on memorials marking adornments at the shrine. They are people who have not simply "talked the talk" but also "walked the walk."

They were joined by the professional architects and the artists, who together comprised the shrine committee while the building was being developed. The meetings they attended were many, the time they donated was beyond any compensation, and the result of their united experience and wisdom stands for all to see. It is worth mentioning again that these people made major sacrifices, spending on occasion from evening well into the wee hours in discussions on how to bring into reality the Shrine of Mary, Queen of the Universe.

Once building operations were complete, the committee (minus the contracted architects and artists) continued to meet frequently, sometimes as often as twice a month, to review progress, deal with financial developments at the shrine, and lend their wisdom to its governance. Without their advice, I never made a major decision, and every new venture of the shrine, irrespective of its nature—whether art or fund-raising or maintenance improvement—came only after the committee had first approved.

The story of the "three hundred" who assumed responsibility for the construction of Mary's Shrine in southwest Orlando should never be forgotten. It is a story of people with a burning love, founded on faith and the desire to play an active part in the spread of God's kingdom. In many ways it is very much like a fairy tale that people find hard to accept. But it is also, in every way, a commendation of the ideas of Vatican Two and what the Holy Spirit can achieve through those whose lives belong to Him, and who are invited and allowed to take an active part in the spread of God's Word.

And on a concluding poignant note, since my retirement, Marcia Pietrzak has been replaced on the shrine committee. I don't know the reason, but it saddens me greatly that her faith-filled enthusiasm and wise counsel are no longer available to the project to which she gave so much time and energy. Her fiery zeal and peerless fervor for the spread of Christ's kingdom helped keep my own spirit in quest of the goal.

A couple of others have been replaced as well. But all can live with the memory of a task well done for the Lord and know that His gracious Mother will long remember their efforts and ambitions on behalf of her divine Son. We live in a transient world, but in the annals of God's designs our destination is eternity. The efforts of all those people must surely be written in the heart of the Lord, never to be effaced. They are surely among the stars in Mary's crown!

Shrine Advisory Committee During the Building Years

Thomas J. Grady
Bishop of Orlando 1974-1990

Norbert M. Dorsey
Bishop of Orlando 1990-2004

Fr. John E. McMullan

Dick Kelley
Chairman

Jack Larkin

Marcia Pietrzak

Wade Hargadon

Jim Nagy
AIA

Bill Brown
AIA

John Dragash
AIA

Jack Rogers
Designing Architect

William Kramer
AIA

Libby Yost
Secretary

Chapter Fifty-Seven:
Mary's Shrine a Landmark

᷂

radually the new Marian Shrine church began to tower higher and higher over Interstate 4. It was destined to become a landmark along this busy corridor. Those were interesting times, flavored with the excitement of daily progress, the urgency to raise the necessary funds to pay for the work, and high hopes for the institution that would surely bring glory to God. There was a feverish amount of activity in our administration offices as we planned, wrote letters to our benefactors, sought new benefactors, all the while trusting that the Mother of the Lord would always be with us in our effort.

We got the help we needed. "Our people" throughout the United States (who had once come to fulfill an obligation and find the Lord at a hotel Mass or within the temporary building) thoroughly understood what we were about. They had visited Cinderella, seen her castle, and enjoyed their visits to the theme parks. But a vast spiritual area of their lives was still empty. The God within them cried out for attention, urging them to find a place of peace in which to recreate their spirit and so be able to return home with the wholeness for which they had longed. They shared our vision of a future oasis where God would reign, they could pray, receive the sacraments, and take time "to find a quiet place and rest awhile" with the Lord.

Not only that, but great numbers coming to Orlando were young parents, giving their children a treat of a lifetime (and making unknown sacrifices so that children might have wonderful memories). They were concerned about their children's future. In the rapid passage of time, those same children would, one day, bring their own offspring to Orlando. And when they got there they would find "their own" church and remember the great parents who had fostered in them the love of the Savior.

And the Lord of Love always takes preference to Cinderella! He would be there for them and their children in later years. When we emphasized church evangelization, they were pleased and wanted to be involved in spreading the Gospel message in the place where millions gather for family relaxation. And as we worked and the masons worked on the building, more people came to our aid and wanted to be a part of what they saw as a great tribute to the Mother of God.

By October 1992, the roof was in place. It was time to attach the cross to the top of the building. That ceremony took place on the afternoon of October 20, 1992. Bishop Dorsey blessed the cross, and as the crane lifted it to its permanent position high on the gable end, the large crowd that had gathered began to sing the hymn "Lift High the Cross." The event did not go unnoticed by drivers on the adjacent highway, Interstate 4, many of whom slowed down to take a peek while others parked their cars on the roadside and climbed the fence to be a part of what was surely a memorable event.

I recall these incidents particularly, as there was something almost mysterious about them! Drivers pulling off the freeway and climbing a roadside fence, not only to see what was going on but to be a part of it, is not a common occurrence. Quite a number simply abandoned their cars! Extraordinarily enough, the clouds in the sky that late afternoon were in numerous and varied formations that looked like painted angels' wings that could have been done by the Murillo school itself. The lowering sun lent a red tint so as to embellish the glowing wings that seemed innumerable throughout the evening sky. The Lord was sending a message to all that the shrine church in honor of His Mother would be under the future protection of Divine Providence!

Again, please forgive me when I recall the words of a favorite psalm, the ninety-first psalm: "For to His angels He has given command about you, that they guard you in all your ways. Upon their hands they shall bear you up lest you dash your foot against a stone." It wasn't the first visit of angels to my life—nor would it be the last!

The construction of the new Marian shrine reached conclusion without any major problems. Soon we were looking at the possibility of a joyful opening with a first Mass in the building. That day came on January 31, 1993. It was Super Bowl Sunday! The Dallas Cowboys were playing the Buffalo Bills. Coincidentally enough the Feast of Saint John Bosco occurs on the same date. Saint John Bosco was the founder of the Salesian Fathers, who had rendered wonderful service as weekend helpers in our tourist ministry. The selection of the date would pay tribute to them too, marking their involvement in the work. There were of course protests that the time of Mass coincided with the kickoff in the big televised game. It didn't really matter! (Pews had not yet been installed, but would be shortly thereafter).

Every chair was filled, and many people were standing. Bishop Dorsey was the main celebrant and spoke glowingly of the importance of the newly constructed shrine and the opportunities it would provide for every aspect of Catholicism. We had printed a newsletter that gave a slogan for the ministry that is used to the present day. It came from the remark of the church father Saint Ignatius of Antioch on his way to martyrdom: "The song we sing is Jesus Christ." To Him may praise be given!

Spring and summer would pass quickly. Benefactors of the shrine looked forward to the dedication day, which was set for August 22—exactly three years after the ceremonial beginning of construction. I looked forward to it with more than a little nervousness. There was so much enthusiasm about the dedication ceremony that I feared we might not be able to match people's expectations. I had made pilgrimages to the Grotto of Our Lady of Lourdes in France every year, taking with me the petitions of our benefactors, and this year would be no exception. While there I sat at the grotto every day and asked the Mother of God to be with us in our preparations for the great event and also on the day itself. As always, she was listening.

August 22, 1993, was a beautiful Sunday, with the hot Florida sun shining on the crowds who came to celebrate a happy event. We had decided it would be best to lock the doors once the attendees had vacated after the morning 11:30 Mass. The ceremonies were scheduled for 3:00 p.m., and by 1:30 the eager participants were gathering in force. It was indeed a ticketed affair; it had to be. But many wanted to make sure they got seats as close to the altar as possible. (This was one of the few times in my life I saw a rush for the front seats of the church!) After the doors were opened, the church was almost filled in minutes.

With two cardinals (one from Rome) and many bishops present, the Diocese of Orlando and its people took time to rejoice in their faith and in their service to visitors from all over the world. This shrine church would stand in testimony not only to the faith of a people but also to their dedicated resolve to bring Christ to persons from "the end of the world."

Early on that Sunday morning, Bishop Dorsey sent me a telegram that said, "Congratulations. You have worked a miracle." It was indeed a miracle of faith that only Divine Providence could bring about and in which so many people from throughout the United States and beyond had been involved. The Lord had fed the five thousand again! And here in this church in future years thousands would come to participate in Eucharist and be fed the Body of Christ and the Lord of Love Himself. And of course it is always encouraging for a priest to receive acknowledgement from his own bishop of the work he has completed. This would be, please God, a work that would have far-reaching results for God's kingdom.

Chapter Fifty-Eight:
A Pilgrimage and a Gift

✧

Mary's shrine had come to be! Thanks of course to God and Mary, His Mother! I could now look back with satisfaction on the early years. I remembered my first masses in hotels, the multiplicity of those masses, the efforts that were made by volunteers. Yes, I also harked back on the remarkably good advice that was given me by some friendly fund-raisers free of charge, the efforts I had made to raise the needed monies, as well as some of the failures I had experienced, failures from which I learned.

I well remembered my trip to New York, to an association there and the question that confronted me: Why should anyone living in New York support a shrine in Florida? That expedition raised fifty dollars. On a happier occasion, when a noted fund-raiser came to examine our incoming funds, he made the encouraging remark that his services were not needed. All we should do, he said, was continue in the direction we were going. But I think my successes and failures were Mary's way of allowing me to establish that I was sincere in the work I was engaged in for Jesus the Lord under her own mantle. And perhaps there was a message too that "nothing is impossible with God" as long as we allow the Lord to work through us!

Wonderful lovers of the Lord came along. Many made major gifts and gave the kind of encouragement that can only come from true and eager believers. Some remembered the shrine in their wills. Some came with pen in hand to write a check. All of it was a fulfillment of God's providence.

At this time, only two stained-glass windows were in place in the new church. I should narrate the story of how the second one got there. (Recall the first had been demonstrated in the original temporary Mass building). One day a visitor asked for me. He was visiting from Pittsburgh, PA. I had never met him before, but he had attended my masses in the first building, where I told the faithful about our dreams for the shrine. His first words to me were "Father Harte, when you build this church, if you ever build it, will it have a number of stained-glass windows?" When I replied in the affirmative, he asked if I might have any plan for the windows. I told him yes! Then I proceeded to pull from my desk the file that outlined the plan with a name of the subject for each window. "That one there," he said, pointing to the window entitled *The Saints of the North American Church*, "has that been taken?"

"No," I replied, "it has not."

"I am taking it" was his immediate response.

The good man had not even hinted that he was interested in knowing the proposed donation for the window. I now had a problem. How to tell him he was in the $55,000 donor bracket? (Classic stained glass is not inexpensive, and furthermore, we always added a percentage of cost for the shrine itself, as well as to cover any future problems that might arise with the window during installation.)

I had to think fast. Keep in mind that I didn't want to create a heart attack for him by blurting out the costs on which he seemed ready to embark unknowingly. I was afraid that perhaps he might have estimated that he was somewhere in the $10,000 bracket or below.

I decided to tell him what we had done previously, that we had sectioned a few windows at a particular donation for each section. As I recall, the sections were in the region of $8,000 per section. When I had finished, he lifted his head slowly from the diagrams in front of him, looked me straight in the eyes and remarked, "Father Harte, did I say anything about sections? I want the whole window. My wife died a few months ago, and she certainly was a saint of the North American Church. I'll give you a check for $10,000, now and as soon as the window is under way, I'll give you the remainder."

This good man was called to his eternal reward some time before the completion of the window, but his family took over his responsibilities with the same classic generosity exhibited by their father. Those visiting the shrine today can see the plaque bearing the name of his beloved wife, his own name, and the names of his family members—a lasting testimony to their dedicated father and the faith both parents had imparted to them.

The Saints of the North American Church was duly completed. Stained-glass windows are initially laid out in cartoons on a paper the size of the window itself. When the cartoon was delivered to the shrine for approval before the work in glass began, we found one well-known saint missing. Saint Elizabeth Seton had been overlooked. I called the artist, Walter Judson, and told him the bad news. He was distressed and told me the error would delay the installation of the window seriously because another cartoon would take much time and effort. He suggested that since the *Second Coming* window was not yet installed and indeed still not even subscribed to, we might put Saint Elizabeth Seton in a panel of that window. The committee and I readily agreed to his suggestion.

After the *Saints* window had been installed for several months with still no prospective donor for the final window, I was walking toward the Adoration Chapel one Sunday morning after Mass had concluded. A lady was standing in front of the newly installed window. As I passed. she reached out her hand to my shoulder. "Where is Elizabeth Seton in this window?" she inquired. I told her the story of what had happened, adding that Elizabeth Seton would be featured in the *Second Coming* window. "Has it been taken?" she asked. When she heard that it had not, she immediately responded, "I am taking it," in almost the same way as the *Saints* window donor some years previously. Divine Providence has its own way of helpful intervention. There are many people who have this kind of love for the Church and its effort to spread the Gospel. I keep reflecting on the Annunciation passage in Saint Luke's Gospel, where I read that "nothing is impossible with God." He touches generous hearts in His own beautiful way.

One final story in this regard. While the first building was under construction, I received a phone call from a lady who said she wished to see me to discuss a religious book she was reading. It turned out she was indeed a prodigious reader. (I do not give her name because she expressed a wish to remain anonymous in her giving.) In the course of our conversation, she asked if I had ever heard of Medjugorje. When I told her I was familiar with its story, she asked me if I might like to join her on a pilgrimage there. Not having been to the site of the reported vision, and being curious about Communist-run Eastern Europe (the Berlin wall was still in place), I agreed.

I have very happy memories of the journey. Our plane was delayed for four hours in Orlando, necessitating a very late arrival in Frankfurt (an airport that rivals in perplexity and commotion anything the United States can boast!). All planes to Dubrovnik, our final terminal for Medjugorje, were long departed. We could be accommodated on the national airline of Yugoslavia, which would leave late in the afternoon. And so we flew on Yugoslav Airlines, making visits to airports of cities I had never thought I would get near, such as Belgrade and Budapest. The service on the plane was surprisingly good.

While on the ground for more than an hour at Belgrade, we visited a small airport restaurant. The lady who served us looked like tiredness itself, although she was friendly and unable to speak English. My friend took the bill for the meal, at the same time slipping a sum of money into the hands of the waitress as a tip. Her face beamed, and she looked like a new person! The tip, whatever amount it was, had made her day. I won't forget her smile as we got up to leave.

The Medjugorje experience was very positive. We stayed a short walking distance from the Church of Saint James. I was fascinated to see farmers in the fields wielding sickles and other such tools that had disappeared from the free Western World decades ago. Communism had done nothing for its people. The home in which we stayed was a far cry from modern times, something that showed up in sharp relief the next morning when I headed across the corridor for a shower. The entire floor adjacent to the shower was an inch deep in water that reached almost to my bedroom! But the gentleness of the people more than made up for lack of more perfected facilities.

I was asked to hear confessions at the gable of the church with a sign that said "English." I am sure that the many priests and some bishops who had heard confessions at Medjugorje all tell the same story of grace-filled conversions and the desire for Christ that is granted after a special pilgrimage.

I am always saddened when I hear uninformed comments about Medjugorge. Does it matter whether there was an appearance or not? Is it fair to accuse the visionaries of deceitfulness? Where grace flows freely, it surely is for the good of souls. Having returned home, the good lady who had journeyed with me committed to a gift of one million dollars toward our work. And from another source, a person totally unknown to me sent a gift of a statue of Our Lady of Medjugorje that I keep with great affection and gratitude. For me the message was clear: the Mother of God was promoting her shrine in Orlando. And she was indicating that she was pleased. When I look at that statue, I remember another great lady who journeyed on pilgrimage with me and her keen desire to know Christ better. She passed away some years after the completion of the main shrine church. Our friendship never waned, and with her passing I felt I had lost a true friend. But I remember her at Mass every day.

The first phase of the shrine had been almost completed when I made that first journey to Medjugorje. I went with an open mind, glad to visit the place where so many extraordinary happenings were being reported and to which so many people were journeying. My experience of hearing confessions there was memorable from the fact that there were so many people going to confession from all over the world. People from Australia, New Zealand, and the United States were among those who came seeking reconciliation with the Lord. Quite a number had not been to receive the sacrament for many years. Many were repenting their previous stance favoring modern issues that are a perversion of Christianity.

I have returned to Medjugorje on other occasions, and I have witnessed the same euphoria of faith. People pray unabashedly on the streets as they head for the church, and rosary beads are everywhere in evidence. The multilingual Mass in the evening is something to remember, marked by people from so many different places and cultures singing the same hymns in different tongues—a sort of Pentecost in the present. The masses were crowded. There was not much organization for distribution of Holy Communion—there probably couldn't be. At communion time priests simply scattered through the church placing the Lord in outstretched hands whose bodies were frequently hidden behind others. The Adoration Tabernacle at Mary's Shrine in Orlando owes its artwork to my memory of Medjugorje. I described my experience to our artist Jerzy Kenar, and he felt he wanted to place the symbolism of the outstretched hands on the tabernacle door: "Lord, give us yourself."

The thrust of the messages allegedly conveyed by Our Lady to the visionaries at Medjugorje is a call to prayer, conversion, and fasting. This seems in keeping with other messages of Our Lady in other apparitions. However, for many, myself included, the fruits of Medjugorje establish the story of the alleged visitations as, to say the least, extraordinary. I have heard many negative criticisms of Medjugorje but always from people who have never been there. And let me say that every time I was there, I have seen a bishop or two from different areas of the world take part in the liturgies. Many people pray to the Lady of Medjugorje. The title does not call for belief in an apparition but only signals love for the Mother of God. Whatever and whenever the outcome of the Church enquiries, I am sure the title Our Lady of Medjugorje will remain dear to the hearts of many people. It was there they found conversion! The statues of the alleged Medjugorje apparition, sent me by a friend, still adorn my sideboard as a reminder of God's loving providence and of His Mother's care of all her children.

For a number of years at the Orlando Shrine we had the privilege of serving devotees of Our Lady of Medjugorje in a recurring three-day conference that focused mainly on peace and on devotion to the Mother of God. These conferences brought about the same phenomenon as witnessed in Medjugorje. They were attended by thousands of people each year, and I have memories of the Sacrament of Reconciliation being administered for hours on Saturdays by five or six priests. I took part in those reconciliation sessions myself, and I can attest to the fervor of those seeking the sacrament as well as the conversions of grace that took place.

Chapter Fifty-Nine:
Signature Statue Arrives

❧

Priests don't normally reveal their innermost relationship with God. Indeed, I have heard it said, sometimes jocosely and sometimes with some cynicism, that the last place to look for a priest is in church! In fact, apart from the varied and multifarious activities of a priest's life, the church may well be the last place to which he goes to pray!

Let me explain the seeming contradiction. If I had counted the number of times I have been interrupted at prayer in the church in my lifetime, the number would be astronomical. Could I ever pray publicly in church? Almost always someone would come to inform me I was "just the person" they were looking for, and could they have a few minutes of my time? How does a priest turn down that kind of request? I have known many priests who got before the Blessed Sacrament very early in the morning because the rest of the day would be taken up with the main function of a priest—taking care of his flock.

Somehow or other, it had been ingrained in my mind in seminary that the morning was the very best time to pray. There has to be a certain amount of self-government to make this a daily practice, and as one grows older, it is easy to find excuses. But here we were in the mid-nineties with a growing ministry, many more people to attend to, and a growing financial challenge both to pay our bills and to complete the dream. How could it all be kept afloat? Looking back, I realized that what had happened up to this point was mostly providential. I came to a definite understanding that with God on my side I needed very much to stay by Him. I needed Him in my life.

Once within the work surroundings after the day had begun, I had little time for personal prayer. When the day at the shrine concluded officially, there were still lots of chores to be done: letters to be prepared, a newsletter to be published twice a year, benefactors to be called, and a host of other assignments. I found myself at times with my breviary still unread at ten o'clock in the evening. It was time to reform. God was taking care of me in my labors, but where was He in my life? I had to get back to basics.

There was only one thing to do. So for a long time thereafter I arose around five in the morning and sat with the Lord until breakfast time around eight o'clock, this latter depending on the Mass schedule of the day. I believe this time with the Lord was fruitful to the utmost, and from it many blessings would flow in the following years. What this meant, of course, was that when I arrived at the shrine, the Lord and I had already spent a considerable part of the day together, and I could be unselfish in my dedication to the tasks and problems of the day.

When the shrine was dedicated, it was bare of statues. If the shrine was to be "a place like no other," then its furnishings and artwork had to be distinguishingly different too. We also wanted the artwork to be inspirational, one of a kind, raising minds and hearts to God. As far as the committee and I were concerned, the Renaissance that embellished the churches of Europe in ages past would be our guide: we did not seek "art for art's sake" but, as in those bygone days, "art for the glory of God."

Uninformed visitors who saw the still incompletely furnished shrine church occasionally expressed their dissatisfaction with the lack of statuary. In the years previous to the installation of the signature statue of Our Lady, not a few letters had arrived, complaining about the absence of a statue, some expressing grave dissatisfaction that Our Lady's shrine did not have any statue of its patroness within the church. Oddly enough, when we responded to those letters outlining our future plans, not a single reply was received from any person wishing to associate with the project. In my years of priesthood, I have found that those who complain most are those who contribute least or not at all.

I had not been very long fulfilling my resolve of early morning prayer when Mary Queen did send a benefactor to us. Now it was time to find

265

an artist to do the work. There was a general air of excitement among all shrine members far and near. The image of the Queen was destined to take its place in a prominent position within the shrine church. A marble ring in the floor just outside the sanctuary denoted the place where the statue would stand.

We contacted a number of highly recommended artists, and from the responses received, five were chosen for interview. We added to our shrine committee for the occasion the renowned Marian and Carmelite theologian, Father Eamon R. Carroll, since deceased (RIP). Father Carroll had been on the icon committee at the Basilica of the National Shrine of the Immaculate Conception in Washington when it was being constructed. His writings too had inspired many, and we felt he was a priest whose theology of Mary would be a guide toward a sculpture that would make a special statement on the Incarnation.

Bishop Dorsey took part in the meeting. Father Carroll led the discussions with insight and prudence. He listened to each person's opinion and became very much a part of the committee. He remarked afterward that this committee was the finest committee in which he had ever been involved. He was impressed with the intensity of purpose they showed, their respect for one another's opinions, and the ability of each to listen and respond to opinions expressed.

Father Carroll spoke of the work we were undertaking and reminded us that we were about to commission a statue of a most unique individual, the one on whom was laid the greatest of all graces ever conferred by God on a human being. Because God chose her to be the Mother of His divine Son, He had prepared the foundations of all else that the Church attributes to her. In his prefatory remarks, Father Carroll also drew upon the beautiful Marian letter of Pope Paul VI, *Marialis Cultus*, which by coincidence I had read prior to instituting the mission of the shrine. He noted a memorable passage quoting the pope's words on Mary's exemplary greatness which came about "because she heard the word of God and acted upon it and because charity and a spirit of service were the driving force of her actions." The ministry of Mary's Shrine here in Orlando, he said, saw itself serving the thousands of visitors each year. The proposed statue would remind them of Mary's place in salvation and would urge all involved in the ministry to render faith-filled service.

I had personally sent a preparatory letter to each designated artist. In the letter I explained what we wanted, without of course encroaching on the artist's creativity. It had been decided that the material used would be at the discretion of the artist. But even though the shrine was titled after Mary, Queen of the Universe, the committee felt that she should not be wearing a crown, that she was more mother than royalty, and that these choices would give the statue a greater appeal. My letter stated that we wanted "a statue of the simple maiden of Nazareth" holding the divine Infant in her arms. One artist took time to reply by telephone and discuss the letter in detail. Not a Catholic herself, she said she liked the idea of "the simple maiden of Nazareth" and was looking forward to the interview.

A letter I had sent to our shrine supporters had also included an invitation to send their most ardent spiritual desires for inclusion within the base of the statue. The response was astounding. But I could understand it. The Mother of God is special to every Catholic. Here was an opportunity to "connect" with her in a seemingly perpetual way. Indeed, for me, this statue encased all my hopes and desires for God's providential care on the future ministry of the shrine and on all who would continue to be involved in it. Hundreds of names of shrine benefactors are included within the base of the statue, to remain there for as long as the statue stands in its place of honor.

Of all the interviews we have held for various projects at the shrine, this one stands out most clearly in my memory. How does a group of unsophisticated people sit and question those with talents on the subject way beyond anything that group can conceive? But it had to be done. I asked Mary Queen to be with us. She certainly was.

Artists are unusual people! This group matched their renowned artistry with a wonderful sense of good humor and refinement. Questions were asked and answered, ideas were set forth, and the presentation of two artists in particular rose clearly above the surface. One was Jill Burkee, the other Bruno Lucchesi. Jill Burkee set forth a wonderful picture of a shining white marble Mary standing near the sanctuary, highly visible to the majority coming in. Bruno Lucchesi, on the other hand, actually demonstrated in clay what his ideas were. His statue would be bronze.

It took no time at all to decide on the selected artist. Jill Burkee would create the statue of Our Lady, and Bruno Lucchesi would be commissioned for the statue of Saint Joseph whenever a benefactor might come forward.

Twenty-five minutes or so north of Pisa in Italy lies the Carrara marble territory. From here have come marble presentations that adorn churches and monasteries across the Catholic world. And it was to this place that Jill Burkee moved to begin her work.

Finding a piece of marble for a statue looks easy. But this was going to be an exceptional statue, without blemish. And so Jill got to work searching for the stone of her dreams. It took a while for her to find it.

Summer came, and still it had not been found. Some members of the shrine committee decided to go to Italy at their own expense to see the area and learn about the marble. For all of us, this was an enlightening journey. In my own simplicity I had always thought that marble would be quarried just like limestone—by digging into the base of the hill or mound. I had seen this often in my native land as a youngster when limestone was quarried. But to my surprise I found that the marble was procured from the top of the mountain, that huge marble quarries had been burrowed into the mountaintops around Carrara, and that narrow roads frequented by large marble-carrying trucks led to the spot where the marble was found.

Michelangelo had worked in this area. It was from here that he had both quarried and carried the marble from which he had developed his renowned *Pietà*. As we drove ever upward in our air-conditioned car, I was reminded of this genius of less developed times guiding his oxen down the mountain as they pulled heavy slabs of marble toward his workplace lower in the valley. Today huge and imposing machinery quarries the marble with sharp saws cooled by water. And then the heavy trucks do the rest of the work to get the marble to its destination. Visitors to the Vatican mostly overlook the very laborious work done by those famous artists as the talent that produced such overwhelming art fascinates them. For Michelangelo, the journey down the mountain with his chosen block of marble had to be both fatiguing and extremely dangerous.

Toward the end of the year, Jill found the stone she wanted and got to work carving out the statue. It took a long time, and despite our desire to see the statue arrive, we had determined not to hurry the artist. Her work would reach far beyond our own time, and the time she took would be but a speck compared to the years ahead.

The following summer, I returned again to Italy to view the almost completed work. It looked impressive. We celebrated Mass at its foot, asking God's blessing on all who might one day look upon or pray before this statue. And as the Mass ended, we prayed for God's blessing on the hands that had crafted this work of art. As I offered the prayer, I noticed a tear in Jill's eye.

There was excitement among shrine members when the statue arrived in Orlando. It had come by boat from Milan to Miami and thence by freight truck to Orlando. It weighed eight tons. The base on which it would stand weighed four more.

Getting two articles of eight and four tons off a truck is a challenge in itself. Jill was present when it was loaded in Italy. She had to leave its unloading in Miami in the hands of the Lord, but she was at the shrine on the morning of its arrival. A forklift lowered the cherished works from the truck. Now the question: How do you get four tons of marble and eight tons of marble to their place within the church? How much damage can you do in the process?

There is an exit door near the sanctuary area just outside where the statue would stand. First the forklift loaded the base through the door and as far inside as could be reached from the outside. Then a large crane was driven through the main entry doors, right up the center aisle. I was fretful the crane would somehow damage the pews or the marble of the sanctuary. I need not have worried. The crane driver was both accomplished and careful. He touched nothing other than the statue and its base. First he reached the nose of the crane across the front pews, picked the base from the forklift, and gently placed it in its correct position. This took time, as the base had to be carefully maneuvered to the exact spot. And now for the challenge of the statue itself! In similar fashion as before, the crane lifted the statue ever so gently over the pews and brought it to rest safely on top of the base. The entire operation was completed in about four hours. At last Mary Queen was seated in the shrine dedicated in her name!

Naturally, the newly arrived statue drew a lot of attention. People have a tendency to touch a work of art. This magnificent representation of Mary, Queen of the Universe, was dear to people's hearts, so much so that they wanted to touch it constantly. Many wanted to kiss Our Lady's feet or reach to her hands or the foot of the baby. In a very short time, lipstick marks were visible on the statue. The feet of the Queen were losing their original sheen.

I spoke with Jill Burkee about the problem. Since marble is a soft stone, she was of the opinion that once the red lipstick made its way into the statue, it would be almost impossible to remove it. She felt that without protection the statue would be disfigured in a short time.

There was only one thing to do: surround the statue with a Plexiglas shield that would prevent viewers from touching it. The shield, not originally planned, protects the statue to this day. But visitors to the shrine can gaze on the wonderful statue of the Mother of God holding a happy child in her arms and be reassured of her motherly protection throughout all their life journeys.

And a happy footnote: Jill Burkee was thrilled to be given the commission for the statue. She was not Catholic, but at first, as she sought the proper marble and later as she carved the image of Mary, she found herself making more and more inquiries into Catholic devotion to the Mother of God. Some time after the installation of the statue, she wrote a beautiful article in a New York sculptural magazine on the work. And on September 8, 2007, I had the distinct privilege of baptizing Jill *Mary* Burkee into the Catholic faith. The ceremony took place in a little village high in the mountains north of Forte dei Marmi in Italy. She has spent much time in Italy going about her work, and during the baptism I noted many wet eyes among the older members of the congregation. I think the Mother of God was rewarding her for the intense and dedicated way she had gone about carving her statue.

Chapter Sixty:
Saint Joseph Statuary

The statue of Mary Queen quickly asserted its established place as expected. Many visitors arrived "just to see" the shrine's newest presentation. They were not disappointed. In the statue they found, as visitors still find, solace. "The Mother of God," they would say, "has a beautiful face"; "She looks so tranquil"; "She seems to be inviting us to come close"; "She appears to want us with her divine Son enfolded under her cloak"; "She is giving us her Jesus who looks such a happy child."

In the circumstances, I suppose it was not surprising that there now seemed to be a missing piece: Joseph, husband of Mary, should also be in the church. His absence was conspicuous, and it may have been this very fact that encouraged a long-standing benefactor of the shrine to come forward, offering to underwrite the costs of putting the beloved saint in place.

Happily, we notified Bruno Lucchesi. He had completed many works of art throughout the United Sates. Extraordinarily, this would be his very first religious piece! He returned to Orlando to express his ideas and listen to ours. The committee had no hesitation in choosing a clay model he had prepared for the interviews of the young Jesus in the workshop with Joseph.

As with all previous artworks at the shrine, this would be an entirely new presentation of the subject. It would illustrate the human side of the Holy Family—a little boy of twelve sitting on his foster father's bench explaining something to a resting Joseph, who looks keenly at the child with an expression of admiration and wonderment. It might indeed be termed "work break."

The statue would be in bronze, and bronze art needs no protection. It was fitting that such an attractive piece would provide the opportunity to be touched by those who came to view it—and perhaps also share the wonderment expressed in the face of Joseph Himself!

In less than a year, the work was completed and delivered in two parts to the shrine. There would be no problem getting it to its place within the church. Bronze is sturdy and less liable than marble to be crushed or disfigured. Bruno was present to assemble the parts as they were taken from the truck, and within a couple of hours he had Joseph and Jesus in the prepared spot. There were far fewer onlookers than had been the case with the Mary statue. But in the years that have followed, the Joseph statuary has won the hearts of innumerable visitors to the shrine.

Visitors note the attention to details, such as the wedding band on Joseph's finger. (Were there wedding bands in those days? Does it matter? The wedding band on Joseph is a reminder of his fidelity to his responsibilities.) Just at the rear of the statue is a stained-glass window of *Rest on the Flight into Egypt*, where the faithful Joseph watches over Mary and the child, as the Mother of God steals a few winks of sleep on their arduous journey to protect the child. Both works create a tranquil presentation of Joseph and the holy family and are especially attractive to younger children, inviting them to a relationship to the divine Child.

Indeed, this statuary of Joseph and Jesus has become a much-loved work of art at Mary's Shrine. The figures are life size and stand at the very top of the church, close to the sanctuary. Once, when I had directed a couple to where the statue was, I had occasion to meet them later in the afternoon. I asked their thoughts on the statue, only to be told they hadn't found it. They must have misunderstood my directions, they said, because when they went over to that side of the church, all they saw at the top were two people sitting having a discussion and they didn't want to intrude! Bruno Luchessi would have been pleased that his figures were so lifelike from a distance. The shrine church and grounds may be a "place like no other," and certainly this statuary is a presentation of Saint Joseph that meets that goal.

Chapter Sixty-One:
Masses Ended at Disney Complex

The years were passing. The dream was approaching completion. Mary's Shrine was fast becoming a landmark for worship and prayer in the Orlando area.

I was in Italy in 2001 when terrorists destroyed the New York towers, with the loss of more than three thousand lives. The United States was about to enter a turbulent period, with its young men and women going overseas and many sacrificing their lives far away from home.

In Orlando, many people came to the shrine for solace on that fateful day forever to be known as 9/11. What better place to be than with the Lord and His Mother at a time when the sky seemed to be falling for the United States. On my return from my vacation the following week, many expressed their gratitude that they were able to come to the shrine, attend the special masses that had been scheduled by our dedicated priests on that mournful day, and find peace and courage to face the world's problems.

The numbers visiting the Orlando theme parks greatly declined for the following months until Christmas. Mass attendance was severely down. People were afraid to fly. With the resulting depletion of income, it became difficult to keep the shrine going. It was a time to remember "on their hands they shall bear you up" yet one more time. My morning prayer time continued, and I recall visiting the Adoration Chapel frequently, asking for guidance and solutions for the problems besetting us. The Adoration Chapel always provided a source of refuge for me when problems grew heavy.

Because of the aforementioned fear of flying, theme parks had greatly diminished numbers. Gradually, life got back to normal and the arrival of Christmas put an end to our troubles. We had been able to pay our mortgages and expenditures, and with the numbers of visitors returning, everything fell back in place as in previous times.

In the story of the shrine and of the tourist ministry, the following year 2002 marked the end of our regular weekly masses within Disney World. The tourist ministry had celebrated Masses within the Disney complex since 1976. Our priests and volunteers viewed it as a special part of their ministry. The Disney organization had changed greatly since that time. Indeed, it was governed by an entirely different board than when I first started, and the leadership had changed hands more than once. On a few occasions, I had made phone calls to various officers within the organization to discuss problems that seemed to be arising. The responses told me the old days were over! After the passing of Bob Allen, it was well-nigh impossible to speak to or arrange to meet anyone higher than a secretary or coordinator. Arrangements and problems with the Sunday masses were discussed with the lower echelon. After the passing of Bob Allen, I was never invited to any vice president's office again.

Bob Allen, while not Catholic, was a man with great dedication to service. He remained true to the spirit of Walt Disney himself, always concerned about his guests and compassionate toward their spiritual needs. His main problem, of course, was that with the celebration of Catholic masses, many other denominations also wished to be facilitated. The Catholic numbers were huge by comparison, and since an ecumenical group had been formed for Protestant services, Allen partially resolved his problem by inviting them also to hold religious services within the complex. However, his solution most likely did not prevent continued requests and complaints from denominations who wished to hold their own religious celebrations.

In May of 2002, Disney World called. Would it be possible to come to a meeting at Disney? They would like to discuss something. I quickly found that "something" was the abandonment of the masses within the complex. There had been hints of this for several months. There were just too many people coming to Mass in the Luau Cove, they told me, and the company was concerned about the "comfort of their guests." No other place was available for Mass within Disney World, they said, despite the plethora of hotels that had been added since the park first opened. (They should, of course, have been delighted at the numbers seeking Mass. Did it not tell them something about the qualities and aspirations of those using their theme parks for vacationing? Wasn't that exactly what Walt Disney wanted, family gatherings?)

The Disney representatives were gracious, as is the Disney practice. It was time, they said, to end the masses at Disney World. The arguments they advanced were non-convincing, none any stronger than the "discomfort" of the guests. It was very clear to me that a decision had been made in higher quarters that the masses were to be stopped. I did of course argue the cause of the Church, being well aware at the same time that my arguments were futile.

They proposed to send people by bus to the masses at the shrine. (I wrongly assumed the buses would be offered without charging a fare.) There was nothing to do but agree. Sadly, I returned to the shrine, realizing that the proffered change would not be good for our people.

My mind returned to the early days of our ministry and our arguments way back in 1975–1976 that Disney's guests were being invited from places all over the world without any mention being made of the distance of the complex from towns or churches. There was a slogan posted within the Polynesian Hotel in its early days. A newspaper stand announced "News from civilization." The Church was making every effort to care for soul and body in a holistic way, even outside "civilization."

Sadly, we left Disney World because we had to. The busing took place for about three Sundays and then was abandoned. Nobody ever thought to notify me. When I contacted them, the Disney people said it was for lack of interest. It was not paying for itself. (Where had all those people gone who came to the Luau Cove on Sundays? Had they disappeared overnight? There used to be thousands of them!)

We soon discovered there were two reasons the busing did not succeed. First, a charge of ten dollars per person was levied on each passenger. A family of four would have to pay forty dollars to get itself to Mass. The other reason was that the Mass bus program appeared to have been poorly announced in the Disney' hotels. Many people who took a taxi to Mass at that time told me they had heard nothing of the buses. But the fare imposed made it more convenient for many vacationing families to take a taxi.

Repeat Catholic visitors to Disney who expected the Sunday Mass as before were upset at the change. I received many letters of complaint at the time, some of them irate. My approach in reply was always the same: tell the truth, and refer the writer to Disney. There was another snag in the arrangement too. The Disney organization wanted masses to be celebrated for their guests on Christmas Day, in itself an anomaly.

Having considered their requests, I agreed to have two masses at the Contemporary Hotel, although I was somewhat surprised and saddened that New Year's Day would be excluded. As I recall, Christmas Day Mass continued until 2004, when Christmas Day fell on a Saturday. At that time, I again pointed out to the Disney people the contradiction of having Mass on Christmas Day but nothing on Sunday. Their only interest was Mass on Christmas Day; as one official remarked it helped "create a nice atmosphere." I tried to make it clear that Catholics go to Mass on Sunday too, even if it is preceded by Christmas Day, and I explained my conundrum of appearing to send a wrong message to our Catholic people, while at the same time asking Disney to reconsider the situation. The Church did not wish to send out a message that it was all right to go to Mass on Christmas Day and skip the following Sunday. The New Year's Day masses had also been dispensed with.

The subject found quick solution when I received a directive from the diocese, who had never discussed the matter with me, to proceed with the Disney request. The matter was out of my hands. I regretted it because I felt that, as on previous situations, the Church would have won the battle had we stood our ground. But nobody had ever spoken to me from the diocese, and I simply carried out the directive. And with it disappeared any hope of renegotiating the return of Sunday masses within the Disney World complex. This time, the Church had surrendered.

I have great respect for the Disney organization. There is probably no organization in the world that takes care of its guests better than the Disney people. I am grateful for executives like Bob Allen whose enthusiasm for the service of people was surely on the pinnacle that Walt Disney himself would have wished for. But as far as I am concerned, the decision to remove the Sunday masses was erroneous and did no good for the company's image. When you inconvenience a thousand or more guests on many a Sunday, then you can't have their best interests at heart. You are certainly not doing them a favor.

Chapter Sixty-Two:
Monsignor

I n August of 2003, a coadjutor bishop was installed in the diocese. He was the Most Reverend Thomas Wenski. The occasion of his installation would create the first major coming together of Church dignitaries from far and wide in a ceremony specifically organized for the shrine. The soon-to-retire Bishop Dorsey had been installed in a basketball arena in the center of the city because no church building was capable of housing the attendees.

We had dreamt of "a place like no other," and the dream had been surpassed in reality! Not only was the shrine a gathering place for vacationers from all over the world searching for the Lord, it was now a recognized edifice in which not only vacationers but clergy from far and wide would gather in celebration of the faith of the Church.

The installation of the new coadjutor bishop would remain in my memory. But for the wrong reasons! So many clergy would be present that diocesan officials in charge decided that visiting priests would vest in an outside tent erected specially for the occasion.

They were correct! Vast numbers of clergy showed up. Visitors were sent to the tent to vest while those taking an immediate part in the ceremony were vested within the shrine sacristy. I had spent a considerable amount of time on the grounds that morning greeting the visitors as had been my custom. When I got to the sacristy there was a surprise awaiting me. I was to vest with the visiting priests and take my place with them in a pew. Many in attendance saw the symbolism of what was happening. There was a great number of shrine benefactors present at the ceremony. Many of them were literally enraged. One or two made their feelings known to the bishops afterwards. The question they asked went unanswered—why should the leader of the shrine ministry be humiliated in the very building his efforts had helped bring about? Was this the diocesan response to his work? Personally, I know now what I should have done. I should have taken a chair to the sanctuary area and seated myself with those participating in the ceremony, and I wish I had done so.

Since we were a national community, so to speak, with supporters in all fifty states and even further afield, it had been our custom to hold celebrations in Orlando every two or three years. The celebrations enabled shrine supporters from all over the country to gather together and rejoice in the continuing success of their beloved project. The celebrations involved a Mass at the shrine followed by a celebratory meal in a local hotel. It afforded people an opportunity to get together to give glory to God for the success of the shrine ministry and the miracle of faith taking place in central Florida. It also provided them the chance to make and renew friendships with each other. All shared the same objective and were proud of their association with Mary's Shrine in Orlando.

It is well to remember that the shrine was born from the desire of people to celebrate Eucharist, the nourishing meal given us by Christ Himself. It is interesting to note in the Gospels how many times Jesus took part in meal celebrations. From the feeding of the five thousand to His last meal before His crucifixion, Jesus showed a willingness to join in a meal—more than that, even a desire. He performed His first miracle at the marriage in Cana; he rebuked one host for not offering water to wash His feet and at the same time forgave "the woman who was a sinner." Saint John has several chapters of His farewell to His followers on Holy Thursday evening. After His resurrection, Jesus would entertain some of His disciples to breakfast by the shore. It has been said that Jesus loved a party! And not without reason!

Supping together creates a bond. Some of my own best childhood memories center on family meals. And was there anything as good as those scones my mother created for the Sunday evening meal? I'll bet every member of my family remembers them! At the shrine, our "banquet celebrations" were always well attended and indeed remarkable for the distances benefactors traveled, from places as distant as California and Colorado. On occasion too the great friend of the shrine Pio Cardinal Laghi would travel from Rome to be with us, always emphasizing the support of the Universal Church for the work of God's people in Orlando. He always brought greetings from the Holy Father, Pope John Paul II.

One such celebration had been scheduled for a date in November following the installation of our new bishop. Cardinal Laghi was with us and presided at the liturgy that Sunday. After Holy Communion was distributed, the cardinal addressed the congregation. He had always done this in previous times. But this time he had a surprise for us.

The cardinal was carrying a large envelope in his hand. "The shrine," he said, "is an important work of the Church, and the Holy Father is pleased. I was visiting with the Holy Father before I left Rome, and he told me he wants to bestow the title *monsignor* on the rector of the shrine." The cardinal then opened the envelope and pulled out a purple sash, saying good-humoredly that he hoped it would fit.

The announcement, of course, brought great satisfaction to those present, although, to be honest, I was in total shock and had no idea how to react. I think my obvious confusion added to the general excitement. The honor was particularly significant in that the title had not been bestowed on any priest of the diocese since its foundation in 1968. I would be the very first monsignor since the inception of the diocese in all of those years! The Holy Father had dispatched the title directly through an emissary. He must have been pleased indeed with the work of the shrine and with all who were involved in the proclamation of the kingdom.

The title *Monsignor* is significant in that it is bestowed in approval of a priest's work. It comes from the Latin for "my lord." In Italy, particularly, the title is applied to bishops. But worldwide a monsignor is a minor prelate, who is not, however, being raised to the order of bishop.

Frankly, I had never set my sights on anything other than carrying out God's will. I had no doubt the Lord and His Mother wanted me to get the shrine completed for ministry to generations to come and the proclamation of God's kingdom, and the service of the numberless good people who sought out their Lord while vacationing in Orlando was uppermost and, in fact, the only objective in my mind. I can honestly say I always sought God's glory, not my own.

I'll let you in on a secret: It had always been my custom while processing from the narthex to the altar for Mass to look at the hanging crucifix overhead and ask the Lord to help me proclaim His kingdom to the very best of my ability. In one of his writings Saint Leo the Great had referred to "the supremacy of Christ crucified," and in the passage he had uttered the prayer, "Lord, you drew all things to yourself so that the devotion of peoples everywhere might celebrate, in a sacrament made perfect and visible, what was carried out in the one Temple of Judea." This indeed must be the desire of every priest going to the altar. The calling of a priest is to walk with the Lord in the proclamation of the Gospel.

The people in the pews were and are there to be nourished by the Lord of the Eucharist, to bear Him in their souls, and to hear the divinely inspired readings explained. I never once doubted that the Mother of the Lord had led me to this ministry to be involved in the extension of the kingdom of her divine Son. If I could help the worshippers leave the church with a better feeling of closeness to God and a better awareness and desire for His kingdom, then that would be my joy.

The honor bestowed on me by the Holy Father belonged in truth not to me alone but to all the faithful volunteers who had labored so unselfishly for Christ's kingdom. "No man is an island," and the shrine church—the community of the faithful—could not have made progress without the faith and physical support of the many wonderful people, who had surrounded me with their zeal. For them I accepted the honor—an honor for all of us and a reminder too that the establishing of the kingdom must continue on a daily basis.

A short time after the honor had been conferred, I had reason to call a diocesan pastor to get some information. His secretary answered the phone and told me the pastor was not at that moment available but would get back to me. "Who should I tell him to call?" she asked. I foolishly (it would appear) answered that I was Monsignor Harte in Orlando and gave my phone number.

A couple of hours later the pastor did call back. The conversation was surprisingly unfriendly. I received a sharp reprimand on the idea of calling myself "Monsignor" and a bloviation that lasted several minutes on how inappropriate the title is for any priest. (This despite the conferring of the honor by the Holy Father!) There is indeed an ongoing debate among clergy on the subject—a debate, I may add, that has no solution. Titles that have been bestowed for centuries must have some good reason for the development of the custom. Naturally, our conversation was brief, and I put down the phone with a lot of unanswered questions on the subject teasing my brain. All of which, I suppose, tells us we are living in a very mixed-up world!

This priest apparently saw nothing good in my reception of a titular honor. He did not congratulate me. He did not of course know anything of the work being carried out by the laity of southwest Orlando. One of his remarks was particularly offensive. He chose not to ask why I thought the Holy Father had granted the honor, because honor it was. As priests we have a tendency to become very involved in our own ministries, and that is indeed very good. But what would be wrong with taking time now and again to encourage each other in acknowledging the successes of our work for the Lord? Saint Benedict surely would have done that. His admonitions to his monks were always filled with urgings to recognize and love each other. No priest is an island—not even a new monsignor!

I think Saint Benedict would have recognized me with love.

Chapter Sixty-Three:
The Gates of Paradise

Work on construction of bronze portals for the shrine had been under way for a short time previous to my heart illness. (I will tell you about that problem shortly). As with most works of art, progress was slow and tedious. The portals would be adorned with literally hundreds of three-quarter-size completed statuettes. Mosaics were planned to adorn the spaces above the doors of the three entryways. At the outset, we knew it would take several years to complete this project that had been undertaken with the equivalent of a "pay as you go" agreement. (The only mortgage on the shrine was for the building itself.)

I often hear the question, "What inspired the bronze portals?" At the time, it was not unusual to be asked, "Father, why do you want to do this? What is wrong with the wooden doors?" Let it be said here, the wooden doors had their problems. Facing the early sun as they did, it was difficult to keep them varnished, and the constant refurbishing in itself contributed to an unwelcome recurring expense. However, there was indeed a much more inspirational motivation.

From the start, the dream for this shrine was that it would stand out in artistic excellence, a place like no other. Historically, the promotion of art by the Church gave birth to the Renaissance. The many magnificent churches of Europe give testimony that the inner thoughts of the mind can be portrayed in a way that allows viewers to learn and to have their own thoughts uplifted and inspired to the sacred. Occasionally the soul-less will opine, "This could have been given to the poor." The Church is about the salvation of souls (as well as bodies), and obviously the majority in past ages believed that to spend on artwork that would "save souls" was important and might even contribute to the well-being of the body.

Personally, on my visits to some of the well-known artistic locations of Europe, I have always come away with elevated perceptions. At Chartres, for example, it is difficult not to be touched by the faith of previous generations who struggled so hard in adverse circumstances to bring into being not only the beautiful cathedral but the magnificent stained-glass art that adorns it. The glass, the tour leader will tell you, was introduced to educate an illiterate people and bring them the message of Jesus and His Gospel. Indeed, it is scarcely likely that the artists themselves had any inkling that their work would later stand as the epitome of stained-glass art and create a place to which people from the world over would travel to view and enjoy its brilliance and pleasing amalgamation of colors while at the same time absorbing the Gospel narratives. And if you journey to Ravenna, you can see the first Christian mosaics. Created in the fourth century, they still remain, exactly as when created, to illumine the minds and hearts of the onlookers.

It all took time, and effort—and most likely opposition and harassment from within and without! But the burning desire to make known the inner workings of the heart prevailed, and those artists have contributed to the spread of the Gospel message more powerfully than they could ever have foreseen. What was it about those people, the cathedral builders, the artists of marble and glass and wood and bronze? I think the answer is that not only did they love their work, but they also loved Him who inspired them, and in their inner being they wanted to proclaim Christ's kingdom. They were supported by people of similar goals. Today, their works stand as a testimony to a zeal that was the driving force of their lives.

In Florence you can be overwhelmed by the grandeur of the spectacular bronze portals of the Baptistry of Saint John. You can also sit within the baptistry and be transported to another dimension as you gaze upward at the mosaic ceiling that crowns the building itself. (And if your life is not at peace with God, you may be enticed to reformation, or frightened into repentance, as you view the *Last Judgment* depicted just above you!)

Every year millions of visitors come to view the baptistry doors. One has to assume that even though many may not be Christian, they are nevertheless being educated in the truths of Christianity. The bronze portals of Andrea Pisano and later Lorenzo Ghiberti have stood the test of time since the thirteenth and fourteenth centuries. Michelangelo referred to these doors as fit to be the "Gates of Paradise"—a name that remains with them to this very day.

At the "Gates of Paradise," one must encounter God! The Shrine of Mary in Orlando was to provide an opportunity for people to commune with their Creator. To bring this about, we had all agreed to try the impossible! We knew from the start it wouldn't be easy! Many moons had come and gone, many suns had set since the majority of the wonderful pieces of pre-Renaissance and Renaissance art had been developed. Why not allow the same sun and moon to shine on artwork of the new world in Florida? Could we too be influential in bringing the story of Christ to the millions not only in our own time but in the ages to come? Our committee was sensitive to the idea of evangelization. This had been a primary motivation for the shrine. Here again, as so often in the past, Marcia Pietrzak's love of art gave birth to a bold idea. We should install bronze portals that would bring an ageless appearance to the new shrine church.

I shared that ambition myself but had some negative feelings too. "How would we pay for the doors?" I asked. When the subject was introduced, every member of our committee was surprisingly positive. Many members of the committee had vacationed in Italy and had the opportunity to witness the beauty of the famous Florentine baptistry portals. To emulate them was a challenge, but we had already dared to be great. Greatness is achieved in the proclamation of the Lord's kingdom. Why not keep up the good work for the Lord and His Mother? The bronze portals would proclaim the greatness of the Lord to generations long after us!

It took several meetings of the committee to reach complete agreement to go ahead with the project. We were embarking on a major expense. The desire to start the project and its foreseen evangelistic results inspired every discussion. We invited prospective candidates for interview, some new, some familiar. Jill Burkee and GianCarlo Biaggi teamed up as one entry for consideration. We reminded them that, if perhaps they had taken their cue from the doors of Florence, there was also a downside to that! The completion of the Florence doors had been assigned to two artists also, Ghiberti and Brunelleschi. They had fallen out, however, and the work was completed in its totality by Ghiberti, but it took him twenty-one years to reach completion and installation. We could hardly wait that length of time! Our artists assured us they were in harmony, and since we were well aware of their gifted talents, the committee had no problem in awarding them the commission to begin. If you have viewed their completed work in Orlando, I think you will agree it was a wise decision.

The artists couldn't begin their work, however, until the finances were available. Meanwhile, we took time to plan and to discuss the subject matter of the portals with the artists. What they did was begin to reflect on their project and choose suitable biblical stories with which to embellish the portals. All the while, the word of our new undertaking had to be spread abroad. We reminded the faithful that the artwork on the portals of the shrine would be equivalent to "The Bible in Bronze." They would be promoting the message of Jesus even when the doors to the facility were closed.

At one of our meetings another idea was set forth. Since the front of the portals would constitute the opportunity for larger giving, why not afford the less wealthy the ability to contribute also by having their names on the inside of the portals? This would be a lesser amount, yet make involvement possible for many more persons. The idea was adopted. Today, the inside of the doors contains the names of hundreds of people who were delighted to become a part of the church's effort of evangelization. Extraordinarily, when you now approach the doors from any distance within, the names seem to tie together as if forming one whole meshing of script that adds to the magnificence of the entire structure.

As with previous projected works of art, the response to the appeal for the portals was overwhelmingly effusive. The center portals could be commissioned almost immediately. When the work was begun, we were secure in the knowledge of our ability to pay the artists. Within a few months, the center portals were completely subscribed and hundreds of names were already coming in to be added to the inside of the portals.

The artists in their enthusiasm had promised us completion on a date less than two years hence. A celebration was planned that was attended by many from throughout the United States. But the portals had not been installed when the time came, so we celebrated a future happening. We all knew the portals would arrive! (We did of course remind the artists they would still have to be a little faster in delivering the work than Ghiberti.)

Indeed, the center portals did arrive six months later and were installed without any problem. The remaining portals came about three years following. The completion of the project gave all of us a feeling of satisfaction, and I can at least speak for our committee and myself when I say we felt a sense of gratitude to the Lord, who allowed us to be a part of a wondrous Catholic evangelization program where tourists roam. "The Bible in Bronze" will long be a feature of Mary's Shrine in Orlando. It will be "read" by thousands of people throughout the coming years. I believe the bronze portals are an outstanding work of art that will be celebrated in Orlando for years to come. They are the jewels that exhibit the beauty of what is within, indeed another reflection of the "Gates of Paradise."

The remarkable flurry of contributions toward the bronze portals serves to illustrate that our people still enjoy art in their churches. They are also glad to be a part of evangelization and will make the sacrifices necessary to provide instruments that will bring the message of Christ to the world. I was indeed a little scared at the beginning of the portal project, but I quickly found, as in all matters relating to the development of the shrine, that our Catholic people respond enthusiastically when presented with genuine opportunities to promote the cause of Christ.

Today, while approaching the shrine from the parking lot just over the bridge, it would be impossible for the visitor to understand the amount of time and effort that went into the completion of the magnificent bronze portals, Orlando's "Gates of Paradise." They proclaim the greatness of the Lord, and hidden somewhere in the proclamation is the fervor and love of all those who sacrificed for them. True love is forever. Surely the Lord and His Mother will accept that love and return it fourfold! I salute each and every person whose sacrifices made them possible.

Chapter Sixty-Four:
Facing A Health Crisis

✑

nce upon a time, I had a coworker who used to say humorously that I would never suffer from blood pressure or heart problems. Instead, she would joke, I would give them to others! She wasn't entirely right, as time would tell, and that time was here!

Looking back, allow me to advise everyone that time takes its toll. They say time and tide wait for no man. Yes, and the tide comes in long before it was expected. Beware! Day by day we grow older, and the more one enjoys one's work, the faster time rolls. It had been a long time since that morning in 1975 when I first began the tourist ministry. But it all seemed so short, and I had aged. There had been a lot of "battles," and though I had never intended to retire, I was soon to find that every skirmish takes its toll, that the older years make for a less receptive physicality, and that stress increases with age. ,

There was more stress ahead for me. The roof of the shrine church failed. There was no alternative other than to replace it. After less than ten years, its leaking problems were found to be irreparable. The roofing contractor had gone out of business, and the main contractor wasn't about to help us out. In fact, his representative insulted us with charges that we must have had somebody walking on the roof because many tiles were broken. Nobody, of course, had gone eighty feet up on the roof; later on would come the disclosure that the roofing process had not followed the architect's directives, and installers had used power tools to drive nails and broken many tiles that were then left in place.

Replacing the roof would cost the better part of $1.5 million—which we didn't have. You will recall the roof tiles that had been the foundation of our fund drives early on. At this time, it would take forever to garner the required funding. How might it be found? The necessity of the new roof was underscored by the collapse of an outside walkway at an Orlando church, resulting in injuries, some of them serious. Trusting in God, we went ahead anyway and arranged for the work to be done.

I think it was at this stage my aforementioned coworker's belief in my durability began, like the roof, to show some leaks. Another million and a half? And in short time? Without a local community! How could it be done? I certainly wasn't ready for God's plan, and I am afraid the stress began to take its toll.

It might be well here to share something about our financial operations of the time. Over a number of years, the diocese had used the services of a very competent chief financial officer who was both compassionate and friendly to the clergy. One of his favorite sayings was "You priests keep me on my feet trying to steer you away from trouble." He had arranged for a separate mortgage for the shrine through one of the local banks—a mortgage that we faithfully honored every month with on-time payments. This, he explained, would help the diocese too, since it would not have to find the money from its resources for the five-million-dollar loan the project required—a goodly sum, one might readily admit. When written up, the document had been sent to me for my signature. Legally it was not required, but the procedure gave me a certain amount of ownership of the loan and the subsequent responsibility to live up to the agreement that was being made.

We had floated the loan in 1993. It was now 2003 and the loan had been reduced without fanfare to very manageable proportions. It had been practically halved. The ministry had been doing very nicely indeed. Looking at the statistics, our committee concluded that we should simply take out another loan from the same bank. There would be no problem, and the bank already knew our history. In order to accomplish this, we first had to meet with the diocesan finance committee.

Let me add here that I longed for the days when John Wettach, the aforementioned comptroller, was in charge of diocesan finances. John understood the administrative procedures of the shrine. Unfortunately, his successor had no such understanding. He had not once visited the shrine to see its operations. Not only did he not understand, but he appeared to believe that somehow monies coming into the shrine flowed like milk from a newly calved cow. From diocesan officials, I had heard the term "cash cow" applied to the shrine. With the roof repairs there was nothing we could do but proceed, to make sure there would be no catastrophe. A new roof was the only solution. If the diocese would not help us, God and His Mother would!

It didn't take us long to learn there would be little sympathy from the diocesan administrators. Having presented our case at a meeting with them and put forth suggestions of a further loan from the local bank, we were met with positive refusal. The diocesan bank would make a loan of $800,000, but the rest we would have to find for ourselves, and worst of all, the money was to be repaid in a period of three years. It seemed more like a punishing verdict than an offer of a helping hand. I knew that, short of a miracle, such demands could not be met. There was nothing to do but proceed. Lives might be at risk. (The miracle would indeed come too!)

During the time the repairs were taking place, in early June of 2004, as I exited from a hospital where I had visited a shrine volunteer, I suddenly found it difficult to breathe. Being at the hospital, I should have returned to Emergency, but instead I spotted a bench nearby and sat down for a little while. My breathing returned to normal, so I went back to the shrine and my work, but I knew my body was telling me there was a problem.

Two days later, a heart specialist confirmed my fears. I would need open-heart surgery, he believed. He would confirm that with a further test at the hospital the following Friday. Naturally, open-heart surgery was repugnant! I had never had any heart problems, nor was there any history of heart problems in my family. My first inclination was to reject the surgery even if the need was confirmed and "take my chances." A doctor friend I had known for a long time advised me that would be foolish. She believed the surgery would be worthwhile and could prolong my life for many years. Another physician remarked that it was interesting this was happening just as the roof problems were being resolved and wondered if there might be a connection.

When eventually the need for surgery was confirmed, I was ready to agree. But the Friday in June for which the original test was scheduled saw me far away in Ireland. On the previous Sunday morning, two days after the confirmation of my heart problems, I had received an unexpected phone call that my sister Maeve had died while undergoing a medical procedure in Dublin.

Maeve (Mary Theresa), known in religion as Sister Mary Colombiere, had spent more than fifty years in the Irish Sisters of Mercy. In many ways she was the treasure of our family as well as being the oldest. Quietly contented, thoughtful and kind, she was beloved by all. (She had worked in the Irish civil service for a number of years. On one occasion she declined promotion because she felt someone else deserved it more! But I also believe she knew she was going to enter the convent and wanted another girl who was her friend to get the promotion that might not be offered to her later on.) Our time together during my vacations was special, and in her latter days she had the freedom to travel that had been denied in her younger years. For example, she was not allowed to attend my father's funeral in 1956, although she was given a few hours home to visit him before he died. I recall his statement when she left his bedroom: "Maeve is a saint." She did not have permission to attend my ordination in 1961, but she was allowed to attend my first Mass as long as she was home in her convent by 7:00 p.m. that evening. But my father's sentiment that she was a saint was one that was shared by every member of the family.

I wasn't feeling well, and the phone call announcing her death in the early hours of Sunday, June 20, 2004, came as a shock. My sister-in-law made the call and was a little taken aback when I first expressed my own concern that I might not be able to travel. I had not told members of my family of the problems with my heart. But on the spot I decided I was going, and it was much later my sister-in-law told me she now understood the dilemma I was in. Maeve's funeral in Ballinasloe was a memorable occasion, and the bishop of Clonfert presided at her funeral Mass. I managed to get through the ceremonies, including the homily, without ever letting anyone know my predicament. Yes, the angels were bearing me up, and I knew it!

On my return to Orlando, I entered the hospital on July 9 for the tests on my heart. Afterward, my doctor assured me I was living, as he put it, on half a heart. One side of my heart was completely out of service. Talk about the Lord! Talk about the Mother of the Lord! Talk about the angels! I had flown thousands of miles and could have had a major heart attack at any moment!

My heart specialist informed me that a reputed heart surgeon was visiting the hospital at this time and was ready to do the surgery then and there, if I would agree. Why prolong the agony? I agreed. On July 9, 2004, I underwent a quadruple bypass.

Word got out quickly from the hospital that surgery would be performed before noon. My faithful secretary, Libby Yost, called to find out if there was anything I needed, and with teary eyes she arrived at the hospital before I was taken for the anesthetic. My good friend Father John McMullan arrived too, obviously taken aback at the development. He assured me there was nothing to worry about at the shrine while I was away, and having known him for all those years and his renown from longtime service in the Archdiocese of Seattle, I knew I did not need to worry in that respect.

The shrine staff by all accounts, were in shock. But I am proud of how they reacted. Coming together, they decided that each staff member would take a turn to pray before the Blessed Sacrament all through that Friday and that a staff member would be before the Blessed Sacrament at all times throughout the day. The other staff members would take up the slack for the person missing. And so I had a continual remembrance in prayer at the shrine all through that day. My coworkers were interceding for me. Their decision demonstrated their commitment to the shrine and the faith with which they served. I felt very rewarded about their unilateral decision. It was clear to me too they understood the Eucharistic mission of the shrine.

What about me? What were my feelings before the surgery? What was I thinking? I knew I was surrounded by friends. A good friend who had driven me for the early appointment stayed with me during the three hours or so it took to prepare me for surgery, and while I was being wheeled to the operating room, he squeezed my hand. There was nothing to be said, and each of us knew what the other was thinking.

As everyone does when facing major surgery, I had my hopes that the outcome would be satisfactory. Death could well be staring me in the face, and like the Lord in the garden of Gethsemane, I was not eager to meet it. People kept coming and going and there was little time for deep thinking. But the question did indeed keep recurring in my mind, "What if?" I didn't want to deal with the negatives, and, truth to tell, my friends in the hospital helped keep such disturbing thoughts at bay.

As I was being wheeled to the operation theater, I thought back on my life. There wasn't much I would do differently. I had done my best; the rest was in the hands of God. Oh, yes, there were sins of omission and commission I deeply regretted, but then God's mercy is infinite, and I remembered the crucifix above the altar at the shrine and the little prayer I made every time I went forward in the procession at the beginning of Mass. My life had been about the spread of His kingdom, and I was glad of that.

I remembered what Saint Bernard, a great lover of Our Lady, had written: "My merit comes from His mercy: for I do not lack merit so long as He does not lack pity. And if the Lord's mercies are many, then I do not lack merits. For if I am aware of many sins, what does it matter?" I was sorry for my sins. My trust was now in the Sacred Heart of Jesus and in the ever constant vigilance of His Mother Mary and mine.

I must have been ten seconds in the operating room when everything blacked out. Six hours later I would return to consciousness in Recovery. More than one person seemed to be there and I head the command, "Breathe on your own."

I followed the directive and I heard voices saying, "He's breathing on his own now. He's doing all right." For the moment the crisis seemed to be over. I had always worn a miraculous medal around my neck. It was one of my most precious possessions and a continuation of a mother's love. A miraculous medal had been around my neck since early childhood. My mother made sure of that in my boyhood days. A hospital nurse saw it while I was being prepared for surgery. "You can't have the medal on you while undergoing this surgery," she confided, "but I will keep it safely for you." She kept her word, and more! Later she would make sure that I would have a comfortable room in which to recuperate. She brought back my medal, put it around my neck, and visited me every day while I was still a patient, even though I was not under her care. This book makes several references to angels, and most certainly this wonderful nurse was an angel sent by God to watch over me in my illness. I can never forget her loving care and kindness.

There were indeed other "angels" too who took care of me. Many were non-Catholic; all were gracious and loving. I remember on one occasion a young nurse not of my faith who found my rosary beads on the floor beside my bed. She picked them up, placed them on the bedside table, and remarked, "I'm sure you'll need this, and I want you to know where it is." She recognized the rosary and understood I would be using it. My hospital stay taught me much about the vocation of nursing and the wonderful men and women who serve at Orlando Regional Hospital. They are unique, compassionate, and caring.

After five days, I was released from the hospital. All seemed to be going well—until two weeks later, one Sunday evening, I suffered atrial fibrillation. It was a frightening situation. I thought my recovery was well under way, and here I was again in another health crisis. It was a reminder that God is very much in control of our lives. This little pump we call a heart had gone unnoticed over seven decades of my life. We are all in His hands.

An ambulance duly arrived and took me to the hospital. The medical people informed me that all they could do was wait for the heart to correct itself. Nobody said how long that would take, until after three days a very gracious doctor entered my room, sat on my bed, and gave me the bad news. My situation was serious, he said. There was no way of knowing how long it would be before the heart corrected itself and returned to normal. We would just have to be patient and see, he explained.

Later that day, my own internist, Dr. Frank Leiva came by. He knew me well; he had been taking care of my health for many years and was a man of intense dedication and a great lover of the Lord and His Mother. A knowledgeable and experienced practitioner, he had been both my doctor and my friend for many years. He knew I was not prone to sit around and wait. It was that knowledge that brought him to my bedside on this particular occasion.

He warned me I was "gravely ill" and that I should pay attention to whatever the doctors or nurses wished me to do. In no uncertain terms he told me I would just have to be patient. He was reading me the riot act to keep me quiet, letting me know I was no longer in charge of my own affairs.

I suppose I should have sent for a priest to pray with me. I wasn't thinking about death, though. I thought, *This is ridiculous.* Then I picked up the phone and called one of my coworkers at the shrine who helped Father John McMullan in matters relating to the spirituality and assignment of our volunteers. I knew she would be coming to see me that evening, as she had come every day. I asked her to bring me a bottle of Lourdes water. (I had always kept a supply of Lourdes water in my office for distribution to those who might request it.) When I was settling in for the night around ten o'clock, I took the Lourdes water and sprinkled it over my heart. I made the sign of the cross three times over my heart, and I implored Our Lady to intercede for me with her divine Son. As usual she was listening!

Sleep came even more swiftly than usual, but it didn't last for long. Sometime past midnight, I was awakened by a nurse coming into my room pushing a piece of medical equipment. "I need to get an EKG," she announced.

I replied grumpily, "At this hour of the night?"

"Yes," she replied, "your heart has just resumed a normal rhythm. We have been watching on the monitor. The doctor will need this information in the morning."

Coincidence? Or a miracle? In my mind there was no doubt which. The wonderful Mother of God had intervened on my behalf! She had asked her Son for another miracle! I thought of the kind doctors who visited me the previous morning and their carefully worded prognosis. I knew we are all in the hands of God, and the Mother who brought about the first miracle at Cana, when water was changed into wine, was the same Mother who was still caring for her children and guiding them on their way to happiness with her divine Son. She is always there for us. I remembered Knock and Lourdes and Medjugorje. That night I slept to morning secure in the knowledge of the inspired psalmist, "in their hands they shall bear you up."

Oh! I almost forgot! The new roof was completed and was cosmetically much more appealing to the eye than the one it replaced. And how did we pay for it? Well—another miracle! Continue reading …

Chapter Sixty-Five:
Aftermath of a Problem

Further back we have dealt with the problems of the shrine roof, how it affected my health, and how distraught we all were with the lack of sympathy from the diocesan finance committee and diocesan officers. And there was more to come. Soon we were asked to agree to change our mortgage with the local bank and have it assumed by the diocese.

When this suggestion was made, I met with an officer of the diocese (not the CFO), who assured me it would be a change for the better and would now in fact help the diocese. I didn't understand his explanation, but since it had always been my custom to support the diocese in every way possible, I went along with the suggestion. The diocese would pay off our mortgage and for our part we would assume those payments to the diocese. Thenceforward our monthly payments would be to the diocese, not to the local bank. I was very shortly to find out that my cooperation was a mistake. We should have continued with the local bank loan.

For some readers, I am sure this recounting of financial operations may be uninteresting. I record it here because this is the story of the life of a priest, and the events of this time are still very fresh in my memory. Those memories are part of a story that contributed to my service in the priesthood.

For one thing, I was about to find out that there seemed to be confusion in the minds of diocesan officials about the duration of our mortgage. With the bank it had been a thirty-year mortgage. We received a monthly request for payment, we mailed our check, and that was the end. Now it appeared that there were expectations that the mortgage with the diocese was somehow or other to be repaid in a much shorter time—possibly as little as the aforementioned three years. But no mention had been made of that. And so it didn't take long until phone calls began to come from diocesan offices regarding our debt: How soon would the repayment start on our debt? What plans did we have to overcome our debt? Did I realize the amount of our debt at the present time?

Truly I longed for the days of John Wettach, who respected our ministry and always wanted to help out. I recalled our business relationships with the commercial bank too. They never called us to remind us how much we owed. But John was gone, the bank mortgage he had engineered was gone, and so was the stability we once had in governing our finances. The pressure was steadily being applied, and it even appeared that our situation was being discussed with some clergy and others not involved in diocesan finances. It was easy to conclude that confidentiality was on the brink, and I wondered about the ethics of it all.

It was time to pray. I did. As usual, I found consolation with the Lord and His Mother. I need hardly tell you I was frequently reciting my favorite psalm (91), especially its concluding words: "He shall call upon me and I shall answer him, I will be with him in distress." The words applied to the Messiah, but I was well aware that every follower of Jesus could recite this psalm in confidence.

I recall trying to explain our situation in writing on a number of occasions, but my explanations seemed to fall on deaf ears. My ardent promises that I was sure we would meet our obligations went unheard or possibly unread! But the shrine had no local community, and there was no way these funds could be raised speedily. The goal posts had been moved.

And in the meantime a new bishop had taken over the leadership of the diocese. The bishop knew little about the history of the shrine. He had come from another diocese and was most likely in the seminary when the tourist ministry of the Diocese of Orlando was first commissioned by Bishop Thomas Grady. He had to rely on his advisors, lay people who knew little and appeared to arrive at their conclusions by mere speculation.

He had most likely been assured of the "cash cow" Monsignor Harte was milking. "Nothing succeeds like success" was a saying of my father's, and in my case the apparent success of the shrine and the benefactors it had attracted had given rise to the false notion that somehow or other Catholic tourists had bottomless pockets for money storage!

Our shrine committee's presentation at the aforementioned hearing had been ignored. It was clear to me nobody at the diocesan level understood our predicament or indeed how the shrine had come to be. The project was one of a kind, financed by visitors who had come to Orlando. These were people of deep faith, but they were also involved in their own parishes back home. On a number of occasions, I had received letters from benefactors telling me they were sorry they would have to drop out of their support for our project because they were now involved in a local parish endeavor.

There was no way I could be assured or assure anyone else that we could repay our roof debt or any other mortgage in three years, and I greatly regretted that our relationship with the commercial bank had been ended. That would have permitted us many years in which to clear our debts. It was a frantic time for me—a time during which I felt abandoned by those who should have been helping me.

It was the fall of 2004. I was back at work. My illness had been a reminder of my own frailty, but it had also been an occasion of faith. My sudden recovery from fibrillation had been for me an intimate touch of God's hand. There was work still to be done, and I felt it was important for me to complete the commitments I had made to so many people.

It was a lonely time, and our shrine committee understood. However, they weren't there to face the phone calls and the complaining letters from the diocesan finance offices. Christmas was the peak time of the year for fund-raising, and it was not far away. As the weeks went by, I settled into writing to our benefactors, informing them about progress at their shrine as well as of my own recovery from heart problems.

Then it was Christmas week. Approximately four days before the celebration of the Savior's birth, I was in my office with literally hundreds of mail responses lying on my desk and on the floor all around. I always tried to communicate personally. Hundreds of people were coming to see the manger scene in the day chapel. Many would ask to talk with me, and I made it a point to accommodate them if at all possible.

I had just reentered my office, having visited with a very happy benefactor in the narthex, when my executive secretary knocked on my door. She was carrying a document in her hand. It was a fax message from our diocesan financial offices. It had apparently been previously sent by e-mail but had been returned for lack of a proper address. And so it had simply been downloaded and faxed to me. It didn't take long to note that copies had been sent to three or four other diocesan officials, including our bishop. In handing it to me, my secretary apologized that she had to disturb me with this kind of dispatch three or four days before Christmas when, as she put it, I had "more important things to take care of."

The message from the diocesan office was curt and to the point: *From which account did I wish them to take the monies the shrine owed the diocese?* It didn't matter that we had been paying on the loan, it didn't matter that the three years previously afforded us were not nearly up. It didn't matter that I had returned to work following serious heart surgery just a short time previously. And it didn't matter that, for all of us working at the shrine, this was the busiest time of the year. The whole thing resounded like a hand grenade thrown into my office, coming at a time when lovers of Mary's Shrine were mailing in their gifts to help promote the ministry and making the kind of sacrifices that keep the entire church active in its spreading the Gospel.

It would be impossible for me to describe my feelings at that moment. Here I was, needing to send out letters of gratitude for donations received, letters from benefactors strewn all around me—and a hand grenade was being thrown at me to tell me to hurry up and meet the very responsibilities I was trying to care for.

Perhaps I should have been more virtuous than to allow myself to be so disturbed. But I can tell you now, years later, that I have no apologies to offer for my instant response. I could argue about the state of my health following my heart surgery, but I won't. I must testify that so many years later I am still disturbed by this correspondence that conveyed arrogance toward me personally and an ignorance of the shrine ministry that goes unparalleled in all my relationships with diocesan officials. I am glad of my response.

I felt it was important to respond there and then. I think it was Winston Churchill who once said there are times when it is good to hit when the iron is hot, that there are times when stupidity needs to be met head on. There was no need for this letter on the brink of Christmas. The news it conveyed was that nobody at diocesan financial level believed anything I had told them or written over the previous several months. I wasn't to be trusted, despite the fact that the shrine was already being used for diocesan functions, replacing the cathedral for many events. I was the representative of the bishop in this ministry and this is how I was being regarded?

No diocesan funds had been sacrificed for the building of the shrine. Since 1975, I had been working to bring God's plan to the Catholics of the world here in Orlando. I had been given the task by a bishop. Through God's grace, we had succeeded admirably. Bishop Grady had once told me that if I ever needed help from the Diocese it would be there for me. I never needed that help and of course Bishop Grady was no longer around. There were thousands of people throughout the country who trusted me with monetary gifts large and small. Some of those gifts were on my desk or on the floor of my office at this very moment. But the diocesan officials did not trust me, for reasons known only to them. Worse still, they had resisted discussing the situation with me while it was clear they were discussing it with others. And now this. Merry Christmas, Monsignor Harte!

In my instant response I expressed my surprise at their lack of professionalism. At first they had sent an e-mail to a wrong address, and then sent a fax to a business office of the shrine when that failed—a fax I might add that any worker could read—and with copies to other people. This was a bank? Was our business being discussed with all and sundry? I was very frank in telling the writer I wasn't sure who was working for whom! Was I working for him, or was he working on my behalf? And of course I gave no permission to withdraw funds from any account. In my prayer time that evening, I remembered those persons who were destroying my Christmas and testing my determination to continue to raise funds for God's work.

How did the matter end? Possibly it never did! The gentleman to whom I had written responded shortly after Christmas. Naturally, he didn't like my letter. I hadn't thought he would. We were in the Season of Love, and I wasn't about to be drawn further into animosities. But any kind of friendly relationship with those people was ended for me. They never understood the workings of fund-raising for the shrine. It seemed they didn't want to understand, and further efforts to illuminate them would be pointless. Meanwhile, for me, God's work had to continue.

Chapter Sixty-Six:
Summoning Bells

The installation of the bronze portals completed the outside appearance of the shrine. There was some work to be done still to perfect the dream. The hanging of the bells was one such chore.

The bells had been subscribed to many years previously by a dedicated benefactor from the state of Maine. He had been an early and ardent supporter of the building of a Marian Shrine in Orlando. He had given a substantial gift, specifically toward the bell tower and the bells. Like many older Catholics he reflected back to Sunday mornings when the church bells summoned people to Mass and announced it was but a short time until Mass would begin. We had exchanged stories many years ago about the old days and the call of the church bells.

I had told him the story of my Sunday mornings as an altar boy in the parish of Kilfian when the priest would ask us to go "pull the bell." What he meant was "Go pull the rope." There were normally two of us altar boys, and since we both coveted the chore of ringing the big bell in its own contraption outside the church, we would position ourselves so that, when the order came, we raced the hundred yards or so to the spot. It was first man there wins, and no sharing!

Those were days when almost the entire congregation came on foot or bicycle, and people took time to chat and greet each other both before and after Church. Somehow or other I think I felt great power over those people when I pulled that rope and the bell clanged! With the sound, those who had remained outside the church for their weekly chat began to head inside in a concerted movement toward the church doors. Ringing the summoning bell was an important and enjoyable part of serving Mass. To me at that time, the church bell was just as important a feature of the church as the spire or any other architectural attachment!

Perhaps I was not so far wrong either. After all, the "hunchback of Notre Dame" lived in the bell tower. He loved his job too! Going back into antiquity, church bells probably arrived on the scene some time around the Middle Ages. They were a means of communication between the clergy and the faithful, the chiming of bells reminding the village that something sacred was happening or about to happen.

I was twelve yeas old before I heard the clanging of funeral bells when I first attended secondary school. A student had died, and the slow and plaintive sound of just one single bell being rung at intervals of half a minute or so during the funeral procession to the cemetery somehow brought home the reality that we had lost a companion and that we should take time to pray for his soul—even now, as the bell clanged. It gave reality to John Donne's writing, that piece of literature made even more famous by Ernest Hemingway. Donne had written, "Any man's death diminishes me, because I am involved in mankind: and therefore never send to know for whom the bell tolls: it tolls for thee."

It is interesting to note also that bells were rung when a bride and groom were leaving the church. Originally, this was a variation of bells from large to small, creating a joyful noise. Hence the frequent depiction of bells on wedding invitations. Today, of course, things have changed. Working hours vary; people sleep at wide-ranging times and don't want to be disturbed by any noise. And of course there are nonbelievers ready to protest at any would-be godly sound at all! Gone too are the days when a funeral was an occasion for the entire village, and anyway people today are not all that interested in reflecting on the diminishment of death.

Those memories and thoughts were driving our discussions on that morning years ago. My friend felt that he wanted to be take part in the call to worship. He would have been even happier had he known that a business mall would be developed right next to the shrine bell tower, allowing the bells to remind shoppers of the presence of the Lord.

That was a long time before the installation of the bells. He didn't live to see or hear them in action. When they were put in place, he was already home with God. But with the end of this main part of the project in sight, it was time to hang the bells. He is in heaven, I am sure, but his gift to Mary's Shrine serves to remind visiting faithful of the glory of their faith as well as offering an invitation to come and be a part of Eucharistic worship every day of the year.

Early in the campaign for the shrine, I had hoped to have carillons, but this turned out to be an impractical plan, or one might say "an impossible dream," and so we settled for the regular church bells. This plan fell into place very easily while the bronze doors were being crafted in Forte dei Marmi in Italy. GianCarlo Biaggi had come across a bellmaker in northeast Italy, and so one morning while visiting GianCarlo's home place, we took off to find him. We knew where we were going—more or less. At one juncture of our travels we made a right turn and saw a notice in large red letters that read something like "Stop. Ski Lift starts here. Road Ends. Danger." Eventually we found the little town we sought hidden in the heart of the hills with a bell tower reaching skyward. It was the tower of the manufacturers, not that of the local church, and having spotted it, all we had to do was keep driving until we got there. It didn't take long to strike a deal for the three bells, and indeed I was very satisfied with the financial arrangement reached.

The bells duly arrived in Orlando. Obviously they would need an electrical apparatus to make them ring, and getting wires to the top of a bell tower was a costly business. The apparatus would require a platform on which to house the mechanism. Getting "wired" for the bells and hanging them would eventually cost a lot more than the bells themselves.

While in one of the towns of northern Italy, I had seen new bells on display. They had been ordered for a monument in the town, and before installing them the local authorities had made them available for viewing so that the townspeople and others could see them up close and examine them. How often does one have the opportunity of a close-up examination of a bell that will hang from a tower? How many years will that bell be up there? The idea was obviously attractive to people, and many were making donations in the donation box nearby toward hanging the bells. The idea was so good, I contributed myself.

So while we awaited the preparatory work for hanging the bells, we decided to place them in the narthex of the church for all to see. And of course we also remembered the donation box. It was extraordinary how many people took time to examine the bells—a good 90 percent of those entering the shrine, I would guess! And many who have come back later have commented how small they look now in comparison to their size on the ground.

So many contributions were made toward the bells that we had no fear of the expense of hanging them. But we did need to rent a crane for a day in order to raise the heavy bells almost eighty feet off the ground. In time the work was finished, and each Sunday the bells announce that there is five minutes to Mass time. They do double duty at daily Mass. At noon they announce the angelus while at the same time telling massgoers they have only five minutes to get into church. The sound of those bells encompasses the traditions of the ages: summoning people to God, reminding them of His presence, and calling them to prayer. We hope they will perform their functions at Mary's Shrine for centuries to come.

Chapter Sixty-Seven:
Traditions Passed On

There is or was a church furnishings repair shop in Dublin, managed by a dedicated artisan named Sean, the like of whom is probably difficult to find in the world today. I really have no recollection of how I found Sean or his business. It was sometime in the 1980s, and most likely I was coming out of the Jesuit church in Gardiner Street when I saw the sign and went in to see the operation. Those were the years before the throwaway society had fully established itself. Churches would send articles for repair to Sean, and in time he would restore them to their original state. Sometimes too he might swap the article for some other object that caught the fancy of the client.

Sean and I became friends, and for quite a number of years I would visit his workshop, not only to chat but also to see what hidden jewels were awaiting discovery somewhere among his souvenirs. I found more than one.

Sean had a chest in which he placed articles to be worked on later—if ever. They might have been swapped or perhaps abandoned by some church or other. They either awaited redemption or consignment to the great vacuum that said their purpose was finished. I did some investigation of the chest on one of my visits and brought out an old chalice, blackened with the passage of time and lack of care. It seemed to me that if polished it might look attractive.

On the bottom I found an inscription that said the chalice had been presented to the bishop of Limerick in the mid-1800s. That would have been around the time of the Great Famine in Ireland. Even though the future museum planned for the shrine was still only a dream, I felt I was holding in my hand something that reflected faith and history. This chalice announced that even in those dark days people loved their Church and their faith, and here was testimony to a faith that would survive through tragedy and the shackles of depression and desperation. Designed to hold the blood of the Savior, this chalice was held aloft so that congregations in generations past could give witness to their belief in the redemptive act of Jesus on Calvary and their firm assent to it. Here was something worth retrieving.

I asked Sean about the cost. We had no problem arriving at a fair price, and the chalice found itself in the New World, on a new mission, a few weeks later. A chalice and I!—each thousands of miles away from our birthplace beyond the ocean, each in a land seemingly not destined for us in earlier years, and each testifying to the glory of the Blood of Christ. Today that chalice is among the artifacts in the museum at Mary's Shrine in Orlando, and the attendant there relates its story to the many who come to be rejuvenated in the faith of our fathers

The museum was opened on December 8, 1999. It had been part of our plan of evangelization: like all museums, a reminder of the past but also an inspiration for the present. The objective of the museum was to breed a sense of pride in the viewer—a pride in belonging to the same Church that had used those antiques in bringing people to the knowledge and love of Jesus Christ. Bishop Dorsey blessed the museum, praying for those who would visit and asking God to constantly watch over them. Even though we were getting close to Christmas, about four hundred persons from throughout the United States traveled to be present at the ceremonies and the celebration dinner that followed.

Within the museum is a relic of a bone of Saint Desiderius, a French martyr from the mid–sixth century. Desiderius was a courageous bishop who spoke vehemently against the immoralities of the reigning monarch, Queen Brunhildis, and her court. The queen's grandson came to her defense and arranged that the bishop be murdered while in custody on false charges that had been brought against him. Ben Stadelmaier of Nijmegen in Holland had come across the relic in its relatively large container and had provided it for display at the shrine museum.

On the day of the museum dedication, the *Orlando Sentinel* carried a centerfold story of the museum, with special reference to the reliquary. A few days later I received three pages of names to be remembered in prayer with a special petition that I pray before the reliquary and mention all the names. The letter was phrased something like the following—"I am not a Catholic, but I am a Christian, and I too would like to have my friends and myself prayed for before the relic of such a wonderful person of God." Sometimes I think we Catholics take the handed-down gifts of our tradition for granted. As is noted at the museum, relics are not magical instruments but simply reminders to seek the intercession of the particular saint before the throne of God. Every prayer we make is truly a prayer to God Most High.

The centerpiece of the museum is a painting by Murillo of the Assumption of Our Lady into heaven, although some sources call it a painting of the Immaculate Conception. Here again there is a story. Missionaries coming to this country in early times always brought with them a replica of the Mother of God. Their mission and ministry were dedicated to her. This painting was brought by the Marist Fathers, and a few members of this Society had served at the shrine in its infancy. Their congregation decided there was no better place in which to display it than at Mary's Shrine in Orlando.

From this snippet of history we gleam the dedication of European missionaries coming to the New World and their confidence that the mother of God would assist them in the proclamation of the kingdom of her Divine Son. It would have gladdened their hearts if they might have known that one day the American bishops would place the United States under the patronage of Mary Immaculate. Perhaps that early devotion too may have helped to instill the wonderful love for the Mother of God that is borne in the hearts of American Catholics.

From Sean's workshop in Dublin came a second item of historical importance. We were just moved into our first temporary church building. Over in a corner at Sean's I saw an old candelabrum. It held about twenty candles, and it surely brought back memories of my mother, who could never leave a church without first lighting a candle. She didn't want only to pray! She also wanted to leave her prayers to continue to be represented in the burning candle! On the front was a brass image of the Sacred Heart of Jesus. Sean couldn't remember where the piece had come from, but I envisioned that it had been the promoter of many prayers. I was aware that our Catholic people like to light candles and leave their prayer ascending to God when they depart the church. And wasn't the Sacred Heart picture in our kitchen among my earliest introductions to the humanity of Jesus? Mary's Shrine in Orlando, I decided, must provide the same opportunity for its visitors.

Weeks later I drove to Orlando International Airport to pick up the candelabrum and bring it home in the trunk of my car. We placed it in the temporary church, and there it remained for five years until masses were moved to the main shrine church that meanwhile had been completed. In the church it was placed at the mosaic of Our Lady of Guadalupe.

Permit me to digress a while from the candelabrum, although the story I write is still very much related to the lighting of candles. One of my nieces married shortly after Christmas. While back in Ireland for the wedding, I took time to go around the city churches, visiting the Nativity scenes. One in particular struck my fancy. It was a "walk-in." It had been built so that the visitor could actually enter the stable and pray under the same roof that shielded the Infant Jesus.

After I had returned, I proposed the idea to our shrine committee. Would it be feasible to turn the weekday chapel into one large stable for the Christmas period? The idea was approved, and the following Christmas saw a Nativity scene at the shrine that has been repeated every Christmas since. Many staff members got to work, unscrewing the pews from the floor, removing them to storage for the time being, and building an unrivaled crèche scene. The scene included many bales of hay on which people could sit while on their visit, and of course hay was strewn all over the crèche floor too. It is very likely that this was the only time in their lives when numberless people had the opportunity to sit on a bale of hay and transport themselves in spirit to the Bethlehem birthplace of the Lord. A remarkable facet of this work is the enthusiasm with which the shrine workers went about their tasks year after year.

Now we had a problem! Very obviously the candelabrum before the Guadalupe mosaic would have to be removed. Open flames and hay do not go together. We moved the candelabrum away from the crèche and placed it at the furthest wall across the narthex of the church, where there would be no danger of fire.

The first Sunday it was there, all the candles were burning. Many people came asking if there might be another candleabrum somewhere within the shrine. We quickly enquired with a church supply company, and two more candelabra were shortly in place. And it didn't end there! In time all the candelabra now in the shrine today had been installed, and had we the room, we probably would have obtained more! Then at a committee meeting, one of our architects suggested placing a brass backing on the candelabra so they would reflect a glow—the light of Christ—to those entering the church. In time that was done too.

Later, favorite saints were chosen—Saint Anthony, Saint Jude, Saint Theresa of Lisieux, Saint Francis of Assisi, and Saint Raphael. Jill Burkee, the carver of the statue of Mary Queen, then created bronze plaques of those saints to hang over the candelabra. Benefactors were quickly on hand to underwrite the costs. The original candelabrum never returned to the day chapel. It is to be found just opposite the Brian Hanlon artwork of the Sorrowful Mother. Most people will associate with the above mentioned saints, except perhaps Saint Raphael, the archangel. Did you know he is the patron saint of travelers? For further information read the short book of Tobit in the Old Testament.

In both of these items tradition comes to the fore. In many Catholic churches today, the practice of lighting votive candles has almost disappeared. Many new churches are carpeted, and the candle creates a danger of fire. From my experience at the shrine I would encourage providing a place for votive lights in every church, if at all possible. Not having the opportunity denies the faithful the satisfaction of leaving a prayer to be continuously offered to the Lord during the duration of the candle's life. While we give up on our votive candles, many department stores are offering votive candles for purchase. This is surely an indication of the desire of the faithful to express their innermost devotional feelings in a more prolonged prayer than they have time to offer. I remember, of course, the little red lamp that always glowed under the picture of the Sacred Heart in our kitchen as a child. I am sure the Lord remembers too.

It could be argued there is nothing in scripture about glowing lamps or candles. But we are a church finding our roots in scripture and tradition. The lighting of candles goes back a long way in our Catholic faith. The candles burning on our altars at Mass remind us of the Light of Christ that we pray will enlighten us and all peoples. When the Mother of God carried the baby into the temple at the presentation, she was carrying the Light of the world in her arms. How we long for that Light in our hearts.

Votive candles remind us of our true desire for the kingdom of God. If we think of it, they bring us back to our baptism, in which the baptizing celebrant always reminds the candidate that "you have been enlightened by Christ. Walk always as a child of the light, and keep the flame of faith alive in your heart." We may not always remember it, but we are Christ's light to the world!

It was not unusual while I was at the shrine that someone would come to me after Mass asking for "permission" to light a candle "because I am not Catholic." I particularly remember a group of high school students who attended a Sunday Mass. They were friendly and delighted to be at the shrine. Quite a number of them were not Catholic. When they saw their Catholic companions go over to the votive light stands, two of them came to me and asked if they might light a candle too. Christ's light shines everywhere, and it is indeed the longing of many hearts!

The tradition of the Christmas crèche goes back a long way in Catholic history too, to the time of Saint Francis of Assisi. That's more than eight hundred years. I don't know what the regulations of Francis were regarding the crèche. His motive was to promote a devotion to the Infant Lord and Incarnate God and help keep alive the circumstances surrounding His birth in poverty. My mother loved the crèche, and there was something poignant about her coffin lying beside the crèche at her funeral Mass. And I have great memories of her sending me—aged about six—and my older sister on the bus to Ballina Cathedral so that I might be able to see the big crèche that was always in place there at the Christmas season.

As I reflect on the enthusiasm of our shrine workers in erecting the crèche every year, through laborious work and giving of themselves in extra measure, I cannot but reflect on the desire for the divine Infant that surely rests in the heart of every faithful Christian. Sometimes liturgists make regulations, and sometimes regulations by non-liturgists are attributed to liturgists. Mary's Shrine in Orlando is host to visitors from all over the world. The crèche was always installed in early December. There were always the few who protested—either that the crèche was on display at all or else that the baby was "too early" in the crib scene, that He should not be placed there until midnight Mass.

The shrine is not a parish church. Those who visit may be back again or may never be back. I found that visitors were always enthralled with the shrine crèche, taking photographs aplenty. The old saying that "Jesus is the reason for the season" certainly applies here. Perhaps in a parish it is fine to leave the baby out until Christmas Day. But visitors to the shrine were always excited by the opportunity to share with their family and friends their photographs of the crèche with a complete Nativity scene for all to enjoy. Christ longs to be born in the heart of every Christian every day!

Previously in this chapter I referred to the Brian Hanlon sculpture in the narthex. It could be said that, as in the case of the Sacred Heart statue, the statue of the Sorrowful Mother came into the shrine through the devotion of the faithful. When the shrine first opened, there were niches ready to receive statues. We all knew it would be a while before the statues would arrive, and at that time no particular statues had been designated.

In a short time, a very beautiful painting of the Sorrowful Mother found its way to our art collection. The museum was not yet open, so it was decided to place the painting in a niche within the narthex. That painting drew a lot of attention, and many stood and prayed before it on their visits to the shrine. It remained there until the museum opened and provided a place in which to exhibit it. But not without protest! Its departure brought regrets and questions from many people.

Then and there at a committee meeting it was decided to procure a statue of the Sorrowful Mother to be placed in the vacated niche. By a strange coincidence, Brian Hanlon came to Mass at the shrine very shortly afterward and enquired if he might become involved in any way in the artwork. He received the commission for the statue. With the statue, as with the many other pieces of religious art at the shrine, it is extraordinary and spiritually elevating to watch the personal devotion of the many who take time to pray unreservedly before their favorite object of devotion.

The Second Council of Nicea still contributes to the spirituality of the Church after all those centuries since it first met. That was the Council that approved the veneration of sacred images as reminders of our relationship to the God of Love. And you can find a reminder of that Second Council in one of the shrine windows depicting the seven most important councils of the Church. Our lives are interwoven with the Divine.

Chapter Sixty-Eight:
The Rose Window

The great church edifices of Europe are all adorned with magnificent rose windows. The custom developed during the French Gothic period. The first rose window is thought to have arrived on the scene in the early thirteenth century. The window was intended to represent the focal point of the church, its shapes and variety of colors calling for the attention of the faithful.

Previously, popes had called for the instruction of the faithful through whatever artwork could be placed within the church. A magnificent example of this sort of directive is to be found in the Cathedral of Monreale in Sicily where the entire church floor, walls, and ceilings are covered in mosaics that tell the Gospel story in a very vivid fashion. Mosaic art, of course, came long before stained-glass art, but with the arrival of stained glass, the artistic evangelizers turned to the development of windows that narrated Gospel truths.

In keeping with Church traditions, we had always planned for a rose window. The original architectural plan called for two, one at either end of the church, but in time this was found to be an architectural impossibility if the design plan was followed. Hence, the committee focused entirely on the rose window that now sits gloriously high above the main entrance portals.

This is a large window, much larger than appears from the ground beneath. Creating it entailed the use of a great deal of glass and quite a number of artists working together at the Studios of Domus Dei in Rome.

The window took more than a year to complete and entailed my going to Rome with directives from our committee on four separate occasions. However, I think that once you view the window, you will agree that the work that went into it was well worth the effort. I might add here that the best time and place to view the rose window is early in the day, standing in front of the tabernacle of the main shrine church when the morning sun rushes eagerly through the multicolored glass, creating a prism of splendor for the eye that is akin to experiencing a stunning celestial exhibition of morning glory that must surely have taken place on the first Easter Sunday.

The window is not, however, directly related to Resurrection. Rather it portrays the teaching of Jesus to His apostles on the night before He died, when He said, "I am the vine and you are the branches." In our discussions on the subject matter of the window, a variety of suggestions came up, including having the Lord and His Mother as centerpieces. As the discussion continued, however, and it was the time after Easter, thoughts of the Gospels of the day began to assert themselves. One thought particularly, "the vine and the branches," struck home, and since the entire purpose of the shrine project is aimed at bringing believers closer to Christ, it was decided that this would be the theme of the window.

In His final address to His followers, Jesus could not have chosen a more illustrative example of His closeness to His flock. The sap that runs through the trunk of the tree also extends itself to the branches. As the great Cyril of Alexandria points out in one of his writings, "Like branches growing from the vine we now draw our life from Christ and we cling to His holy commandment in order to preserve this life." In viewing the window, the crown at the center represents the Godhead; the vine, with its many branches extending throughout the window, depicts the unity we enjoy with the risen Lord and the graces won for us, graces that flow constantly into our souls and maintain our oneness with the Savior.

The rose window was by far the most costly of all windows installed at the shrine. The large circle contained regular glass for many years. Occasionally, there were inquiries about the window, but the costs involved caused many an inquirer to beat a hasty retreat! Then one morning, many years after the opening of the new shrine church, a very lovely lady and her daughter came to see me. I had never met her before, and when she told me she would be interested in a memorial at the shrine, I began as was my custom at the lower end. The lady's reply has remained in my memory: "I'd like something a little higher."

After I had listed the normal memorials, I suddenly realized here was a lady who wished for something really special to commemorate her recently deceased husband. I invited her and her daughter to come with me into the narthex, where I explained the possibilities of the rose window. There was little explaining to do! Mother and daughter agreed that they wanted the window.

I narrate the story—which echoes the commissioning of the very first stained-glass window, previously related—because sometimes I am asked how I found all those people who contributed large donations to Mary's Shrine. The fact is I did not find them. They found me! They came to Mass in celebration of their faith and left something of themselves to help others celebrate their faith too.

Did the Lord and His Mother send them? Of course! Many had been on our mailing lists, were acquainted with the ministry, and—believing in its future success—decided to become further involved. Others, like these latter good ladies, apparently knew of the work, and their inner spirits directed them to assist a ministry that had the Mother of God as its patroness. The memorial plaque for this window is located just inside the main doors, to the right as you enter. As with all the other memorials it stands as a testimony to faith and the desire of God's special people to help in promoting His kingdom.

Chapter Sixty-Nine:
Catholic Devotion

here is a stained glass window within the shrine church that portrays our American Saint, Elizabeth Seaton. She once wrote to her Sisters, "Let your chief study be to acquaint yourself with God, because it is the only knowledge which can fill the heart with a peace and joy which nothing can disturb." She wanted her Sisters to be fully attuned with the things of God. From the relationship love grows and with it a feeling of peace and security in the heart of the believer. That feeling tends to govern our lives. We become more zealous for the spread of His kingdom.

In the narthex at Mary's Shrine is a statue of the Sacred Heart. As with the signature statue of Mary, Queen of the Universe, it is sculpted from Carrara marble and comes from the same quarry as the marble for the Queen. An Italian artist, GianCarlo Biaggi, was the carver. The statue stands by the entryway to the day chapel. Jesus stands with hands extended, not pointing to His heart as in the more traditional representation but as in a welcoming and invitational gesture of "Come to me." It is not unusual to see persons in prayer before this statue holding the hands of the Lord as they make their petition.

There is a story too on how this statue came to be. I think you will agree it is strongly related to Catholic devotion. Perhaps the Lord was reminding me I had been forgetful. Did He not make me aware of His presence in younger days when his picture hung on the wall with the little red votive lamp underneath? Throughout my life I had recited the Litany of the Sacred Heart every day in my morning prayer. Our home parish church at Kilfian in Ireland was named for the Sacred Heart. And could I have forgotten "the miracle of the football"?

A couple was on vacation in France and went to see the stained glass at the Chartres Cathedral. While there, they came across an old, dilapidated statue the Sacred Heart. That statue had stood there, unrepaired for God knows how long! I had seen it myself on my visits to Chartres. Like the artifacts at Sean's in Dublin, it seemed to have completed its mission. It wasn't attractive anymore, and pieces had been broken from the torso of the Lord. It had become so unimportant as to apparently stand unnoticed even by those who administered the Cathedral! But there was one more thing for it to do: it would inspire a representation of the Sacred Heart in Orlando.

The couple, familiar with our Orlando shrine, remarked to each other about the neglected state of the statue. It upset them. Their own devotion to the Sacred Heart prompted the desire for a more appropriate statue. When they discussed it, they decided to offer to support the procurement of a statue of the Sacred Heart for the shrine. On their next visit, they sought me out and asked if their dream might be a possibility. As they spoke, many thoughts were running through my head, not the least being that the Sacred Heart Himself had come to me through these good people. They were His emissaries. Our shrine committee discussed the matter, and commissioned GianCarlo Biaggi to do the work. A year or so thereafter the statue was put in place. One might say it was the result of the kind of devotion Elizabeth Seton had fostered and a vessel of that peace and joy about which she had written.

The day chapel at the shrine has a threefold title. It is referred to simply as "the day chapel" but also the Chapel of Our Lady of Guadalupe or the Universe Chapel. The latter title comes from the artful blue windows created by the Kentucky artist Ken VonRoenn. VonRoenn was also the artist who created the crystal-glass windows from the narthex into the church. Originally an architect, he followed his heart into a different vocation, the production of magnificent glass doors and windows.

To produce the blue windows in the shrine chapel, he first took photos of the stars and constellations in the night sky. He then transferred the negatives into the glass windows, bringing about a feeling of looking into the cosmos. We are God's creatures, and since God has created everything, we all belong to Him and are within His net. This netting is plainly visible across the windows, echoing the miracle of the taking of the huge catch of fish the apostles achieved at the command of Jesus in the Gospel of Saint Luke, chapter 5. "I will make you fishers of men," Jesus had promised Peter. In this window all of creation comes under the jurisdiction of an all-loving God.

This Universe Chapel does not have a tabernacle or retain the Blessed Sacrament. Its sacred space is used for daily Mass only and for liturgies with smaller attendances. People are to be found frequently praying there despite the nonavailability of the Real Presence. On one occasion, when one of our clergy saw a lady deeply engrossed in meditation, he thought to remind her that the Blessed Sacrament was not present. Her answer was revealing: "I know," she said, "but I come here about once a month just to sit here and pray, and as I look at those blue windows, all my troubles just melt away." Surely a nice complement to the artist and to the space he helped create.

Within the chapel also is the mosaic of Our Lady of Guadalupe. Since this shrine of Mary is located in the southernmost part of the country, the committee and I wanted to have a representation of our Guadalupe, "Queen of the Americas." Space was left for this artwork in the preparatory design of the shrine.

I spoke to Bishop Grady about our plans. He was fully supportive, not giving any direct command but simply reflecting on his own ideas. This was the same bishop who, in his younger days, had been instrumental in completing the Basilica of the National Shrine of the Immaculate Conception in Washington DC. There he had attended many a brainstorming meeting himself where he had developed the art of listening. His own philosophy was similar to that of Thomas Jefferson, whom he quoted more than once: "He rules best who rules least." On the occasion of our discussion as to how to present Our Lady of Guadalupe, Bishop Grady gave no directive, but something he said stayed with me. "The image was imprinted on a *tilma*," he said—that is, on an Aztec cloak—"and to reproduce it in a mosaic might be the thing to do." I left his office knowing how we would proceed.

In due course, we did indeed have a benefactor, and the work was completed by a firm in Rome, Domus Dei. While the work was being done, I visited their studios and got to see the tedium with which the artist has to work. One little piece of glass after another has to be gently put in place and cemented to the previous pieces. Thousands of glass pieces are assembled in similar fashion until the picture is completed. All of this is done by one single artist working alone. (It is well to remember, as previously stated, that the work of mosaic art had its beginnings early in the fourth century or perhaps earlier). Later on, in the mid-nineties, the pieces now ready for installation were delivered to the Shrine. Then we ran into an unforeseen problem.

I well remember the occasion. The pieces were heavy. Contrary to what we had expected, there was no way of getting them safely into place. To make things worse, the Italian worker who came with them could not speak a word of English, and nobody at the Shrine could speak a word of Italian. The worker saw the problem, we saw the problem, but we couldn't communicate.

But the Lady of Guadalupe herself was smiling over us! Fifteen minutes or so into the crisis, an Italian priest, FatherAl Manni, walked in. We didn't even know he was in the country, as he had been stationed near Milan for several years. He was in the Salesian house in Tampa for a short vacation, and he had decided to come see what was happening at the Shrine. (He had been very much a part of our early ministry to tourists and had proclaimed the future Shrine to massgoers with enthusiastic fervor for several years). We surely needed him now for what was happening at the Shrine.

He conversed easily with the Italian worker, and we quickly learned it would be necessary to ask our building contractor to help us out. Next day four men arrived, ready to take on the task. Suffice it to say that four days later the mosaics were in place, ready for safe viewing by the public. It turned out there was much more work involved than anyone had foreseen. One man had to work in a cavern within the wall itself! When the work was completed, he was cut from within the structure, and the gap caused by his retrieval was then closed with drywall.

Our Lady of Guadalupe is very dear to the hearts of the faithful from the southern hemisphere. I was to learn much about their devotion in the years that followed. For one thing I noted that visitors from "the South" always made a beeline for the Guadalupe image and spent time praying before it. The apparition itself was extraordinarily remarkable in that it brought about the conversion of somewhere between nine and fourteen million Aztecs in Mexico. People who had been involved in human sacrifice and worship of a variety of deities left their primitive beliefs behind in favor of Christianity. And the Shrine of Our Lady of Guadalupe was to become the second most visited shrine of Our Lady in the world. Reading through the history of the apparition, one can see similar comparisons with alleged apparitions in modern times. Even after a bishop had approved the genuineness of the event, a local Franciscan friar denounced it as being farcical and false.

The mosaic was not long in place when World Cup soccer games were scheduled for Orlando. And hereby hangs a tale of woe! The Republic of Ireland had defeated much-fancied Italy and were scheduled to play Mexico in Orlando, on a never-to-be-forgotten date (June 24, 1994)—never to be forgotten perhaps for the wrong reasons! Naturally, every sporting Irish person in Florida was thrilled at the prospect of watching the Ireland team right here in sunny Florida. Irish "natives" of Florida were proud of their team, and we were greatly offended when the local sheriff made some derogatory remarks about Irish supporters in the days leading up to the game. The sheriff was made aware of our anger too. It was a memorable time.

The teams were lodged in hotels distant from each other, with the Mexico team much closer to Mary's Shrine. On the day before the game, a number of the Mexican team visited the shrine, prayed before the mosaic of Our Lady of Guadalupe, and asked the priest on duty for his blessing. The priest, Father Willie Boyle, was an Irishman himself and joked with the players about a "blessing for the enemy," having given them the petitioned blessing.

Next day, Saturday, I had the good fortune to attend the game with Father Willie through the generosity of a good friend who procured the tickets for us. It was a typical Florida day, and temperatures on the field of play flirted with one hundred degrees Fahrenheit. Ireland, playing in what would have to be considered adverse weather conditions, unfortunately lost by the odd goal in three, and we returned home deflated.

Throughout the game, the variety of Mexican banners stood out, not the least frequent among them being a flag bearing the image of Our Lady of Guadalupe. That evening I was scheduled for the 6:00 p.m. Vigil Mass of Sunday. In my customary pre-Mass banter I mentioned this fact, joking that perhaps, if Ireland had a banner of Our Lady of Knock, they might have done better. I soon realized I had discovered a way to offend both the Mexican and Irish followers at Mass, and there were many on both sides. The Irish told me afterward I was hard on them, and one man in particular was quite upset. I had not only offended him, he said, but also the team. "Our players are practicing Catholics too," he said, at the same time indicating that my words made it seem as if they were not! Naturally, I had no such intention, nor had I intended to get into the religious beliefs of the teams in any way, but it was too late to take back what I had said.

On the other hand, a couple of Mexicans who spoke relatively good English told me of their astonishment that I seemed to find it strange that they should be waving a flag of Our Lady at a soccer game. "Don't you know anything about Mexico?" one inquired. The truth was I knew very little. I would find out later that the flag of Our Lady of Guadalupe was almost on a par with the flag of Mexico! In Mexico's war of independence against Spain in 1810, the rebels had marched under the flag of Our Lady of Guadalupe, and there was nothing unusual at all about it being waved about at a soccer game. Our Lady of Guadalupe had become synonymous with Mexican nationality!

The Feast of Our Lady of Guadalupe was first ascribed to December 12 (on which date it is still celebrated) by a Mexican priest who had taken part in the rebellion and later became a member of the new government. The story of the apparition is a heartwarming story. But then, since that first miracle at Cana, the Mother of the Lord has been busy guiding her children to the kingdom of her divine Son, and her intercession as the Lady of Guadalupe and Queen of the Americas has given birth to many wonderful stories indeed. I should have known, of course! Defeat in a World Cup is difficult for any group of supporters. As a Gaelic games fan from County Mayo, I had tasted lots of defeats myself. I should have known better! A sadder and a wiser man I rose the morrow morn.

Chapter Seventy:
Understanding One's Vocation

When 2004 came to an end, I knew it was a year that would remain in my memories; I wouldn't need to consult notes! I had lost my beloved oldest sister, I had undergone quadruple bypass surgery, and I had experienced the "Christmas crisis" that told me of my standing in the financial offices of the diocese. I had spent that Christmas in a haze, but in my prayer life I knew that God was with me.

A priest bears the mark of the priesthood of Christ through his ordination. In ways, it is easy to forget this, with the permanent effort of trying to serve our people as best we can. Christ is the priest's constant companion, and in the life of Christ there is plenty to imitate, especially when things seem to be going wrong.

I have mentioned Saint Paul many times throughout this narrative. One of his great sentences was "Imitate me as I imitate Jesus Christ." Paul was a wonderful example of Christian living, always reminding his readers of how they should live if they bear Christ's name. To the Corinthians, he wrote, "It is no longer I who live, but Christ lives in me." And like Saint Paul the priest is another Christ, called to reflect the Savior to all he serves.

The calling of the priest is to bring his particular gifts and talents to the service of the Lord. Sometimes we don't even know what those talents are, but the Lord develops them in us. Jesus was not beloved of all. Neither will His representative be. Sometimes it is hard to make peace with this. Even those in charge may fault us. At times they may be correct too! It is important to remember our own humanity. There are indeed times when we may be wrong. I have made my mistakes. I have been accused of being "stubbornly Irish" (guilty to a point!) and overheard at a ceremony the statement, "This man never does what he is asked to do." (Not guilty in any way!).

In one way or another a priest must always try to react like Christ Himself and remember the words of Saint Paul to be "an imitator of Christ." The recently canonized Saint Faustinus endured condemnation in her convent, but time has shown that it was those who condemned who were wrong. There are many similar examples in the lives of the saints. In the long run, it all comes back to prayer and our relationship with the Lord.

Throughout the years, I formed the habit of taking special prayer time on Christmas Eve, on New Year's Eve, and on Holy Thursday. On Christmas Eve, I always thank God for my parents, the faith they instilled in me, and the courage they passed on to stand for what is right as well as the social virtues that helped form my personality and my character. I thank God too for the rest of my family, and I always recount the various blessings I have received, not only throughout the year but during my entire life. And sentimentally I reflect on Christmases past and how my faith was nurtured in so many different ways.

New Year's Eve provides an opportunity to reflect on the immediate past and to ask God's blessings on what lies ahead in the coming months. And as on every day of the year, I confide to the Lord and to His Mother all the wonderful people who have helped me in the proclamation of the Gospel. In the Christmas season of 2004, I had plenty to pray about, lots on which to reflect, and plans to make for the coming year at the shrine. I wasn't done yet!

There is a question too about the Passion of Jesus in the life of a priest. The Lord Himself said, "No servant is greater than his master," and He issued the invitation that all who wished to come after Him should take up their cross and follow Him. Celibacy is a cross in itself, and priests learn how to carry that cross. It is a cross we feel we have inherited directly from the Lord—or perhaps a gift we offer to the Lord for the honor of walking with Him.

Personally, I have found that the crosses that come from the situations in which we find ourselves in the course of our work can be much harder to accept, and it is important for every priest to understand that holiness comes with a price. Superiors who make demands beyond the ability of the individual or refuse to listen certainly contribute to the development of holiness. And sometimes they go too far in their demands.

I recall a contemporary seminarian, a man of great faith, who ardently longed for the day of his ordination so that he might be able to go work with the less fortunate and bring Christ to them. Having been ordained, he found he would not be allowed to serve in the very cause for which he had entered the seminary. He later left the priesthood, educated himself as a medical professional, and still works with the impoverished, caring for God's seemingly abandoned people. Most likely this man too had his maligners, but with his departure from the priesthood, a great light went out for the Church. To be able to listen is a great gift, and may our Church leaders, who are normally very aware of their authority, be also filled with the spirit of listening to what is in the hearts of those who represent them in the vineyard of the Lord. The Passion of Christ is lived out in one way or another in every person's life. The priest should not expect to escape what we will later find out was the touch of God's hand helping toward salvation.

An article in the Irish *Sacred Heart Messenger* (August 2007), written by Paul Andrews SJ, touches on this point. His understanding of life's problems for the believer is illustrated here. In the article, he addresses the subject of quiet prayer time, especially where there is a critical situation. Here is what he writes: "But let's face it, if we have the place and the leisure to pray quietly, we are the lucky ones. Most of the time God touches us, not by subliminal messages, but by a wordless touch which can be painful. The Africans have a more realistic perspective when they say: *The Gospels are attractive stories, but the part that matters is the Passion of Jesus. That is what serves us, because most of our life is like that, meaningless suffering. The Gospels are a Passion Story with a long introduction.*"

I was quite upset that Christmas, despite my best efforts at pretending all was well. I had learned too much from the "crisis" incident. Time and again I had to remind myself of the Passion of Jesus. Someone had written that Jesus's priesthood was at its zenith when He was nailed high on the cross. It was a consoling thought. I recalled too the words of the blessed Mother Teresa of Calcutta who once said, "I know God will not give me anything I can't handle. I just wish that God didn't trust me so much."

Indeed, I knew I had to handle my problems. A lot of people were depending on me. I remembered something I had written in "The Way of the Cross," a little publication of mine that had come out some time previously. In reference to Simon of Cyrene helping Jesus, I wrote, "Was it Simon of Cyrene who was helping Jesus, or was it Jesus who was helping Simon of Cyrene?" Whatever help Jesus needed from me was for my own well-being. I wanted to help Him though! And as always, His companionship made my burden lighter.

When the year 2005 began, I had made peace with the problems that were besetting me, and peace too had entered my heart toward those who were causing them. God's work must not be stopped by human fatuity. An anonymous author had written, "Without His love I can do nothing, but with His love there is nothing I cannot do." Another year to work for His kingdom! I recalled the words of the psalmist: "The Lord is my Shepherd; there is nothing I shall want."

Chapter Seventy-One:
One for the Road

nce upon a time, in the far distant past, a couple of persons friendly to our Catholic faith had purchased acreage surrounding our shrine property. Knowing the wife was an ardent Catholic, I wrote them a letter suggesting perhaps they might like to donate a few acres to the shrine. I was much younger at the time, the future shrine church was still only a distant dream, and my energies were at a peak! The vicissitudes of old age were far in the future. I hesitate to give their names because they might not like the publicity.

The couple responded to my letter by asking for a map of our property, something that I duly procured. One of their representatives would be coming through Orlando, and he would pick up the map and take it across the country to them. One Sunday, he attended Mass at Holy Family Church, and I gave him the required document. He was friendly and affable and told me he would get it to its destination, and someone would get back with me. Nobody ever did, and I presumed our request was on the long finger or had been turned down. That was in 1984.

Then many years later I heard that the good man had died suddenly on his journey, and the map's destination was never reached either. We negotiated again, since the property had been sitting there unused. The shrine church itself was now built, and thousands of people were coming there. The property owners were actually in the final stages of completing the sale of the entire lot, and at this time they agreed to donate five acres of their property. I was directed by the owners to go downtown to an attorney's office and choose the five acres—any five acres—I thought would be good for the shrine to own. Accordingly I did so, and knowing the property well and having walked it in years past, I chose what I believed would be most beneficial or our purposes..

Naturally, nothing comes easily! I heard no more for several months, but since a couple of representatives of our diocese were at the meeting, I took it for granted that the usual legal requirements were being gone through and that in time someone would call me. There was no call! Summer passed in its entirety and on to autumn.

Then one morning, I found out through our groundskeeper at the shrine that he believed there were some wagons on our property that were being used as offices for the buildings that were being erected adjacent to us. "Bob," I said, "That's not our property. That's not what I chose."

"I think it is," he replied, "but I'll find out definitely." To my dismay, he found he was correct! A change had been made, deliberately or otherwise I know not, and property I had not chosen now belonged to us.

I was, of course, crestfallen. Half of the new property that had been designated to us was "preserve," meaning it could not be built on without a special permit that would be difficult to obtain. It was also under water, and to build on it would cost more than the bundle we could afford. There was nothing to do but let it sit there for the time being and use it possibly for parking overflows at Christmas and Easter, assuming the ground was dry enough at those times.

Now bear with me, because I am in the middle of a "miracle" story. From a financial point of view, the ground was useless; we didn't have the money to prepare it for use, and if we ever had, would it be worth it? Of course we didn't know that God had His plans too! "O happy fault," Saint Thomas had written about the fall of our first parents. God was induced to become man. And God hasn't changed at all. Neither is anything impossible with God.

Some years before my retirement, I was approached by a gentleman who wanted the property. He would give a million dollars for it. Of course I refused. Five (even wet) acres for that amount would be a giveaway. I stated my price, and he didn't come back—for several months! Then he came again, and again.

I suppose I am a dreamer. I began to dream again. I was not far from retirement. Wouldn't it be wonderful if the individual really gave us the price we had sought? I recall driving in my car and dreaming about it. I felt like the apostles before the resurrection. *Could it be possible this miracle would happen? Jesus had said something about resurrection! Ah, no! Stop fantasizing! But the buyer seems interested, even if he is a far cry from where we want him to be price-wise! Stop your dreaming!*

But it did happen. In the end, we were offered the price we asked. It would not only pay off all shrine mortgages, but it would also allow a nice sum that could be used as an endowment for future shrine projects. Sometime in the future the shrine would be able to offer seminars specially related to the theology of the Mother of God. "The dream" would be completed at my departure from the shrine. And so it came to be! Looking back, I recalled the stress of the new roof. My faith was weaker than it should have been.

Now, I leave it to you, dear reader, to decide where God came into all this. The story is absolutely true, a remarkable testimonial to Divine Providence. "Don't be afraid," Jesus had said! Where His kingdom benefits, He is always at hand to turn the water into wine! That wine was to become His gift of His own blood in the Eucharist. The ministry of the shrine was to bring this Eucharist to thousands of seekers. The Lord was keeping His promise: "I am with you always." And I could go on my way to retirement, reflecting on yet another miracle bestowed on God's work. A seeming error became a handsome benefit for Mary's Shrine! Two and a half acres of wetlands had suddenly become valuable.

I thought of Mary at the wedding of Cana. "Do what He tells you." Well, we had done that. And once again "the water" would become reason for celebration. All mortgages cleared, and something left over for future furtherance of the kingdom. Truly "One for the Road." I could leave at peace with myself. There was an inner smile as I recalled the opposition we had encountered so many years ago when the shrine was proposed. My retirement would be blessed with a miracle! Could even a fiction writer dream up this ending?

Chapter Seventy-Two:
The Rosary Garden

⟶⟵

As part of "the dream," we had always envisioned prayerful surroundings for the future shrine. I had described the dream at a hotel Mass one Sunday morning in the far distant past, and when Mass was over a lady approached me. She was a resident of Miami, a landscape designer, and she told me she was particularly struck by my plan for the rosary garden. When we got that far in carrying out our plans, I was to call her. She was Laura Llerena, and she was to play a major part in what is now the shrine's rosary garden.

When eventually I did call her, she was ready to come on board with her plan, a total gift to Mary's Shrine. Effectively, the plan was for the garden that is at the shrine today. There would be a variety of flowers and plants—mostly native, some annuals—the Stations of the Cross, and a pathway that reflected the fifteen decades of the rosary. (That was long before Pope John Paul II increased the number of decades to twenty.) The pathway would enable the pilgrim to pray the rosary while negotiating the path and enjoying the tranquility of the area. Some very old Florida plants that had established themselves there would not be removed, and the garden would be allowed to retain a natural look. Laura did not want too much manicuring. She wanted the "Florida look" with just a little adornment here and there. Hers was a sage plan in every way. We quickly found that maintenance of annuals, even the small number she had prescribed, was highly costly whereas indigenous Florida plants require little attention.

We had set the date for dedication of the shrine for the Feast of the Queenship of Mary, August 22, 1993. As the day grew closer, it was evident that a concerted effort was needed to get everything completed on time. With a last great drive the work was completed, and finally the manager came to my office to invite me to come see the finished project. It looked nice indeed. He and I walked the rosary path. Everything looked wonderful in our new garden, until I came to the end of the walkway. There were only four decades of the rosary! The fifth was missing! He was unhappy with the bad news, but decided then and there that the problem must be corrected immediately. He got his men to start all over again, remove some of the already placed decades, and make room for a fifth decade. A day later, the job was completed. It was two days before the dedication day.

The rosary garden attracted visitors almost immediately. Some locals made it a place for special visitation, praying and meditating there frequently. The hurricanes of 2004 did severe damage to some of the plants and trees. When I seemed to be dallying—as I dealt with the high cost of restoration—I received more than one inquiry as to how soon we intended to put the garden back in its original shape!

About a year before my retirement, a benefactor left a sum of money to the shrine that his family were glad to put to use for the instillation of the bronze Stations of the Cross. These were also completed in the foundry of Domus Dei in Rome. Their arrival in the rosary garden heralded the completion of a project that had always been in our plans. As the last bronze station was erected, I remembered the good lady from Miami whose dedication had designed the garden and the morning she came to me after a hotel mass so many years ago. Her dream and my hopes were now indeed fulfilled. Today, visitors can pray the rosary within the garden, make the Stations of the Cross, or simply sit in prayerful reflection on one of the many benches provided for the purpose.

The signature statue in the garden is that of Mary, Help of Christians. It is a very old statue, created in cast iron in Paris, France, in the mid-1800s. The statue is reputed to have found its way to Utrecht in the Netherlands, where it sat for many years in a town square, adjacent to a convent. While Holland was occupied by Hitler's forces during World

War Two, the people of the town gathered daily to pray the rosary before this statue. In time, long after the war ended, the convent was closed, and with the advent of more secular times the statue was removed from its long-standing base. It was among the treasures discovered for the shrine by Ben Stadelmaier of Nijmegan. He had it shipped to Orlando, and it was put in place as the main shrine church was being built. It is extraordinary how far faith reaches. The story of Utrecht was completed in Orlando, thousands of miles away!—the same statue, the same faith, the same love for the Blessed Mother of God.

Pope John Paul II died on Saturday, April 2, 2005. I recall offering the Vigil Mass at the shrine on that Saturday evening. The church was almost full, and I have never seen a congregation that was so affected by a death. Many people came into the church crying. When I spoke of his passing and his papacy, hankies were fluttering throughout the church to wipe away tears. After Mass, a young boy of about sixteen tearfully expressed his sorrow that he had not attended the youth assembly in Denver the previous year. The late pope had been there, and the griever expressed his regret for an opportunity lost.

Pope John Paul II had played a personal part in my life too. Thanks mostly to the support of my good friend Cardinal Laghi, I had been afforded the privilege of offering Mass with him on four different occasions within his own chapel. All were memorable occasions, and the first particularly stands out. The Holy Father would receive a few friends with me, and we were to be at the bronze doors of the Vatican at 6:30 a.m. We took a taxi from our hotel through the quiet streets of early-morning Rome and waited patiently with about fifteen other persons for the doors to open. It is hard to describe the feeling as one realizes there is an extraordinary event happening right at that moment. We were conducted into the pope's chapel, and there he was, kneeling before the altar, deep in prayer. Shortly, he would go to the sacristy to vest, and then after we received instructions as to where to stand around him, the Mass began.

I was immediately to the right of the pope at the altar, and a shiver of excitement passed through my body as he turned and extended his hand to me for the sign of peace. This was the Vicar of Christ, his blue eyes seemingly looking through me! After Mass, he inquired about my work and promised to remember in his own daily prayers the development of the shrine and all who would help me. Perhaps the shrine stands as proof that the prayers of a pope are influential with the Lord.

Following my visit, while wending my way from St. Peter's to my hotel, my mind went back to the days when my grandmother explained where the pope lived, but people rarely see him, she had pointed out. Times had changed! Her then six-year-old grandson had just celebrated Mass with the pope, within the papal residence!

Did the Holy Father remember my visit? I think so! Cardinal Laghi would reinforce that belief a number of years later, when he announced publicly that the Holy Father was bestowing the title *monsignor* on me. I would, of course, meet with John Paul II a few more times, all memorable occasions. I feel certain the pope did indeed pray for our ministry and those involved in it, so much so that I pray to him myself. If he could help me on earth, he surely can help me in heaven!

On the evening of the pope's death, a friend called me. He had been aware of my relationship with Pope John Paul II. The pope's promise to pray for benefactors to Mary's Shrine in Orlando had been proclaimed on every shrine offering envelope. "You ought to do something about Pope John Paul II," my friend advised. "Perhaps a bust of the pope in the rosary garden. He was your friend. He was interested in the shrine you were trying to build. He promoted the rosary, and wouldn't it be nice to have his bust somewhere at the entrance to the rosary garden?"

There and then I knew what I had to do. The next day was Sunday morning. I would announce it to the faithful. We would erect a bust of the late pope in the rosary garden. It was the only time in the history of the development of the Shrine that I had acted on my own without consulting my committee. There wasn't time to call a meeting to discuss this attractive idea.

Time proved it was an attractive idea indeed! A major benefactor immediately came forward, himself a member of our shrine committee, to underwrite the project. There were many responses from my appeals at Mass, and through the mailings offerings came quickly too.

A local artist would do the work. She was Loura Dobbs, living in Orlando, though a native of Michigan. I had witnessed her marriage to her husband Gregg and then watched their children grow to adulthood as they attended seemingly every Sunday Mass I had offered since their wedding day! She would donate her time in order to keep expenses down. Her presentation to our committee was quickly accepted, and a few months later the bust of Pope John Paul II graced the rosary garden. It stands on a granite block quarried in the state of Maine.

As with the bricks for the rosary path, there was no easy way of getting the massively heavy slab into the rosary garden. It was eventually lifted by crane and swung over the administration buildings into its place in the garden. Just to make sure, I advised our office workers to vacate their offices and "come and watch" while the slab was being hoisted. It was good for them to see an unusual work in progress, but it also cleared the offices of people just in case of an accident.

And so the bust of a beloved pope—himself a devotee of the rosary—came to welcome all who down through the years might come to commune with God within this rosary garden at Mary's Shrine in Orlando. An inscription on the granite is a summation of Pope John Paul's letter on the rosary—that to pray the rosary is to enter into the mysteries of Christ.

Chapter Seventy-Three:
Ay, Fleeth the Tyme

For thogh we slepe, or wake, or rome, or ryde
Ay, fleeth the tyme, it nyl no man abyde.

—Geoffrey Chaucer

More than three decades had passed since Bishop Grady had assigned me to begin a parish in southwest Orlando that was named Holy Family and to take care of the tourist ministry from this parish. The Lord had sent wonderful faith-filled people into His vineyard with me. Mary's Shrine in Orlando had come of age! The dirt road leading to our project was gone, replaced by a modern tar macadamed street. We had opened the first building in 1986, standing on its own a mile or so from a main road. Now we were on a newly created street with a shopping center next door. A newspaper article about the shopping center told its readers the new center was adjacent to Mary, Queen of the Universe Shrine. The writer assumed his readers knew the location of the shrine. We had indeed become a landmark!

When I read that article, I could not help remembering my many visits distributing information on masses to the hotels, the enthusiasm of our volunteers, and the excitement as each stage of the shrine project came to be planned and eventually completed. They had been busy years and blessed years too.

I recollected our efforts with the local and state authorities for permits to place directional signs on the highway and the apparent animosity with which our applications were treated. At one meeting, state representatives seemed to find what they considered our overly ambitious request somewhat humorous. A few weeks later, I received a letter professing a certain amount of admiration for our determined efforts but at the same time telling me the request for road signs for the shrine would never be granted. "Never" came about six months later! A friend of the shrine brought the matter to the attention of Florida Governor Jeb Bush, and permission for the signs was granted shortly thereafter.

There was still much to be achieved, but time was no longer on my side, and neither was my health. I had reason to be reminded of the words of Chaucer: "Ay, fleeth the tyme." Following my open-heart surgery in July of 2004, I had returned (too soon) to work in early October of that year. Looking back, I now realize things were never the same for me health-wise after the surgery. I had lost some of my earlier initiative. Sadly, the state of my health did not earn any special caring from diocesan authorities. Incidents that previously I would have taken in my stride now created stress. Some of my previous diplomatic assurance had deserted me.

There was now a bigger burden to carry at the shrine too. In January 2006 our bishop included the shrine in a heavy diocesan taxation without consulting with me. This was a first for the shrine, and it imposed a burden that I had neither the initiative nor the ability to carry. Frankly, I could see no way to raise an additional two hundred and sixteen thousand dollars within the year and go through the same effort again and again in the coming years. Heretofore, all gifts to the shrine had been used entirely for its ministry in the service of the visiting faithful. My fears that in recent times the shrine was being seen as just another parish were being realized. It seemed that after all those years of striving to reach a goal and fulfill a dream, the road was getting more difficult to travel when I might have expected it to get easier.

Later that year, I felt severe chest pain again. An examination by one of my doctors found no deterioration from the open-heart surgery, but the doctor advised that I needed to avoid stress, and it was his belief that I should retire from my present assignment. Naturally, it was not the kind of advice I wanted to hear. However, the physician emphasized his opinion that I was beyond the ability to carry this kind of stress in my life.

Still, with the shrine and my dream there remained much to be done. I really had no desire to leave the active arena. Among the unrealized aspirations in the dream were a statue of Saint Peter and the provision of an interactive display where the visitor could learn more about the development of pilgrimage in the history of the Church. I had always dreamt of a Saint Peter statue. On one occasion, while I was visiting Saint Peter's Basilica in Rome, a non-Catholic lady in our party told me she would like to join the queue and place her hand on the foot of Peter. I couldn't help noticing the tears in her eyes as she looked up at Peter and rubbed his foot with her hand. She didn't share her thoughts, but it was evident this non-Catholic lady had the same aspiration as all of us—to be with Christ and Peter in the kingdom of heaven. Since Mary's Shrine in Orlando would be visited by countless thousands too, I felt it would be proper to provide them the opportunity to be reminded of the great saint's faith and fidelity to the Lord and allow them to place their wishes for eternal life in his care. Besides, Saint Peter was a symbol of total authenticity to the teachings of Jesus. This was what the shrine was all about in its service to the people of the world.

How long would it take to bring the statue about? Would I be able to raise the funds quickly enough? I did not want to leave unfinished business behind when I retired! I had hoped that the shrine would have a pipe organ. The building of the organ would take four years, and I felt quite sure the finances could be raised within that time. But I knew too it wasn't going to happen on my watch. The sands of time were slipping away.

I didn't want to retire. I decided to go against the doctor's advice and try to complete the Saint Peter statue and the interactive historical display. After that I would decide.

I proposed the idea of the statue to the shrine committee. There was a long discussion. All were agreeable to go ahead with the idea, and the very first meeting proposed that Loura Dobbs should be given the commission. Loura was delighted to go to work for the shrine once again, and in short order, she was able to make a presentation to the committee. There were further meetings before Loura's presentation was accepted. As was always the case, the committee wanted a one-of-a-kind piece of artwork, one that could be viewed at the shrine and nowhere else in the world. The decision was made that the new piece of art be placed just inside the glass doors from the narthex, with the feet of Peter easily touchable by the people.

There was no problem finding a benefactor. He was "one of our own" again, a member of the shrine committee. But many of our shrine supporters throughout the United States wanted to help too, and so donations came in from many sources. The names of all of those people are included in a disc within the base of the statue itself, to remain there as long as the statue stands. I had already retired from the shrine when the statue was put in place, but on a November Sunday in 2007, I was happy to be present as the statue was blessed during a Sunday morning Mass.

If you go outside to the outdoor chapel at the shrine, you will find the first piece of artwork of this tourist ministry, created by Jerzy Kenar, that of Jesus and His Mother. Then walk just inside the narthex and your eyes will immediately be drawn to the Kenar Holy Water font with its overhead arch towering upwards, symbolic of our journey to God that begins with the waters of Baptism. Then as you enter the Church through the strikingly ornamental VonRoen glass partition you will be greeted by the statue of St. Peter, left hand outstretched towards the tabernacle, seat of the abiding Lord who is the very heart of Catholic faith and worship. Up front is Jill Burkee's magnificent rendering of Mary Queen, and to the left stands the enthralling presentation by Bruno Lucchesi of Saint Joseph and the Child. Add to these the works by GianCarlo Biaggi (*The Sacred Heart*) and Brian Hanlon (*The Sorrowful Mother*) as well as *The Crucified Christ* and the *Resurrected Christ* (both by Jerzy Kenar), plus the *Stations of the Cross* by Frederick Ansele, and you will realize that a lot had happened in the three decades that had moved us from one century to another.

As work on the statue of Saint Peter progressed, time was of the essence. After serious and prayerful reflection, I was beginning to settle on the last day of October 2007 for my retirement date. This would be the eve of the Feast of All Hallows, that had given its name to the seminary that had sent me forth "to teach all nations." In August 2006, I returned to Knock Shrine, in my native County Mayo, as had been my custom every time I visited Ireland since my ordination. My prayer time there in recent years had always been directed toward the ministry of our Orlando Shrine, its remarkable volunteers, and the benefactors of the shrine far and wide. This time though, I had something new to ask Our Lady about. We needed to converse about my retirement. She had brought me full circle.

The author concelebrates a mass at the Apparition Chapel of Knock Shrine, Co. Mayo.

I sat before her statue within the old church itself and debated the situation with her. It had been many decades since that "longest night," away back in 1939. I had aged, Knock Shrine had changed, but the Mother of God was still the same. I came away from my prayer time with a sureness and serenity that was not there when I came to pray. I would retire on October 31, 2007. It was God's will, and His Mother approved. Just as she had heard my prayer as a young boy, I knew she had been listening now too. She and I had come through many a crisis together. There was no need to fear the future when I would have to say good-bye to a ministry that I passionately loved.

Only one unfulfilled part of the dream was really left—the provision of an interactive display room to tell the story of Christian pilgrimage.

With less than a year to go, I decided it could hardly be achieved. There had been a prospective benefactor for the project back in 2005, but then a hurricane destroyed the city of New Orleans, and our possible benefaction was directed toward the recovery of that city and its people. The interactive part of our museum appeared dead—but not really!

Members of my staff, though, were not quite sure about that. One in particular convinced me that we should proceed with the project, and having consulted with the shrine committee, I secured the go-ahead. And so my last year at the shrine was taken up in extra meetings, some of the most enjoyable I experienced in the ministry. We were discussing religious topics, setting them in historical context, looking into dates and happenings, examining and discussing apparitions of Our Lady, looking into the journeys of Pope John Paul II, and getting a lot of facts together that would interest viewers.

The information would be conveyed on attractive wall boards as well as through video screens around the walls. Three actors were employed to bring the reality of historical times to the attention of the viewer. For our meetings, the contracting firm (who specialized in this kind of work) provided a prompter for us, to keep us on our toes! She was a good leader and came with her homework done in advance. There was many a friendly argument as to what should or should not be included, for example "who was the first Roman emperor, and when did he rule?"

The project was completed on schedule, and the display was opened in the summer of 2007. Its arrival signaled the completion of my involvement in building the dream. Someone else would have to attend to procuring the pipe organ.

Around March of 2007, Mary, Queen of the Universe Shrine had come to the attention of the American bishops. It was declared a national shrine, recognizing it as one of the very special devotional shrines of Mary within the United States. Personally, I saw it as a tribute to the Diocese of Orlando that had taken steps to serve its tourist population in the first place. It was also a grateful attestation to the work of the volunteers of southwest Orlando, who had dedicated themselves to the service of their fellow visiting Christians and had striven to bring about the fulfillment of the dream in their service to the many. The result of their work saw the completion of probably the only church in the world erected as a ministry to tourists.

In May of 2007, we were ready for the last hurrah. At this time there was much to celebrate, including the title *national shrine*, the completion of the bronze portals, and the opening of the interactive pilgrimage center. I knew this celebration was, so to speak, the end for me. However, in neither the invitations nor the celebration itself did I refer to my coming retirement. I wanted the celebration to be directed toward the most recent successes that had been granted by the Lord and His wonderful Mother on this ministry. The celebration was to center on progress with this special project of the Lord. Previously, I had informed the bishop of my decision. Following the celebration, I wrote him my letter of retirement. He quickly responded with his acceptance.

Chapter Seventy-Four:
A Fond Farewell

⁓

In September of 2007, I vacationed at home in Ireland, returning at the end of the month. The month of October swiftly counted off its days. With about two weeks to go before my retirement, the bishop called me to his office to announce his appointment of my successor. He had never spoken to me or sought my opinion. I had played no part in his decision, so I would bear no responsibility for the success or otherwise of the new leader of the ministry. I could only pray that he would meet the challenges of his new assignment and continue the traditions of serving the faithful from all parts.

The guidance of the ministry itself was so vastly different from parochial ministry that I had cause to be concerned about a successor who, through no fault of his own, might be entirely uninformed regarding the varied facets of service to tourists. It was evident to me nobody at the diocesan offices understood the ministry of the shrine. But I was quite sure the Mother of God would continue to be as active as ever in the development of the shrine that prided itself on bringing Eucharist and reconciliation to the thousands, a place where God's faithful came to commune with their Creator in idyllic surroundings. As far as I was concerned, she was still totally in charge, and she would continue to watch over the work.

Someone has written that there is a price to pay for nostalgia. I suppose it is human to look back, and when we grow to love our work, it can be difficult to walk away from it. But love of work comes mostly from love of those with whom we work, whether they are creators or recipients of our toil. I had been involved in the ministry of the shrine for almost the same length of time that the Lord was on earth. October 31, 2007, completed thirty-two years and eight months of serving visitors to the area. Many persons had crossed my path since we first began in a hotel ballroom in 1975. I could only hope I had helped some of them, and if their vacation in Orlando was the better for having met my coworkers and myself, then our work was not in vain.

What is it like for a priest to awaken to the morning of one's last day of a life's work? Gratitude should surely be the first emotion. We belong to God; He calls, and we answer. Everything we do is through Him. The priest walks side by side with Christ the Lord. I had been blessed to see not just the beginning of the dream but just about its complete fulfillment. October 31, 2007 would be the last morning on which I would awaken with a responsibility on my shoulders. I hoped the Lord was saying to me, "Well done."

I am sure there was a little sadness too. I would miss my helpers in the vineyard, the volunteers and the shrine staff who had been my rock-solid supporters and companions over all those years. But I knew too that nothing in this world is forever. They and I were about to part, but it would be a physical parting only. My life had been changed by them. They had influenced me in ways beyond their awareness. I had witnessed their faith and dedication. I had experienced their love. I had received inspiration from them that improved my ministering as a priest. They would always retain a place in my heart.

Let me tell you I worked that last day as I had done all the others. Every day of my shrine ministry had seen me take care of incoming mail, visit every office and every office member, and deal with administrative problems and situations so that the day was gone before I had barely begun! My last day was no different. I noted a tear in an eye here and there, but I deliberately took no heed.

Now and again, throughout the day, there were phone calls from well-wishers who wanted to express their gratitude for my work and the establishment of the Shrine. My gallant secretary Libby tested my resolve when office hours ended. She had been with me for many a year, and she took my departure with a heavy heart. I comforted her with assurances of future meetings that we could hold on our own time, when she wouldn't need a notebook and pen. Since it was the eve of All Saints, I had scheduled myself for the Vigil Mass at six o'clock. My good friend Father John McMullan, who had also decided to retire on that same day, concelebrated the Mass with me. The homily was on All Saints, and there were no good-byes.

Following the Mass, the volunteers, Father McMullan, and I completed the lockup of the church. There was no one there to receive the church keys, which I wouldn't need anymore, and since no one was there to take them, I left them on the executive secretary's desk, turned out the lights, and departed by a side door that I slammed after me to ensure it was locked. Forty-six years of active priesthood had come to an end. I was closing the door on a project that had begun so many years previously, one that had tasted great success through the blessings of the Almighty. Outside, a couple of faithful volunteers were waiting for both of us priests to accompany us to dinner at a local restaurant. Next morning would be the Feast of All Saints. I remember recalling my parents' love of the Lord. Tomorrow would be their big Feast Day too, and I knew they would remember their boy in their joy with the Lord.

I had taken the day's mail home from the shrine, not an unusual custom for me. When I opened the first letter at home, there was a surprise for me. It was from a department of the diocese. It announced there had been "fundamental concern about current management practices" at the shrine, and an investigation concerning shrine staff and various administrative procedures at the shrine was set to take place. My gold watch on my retirement day—or was it a barbed wire band for my wrist? A "review panel" had investigated was what the letter told me. And the hearing was held and the investigation would take place at the request of a part-time worker who had been dismissed some five months previously, with good reason. Another hand grenade was thrown into my life from "friendly" sources.

This so called "hearing" with a panel, whose qualifications and names were not revealed in the letter and have not been to this day, had made several decisions without consulting anyone at the shrine. People who, one can assume, knew not the first thing about the shrine ministry had sat in judgment! The letter quoted Jack Larkin (the shrine manager) as having attended a meeting. Jack believed the matter was settled, and though he had mentioned it to me on my return from Ireland, he considered the issue as spurious and was totally shocked when I informed him. The mailing date of the letter would make it appear almost as if its delivery date was planned in advance, giving no time for me to raise questions.

Oddly enough, the letter, while announcing a further "investigation" already contained the purported investigative results, recording a number of requirements future administrations would have to adhere to. To the best of my knowledge, nobody on the phantom "panel" knew anything about the administration of the shrine. And there were clues in the letter that an attorney had been involved in its creation.

I was retired now, I had never had any concerns expressed over thirty-two years of administration of the ministry, and now on the day of my departure I was notified of "fundamental concerns"! Not one diocesan official had ever spoken to me about any such concerns. Both Bishop Dorsey and Bishop Grady had frequently complimented me on the blessings that had come our way, both for the shrine ministry and the Diocese of Orlando at large. Both of those bishops had departed the scene. A copy of the letter had been forwarded to the present Bishop (Wenski) I wondered how this investigation could take place without his prior approval. Two weeks previously he had called me to his office to inform me of my successor. He had not spoken one word about the pending allegations, even though the phantom committee must already have completed its work. His letter accepting my resignation some months previously had expressed his satisfaction of my work at the Shrine. It was an incomprehensible situation. A phantom committee had sat in judgment, witnesses were not called, the accused (me) was not informed and conclusions were arrived at and directions given – even before the pre-arranged investigation. It was comparable to an installment from *The Tudors*, a television program that depicted the vengeful attitude of King Henry V111 on those from whom he wanted retribution.

I had begun the ministry with no funds. Now a magnificent shrine church existed with thousands of supporters from all over the land. All mortgages and debts were paid, and my successor would merely need to maintain what was passed on to him. Nobody had ever called me to inquire why the individual who was making the complaint had lost his part-time job. The silliness of the entire operation began to dawn on me. Somehow I began to realize there was more to this than met the eye! Somebody, somewhere, was sending a message. But for what, I had no indication.

I put the letter down and took up my breviary. After I had completed the portion allotted for that day, I felt calmer. I would take no action. In fact, I began to laugh out loud, to an empty room. Somebody had gone to a lot of trouble, and for what? The person who signed the letter was most unlikely to have written it. There were indications within the document that it might have come from the desk of a lawyer. There was a message somewhere in this, but the only message that came through was one of ignorance and lack of good grace.

Maybe it was meant to be a joke, and that was how it would be treated! The shrine had been built for God's glory, and I had given every ounce of my energies to it. Did it matter what some misguided soul in the diocesan offices was about? However, the investigation did indeed take place, but I have never heard anything from anyone as to the results. The whole farce stands as a stark example of the abuse of power that sometimes pervades the corridors of those who consider themselves infallible in the positions bestowed on them in the accidentals of history. Such persons need frequent remembrance in our prayers.

This affair serves only to illustrate the humanness of the Church to which we belong. God took our human nature for our sake, and while the Church is divinely inspired, it retains all of its human characteristics. We have come across some of those already in this story. Jesus had to deal with the problem even among His apostles, a couple of whom wanted to be Lords of the Domain, one of whom denied Him, and one of whom finally betrayed Him. We should expect the Church to be no different. All of the above personalities are still to be found among our ranks, the notion of service is frequently smothered by the desire for power, and Holy Orders does not exclude from jealousy envy or power seeking. For the lay person, the important fact to remember is that the church of Jesus consists of every member, not just those in authority. Each individual plays an important role in the spreading of the Good News. We cannot allow ourselves to be misled by the deficiencies in character or personality of those who allow their positions in life to make them devoid of Christian love.

I make note of this too because any aspirant to the priesthood has to understand that his first and foremost relationship is in deep humility with Christ the Lord. In that relationship, and only there, will be found the rewards promised to faithful followers. The priest places his own life in the hands of the Master. There is never a time when a priest can sit back and decide he has reached the pinnacle of spirituality. The priesthood will not shield him from false perceptions or the vanity of those among whom he may be called to work. Perhaps the bigger the apparent success, the larger the price paid! In Saint John's Gospel we are told that the raising of Lazarus was one of the immediate causes of the crucifixion of Jesus. Those who align themselves with Him in His ministry should expect to be called upon to suffer too.

It seemed a little strange the day following my retirement, on such a glorious feast, that I had no responsibilities. For many a year, each Sunday and each festival brought its own preparation. It had always been a joy to peruse and reflect on the sacred readings at Mass. For the most part, that was now over. On the other hand, there was more time for personal prayer. On that morning, I simply sat with the Lord and reviewed the various aspects of my life, thanking Him for my upbringing and the many favors He had bestowed on me in so many different ways.

I recalled for Him the audacious dream of priesthood he had planted in my soul. And I surely thanked Him for the extraordinary way in which it had been realized! It included an incredible history of starting a church from nothing and leaving it as a financially well-endowed landmark shrine church. I remembered the words of the psalm: "Not to me O Lord, not to me, but to thy name be the glory." My successor would have no mortgage, only the challenge to keep the ministry alive and well and continue to fulfill the mission of the shrine in the service of tourists. Nor did I forget to thank the Lord for the greatest favor of all—His priesthood. Once again I offered all my days to Him, both those past and those to come. I wouldn't be as busy from now on, but I told Him I still hoped I could contribute to the establishment of His kingdom. "Once a priest, a priest forever." I would always be ready to help out with weekend liturgies if the need arose, and as long as God preserved my health, I would continue to answer His call.

God has been good to me. As in any life, I have experienced my ups and downs. But in all situations the grace of God has prevailed. In my homilies, I frequently remind the listeners of the "power of God in the life of the Christian." The words of the angel in Saint Luke's first chapter are still true: "Nothing is impossible with God." God's power worked through me too.

As a child I wanted to be a priest, long before I knew the sacrifices it would entail. In more mature years, my desire did not change. I am often asked the question, "If you knew then what you know now, would you still have chosen the priesthood?" God has His own ways, reveals Himself to us in accordance with His plans, and affords us the graces to persevere. Saint Paul states it beautifully when he boasts, "In Him who is the source of my strength, I have strength for everything." I cannot see myself as other than a priest.

A priest friend who died shortly after the main buildings had been completed told me that he planned, on the time of his departure from this world, to "fly over the shrine and see it like the angels!" He said, "You were called to undertake this work for God." They were the words of a dying friend, and his insights at that time may have been God-given. They certainly inspired me.

On the morning of the day of dedication in 1993, Bishop Dorsey intimated that I had been involved in a miracle. In his retirement years before his death, Bishop Thomas Grady, who first approved of the plan for the shrine, had expressed his pleasure more than once at the success achieved, and he made frequent visits to the shrine, always making sure he chatted with me. Both bishops were always profuse in expressing their gratitude, not only to me but to the volunteers and benefactors who had worked so ardently to add a jewel to the kingdom of God. Bishop Dorsey was particularly gifted in this way. He never left a shrine ceremony without thanking the volunteers, the choir, and everyone involved in that occasion's liturgy.

Time has flown since a zealous lady resurrected an abandoned Gestetner and with it helped initiate a fund raising campaign that would have far reaching spiritual repercussions. It is many years since a good lady stood up in the congregation to encourage an unsure priest to keep going and not to be afraid to ask gifts for the Lord. Those were occasions of grace that embellished all my endeavors thereafter. There were other graces too. The extraordinary people who came my way, the friendships that were developed, the enthusiasm generated from so many, the very obvious interventions of God that took place so frequently, the great love in the hearts of our American Catholics for the Mother of God—all of these became very much a part of who I am today. I have no doubt I am a different person from the one who began the work! I have so much for which to be grateful. Every time I visit the shrine, I see something that brings back a wonderful memory of how the Lord and His Mother got things perfected and the project completed.

Occasionally, I have a dream that we are still at the beginning. Someone is calling to find out which hotel will have Mass, or I am meeting with the committee to discuss finances, and someone is saying, "Wait a minute. We need to think this out some more." I awaken to a different world and a completed project, and as in the dream, I am grateful that the Lord sent me such wonderful advisors. Yes indeed, he has sent his angels to take charge over me! That has to be the story of every priest who tries to do his best.

At this time, if you attend Mass at the shrine on any weekend, you will realize that the original dream was truly fulfilled! Thousands of persons are receiving Eucharist from one end of the year to the other. The "tourist ministry" of the Diocese of Orlando is known from coast to coast. The "Beacon of Light" that was planned for the I-4 corridor near Disney World is shining brightly. There is a Western song that says, "You can't be a beacon if your light don't shine," and certainly Mary's Shrine in Orlando has shone its light from Orlando to far corners of the world. "The place like no other" envisioned in the original concept has become a reality, and often visitors remark they find a solace and peace there while experiencing God's presence in a special way. In every way the shrine experience of the many is that their visit is enlivened by Christ, and they themselves come away feeling a closeness to the Lord and His holy Mother.

The numbers seeking reconciliation are astounding. In times when priests are scarce and parish activities curtail confessional hours, the public at large are aware that they can find a priest administering the sacrament at the shrine at almost any time of the day, even on Sunday afternoons. Happily, people avail themselves of the opportunity, and shrine priests are glad to answer the call by presenting themselves to render God's saving grace to all who come seeking it.

The great glory of the priest is His call to represent Christ at the altar and to make the Lord present for the congregation of believers. The Eucharist is the lifeblood of the Church. Through it Christianity—in all its branches—remains a vibrant force. The success of the development of the shrine gives testimony to the wonderful belief ensconced in the hearts of our Catholic people that Eucharist is at the heart of Christianity. Priests of the Lord carry out this most important of tasks, not only bringing Christ present on the altar in accordance with His petition at the Last Supper, "Do this in memory of me," but empowering the world through the presence of Christ in the lives of His people.

"You have not chosen me, but I have chosen you" were the words of the Lord at His final banquet. I am glad He chose me, glad I responded to His call, and glad that I walked with Him throughout all those years. Mary, His Mother, whose instant conformance to the message of the angel set an example for every follower of Jesus, has accompanied me every step of the way throughout my priesthood, making sure I had the strength to carry out and "do what He tells you." When I am retiring each night, I glance at her picture over my bed—the one I received on my first arrival in the New World—and I am reminded of her care for me throughout every hour of every day of my life and especially since that memorable evening when I was at the beginning of my first priestly assignment.

For whatever years remain, I am happy in the knowledge that in my life the words of the psalm have been fulfilled and will continue to be fulfilled: "For to his angels he has given command about you, that they guard you in all your ways. Upon their hands they shall bear you up, lest you dash your foot against a stone."

"The Longest Night" dawned into a day of near perfect fulfillment. And the best is yet to come!

Epilogue

On July 16, 2009, word was received from the Holy Father by the Diocese of Orlando that Mary, Queen of the Universe Shrine was being raised to the status of a minor basilica. And on August 22, 2009—only sixteen years after the ceremonies of dedication—a liturgy took place to celebrate that happy event. The Diocese of Orlando was being recognized for its extraordinary care of visitors from the world over.

Previously, on July 6, 2009, Archbishop Antonio Maria Veglio, president of the Pontifical Council for Migrants and Travelers, gave a pastoral message, written in anticipation of World Tourism Day, celebrated September 27, 2009. "Tourism," the archbishop noted, "can be an occasion of dialogue and listening, in so much as it puts people in contact with other ways of living, other religions, other ways of seeing the world and its history." The message also stated, "As a phenomenon tourism gives us the possibility of celebrating diversity and thus can be Christian, an open road to contemplative confession."

The late Cardinal Laghi had expressed his admiration of the tourism ministry of Mary's Shrine in Orlando on many occasions. He had taken part in ceremonies marking the progress of the ministry and had carried the good wishes and blessings of the Holy Father, Pope John Paul II, on each of his visits. He had indeed expressed his opinion that one day this shrine would be raised to the status of basilica. He would have been most happy had he lived to see the day that came so very quickly. There was a time when many people wondered if they would ever see the Shrine completed. Little did they know that they would even see it declared a basilica in their own lifetime!

The miracle continues.

Monsignor Fachtna Joseph Harte was born in the country parish of Kilfian, near Killala Co Mayo in the Diocese of Killala. From an early age he desired to serve the Church. He received his secondary education at St. Gerald's Secondary School Castlebar and St. Mary's Secondary School Athlone. For a short time he was a member of the teaching order of the Marist Brothers, having trained as a teacher at De La Salle College in Waterford City. He departed the Marist Brothers and studied at Mount Melleray Seminary County Waterford and at All Hallows College, Dublin, where he was ordained to the priesthood in 1961. He enhanced his education by completing two master's degrees, one in education from the University of Portland in Oregon and the other in religious education earned at Barry University in Miami.

Father Harte began his priestly ministry in the Diocese of Yakima, Washington, where he taught high school for nine years. In 1970, he transferred to the Diocese of Orlando at a time when Walt Disney had set his sights on the opening of a new theme park. In 1975, Father Harte was commissioned to begin a ministry to tourists in fulfillment of a need that had developed through the resounding success of the new theme park now opened. He developed Holy Family Parish in southwest Orlando and proceeded to commence the building of Mary, Queen of the Universe Shrine on the outskirts of the Walt Disney World Resort complex. This church was to become a landmark, not only in the state of Florida, but throughout the United States and in countries abroad.

In 2004, Pope John Paul II recognized this work by personally conferring the title *monsignor* on Father Harte. Later, the church would be designated as a Minor Basilica in recognition of the architecture and ministry to tourists.

Monsignor Harte is now retired and alternates between Orlando and his native place.

Open Book Editions
A Berrett-Koehler Partner

Open Book Editions is a joint venture between Berrett-Koehler Publishers and Author Solutions, the market leader in self-publishing. There are many more aspiring authors who share Berrett-Koehler's mission than we can sustainably publish. To serve these authors, Open Book Editions offers a comprehensive self-publishing opportunity.

A Shared Mission

Open Book Editions welcomes authors who share the Berrett-Koehler mission—Creating a World That Works for All. We believe that to truly create a better world, action is needed at all levels—individual, organizational, and societal. At the individual level, our publications help people align their lives with their values and with their aspirations for a better world. At the organizational level, we promote progressive leadership and management practices, socially responsible approaches to business, and humane and effective organizations. At the societal level, we publish content that advances social and economic justice, shared prosperity, sustainability, and new solutions to national and global issues.

Open Book Editions represents a new way to further the BK mission and expand our community. We look forward to helping more authors challenge conventional thinking, introduce new ideas, and foster positive change.

For more information, see the Open Book Editions website:
http://www.iuniverse.com/Packages/OpenBookEditions.aspx

Join the BK Community! See exclusive author videos, join discussion groups, find out about upcoming events, read author blogs, and much more!
http://bkcommunity.com/